CW01597066

The Legend of Dave the Villager

BOOKS 31–35

by Dave Villager

Second Edition (May 2024)

Website: davethevillager.com

Email: davevillagerauthor@gmail.com

CONTENTS

Book 31: The Trident of Emeros	5
Book 32: Mad Mulligan	89
Book 33: Mad Mulligan Strikes Back	173
Book 34: The Battle for the Badlands	261
Book 35: Boggo's Wedding	353

BOOK 31

The Trident of Emeros

The Story So Far

Dave was a villager who dreamed of being a hero. After discovering the secret to finding end portals, he set off on a quest to reach the End—a mysterious dimension that no-one has been to for thousands of years. His search took him to many different lands, and he fought villains and monsters along the way. He also made some really good friends.

It's been several weeks since Dave defeated the evil Herobrine by trapping him in an alternate universe, and Dave and his friends have been heading west, following the path shown to them by the eyes of ender, traveling from biome to biome in search of an end portal...

CHAPTER ONE
The Journey Continues

"Stop trying to hit me and hit me!" shouted Spidroth, thwacking Dave across the side of the head with her wooden sword.

"What does that even mean?!" said Dave.

"It means you're a noob," said Carl. "A noob with a sore head."

Dave was about to respond to Carl when Spidroth poked him in the stomach with her wooden sword, and he fell backward, landing hard on the red sand.

"Ow," Dave groaned.

"Get up," Spidroth demanded. "Your training isn't done yet."

"I think the poor chap has had enough," said Porkins.

"It's okay, Dave," said Alex. "It can take practice to get good at fighting. Although, when I was born, I was already much better with a sword than you are. No offense."

Dave pushed himself to his feet and held his wooden sword out in front of him. He was battered and bruised, and he felt like going to sleep, but he forced himself to keep going.

"Good," smiled Spidroth. "For a moment there, I thought you'd given up."

"Dave, it's okay to admit that you're a noob," said Carl. "A lot of noobs go on to live happy and fulfilling lives."

"Shut up, Carl," said Dave.

"Ignore the creeper," said Spidroth. "Use the Sight. Try to predict where my next attack is coming from and block it."

"That's what I've been trying to do," said Dave.

"Well, try harder," said Spidroth. "Don't look with your eyes; look with the Sight."

"Look with your butt," said Carl. "That's the key to being a mighty warrior – you must use the power of your butt to vanquish your foes."

"Carl!" snapped Dave.

"Think fast!" shouted Spidroth. She ran towards Dave, moving so fast that she was a blur.

Without thinking, Dave raised his wooden sword.

CLONK! Dave blocked Spidroth's sword with his own. They'd been practicing for hours now, and this was the first time he'd managed to block a hit successfully.

"You did it, Dave, you did it!" shouted Alex.

Spidroth swung her sword back and aimed another blow at Dave. Again, he blocked it.

"Good," grinned Spidroth. "Now, keep it up."

Spidroth kept trying to hit Dave with her sword, hitting him from every direction. Somehow, Dave was managing to block every blow. It was like a magical force had taken control of his hands. He could see Spidroth's blows coming before she even moved her sword.

I'm doing it! Dave thought. *I'm using the Sight!*

THWOCK! Spidroth kicked Dave in the chest, and he went

flying backward, landing on the sand.

"You're getting the hang of it at last," said Spidroth, "but you've still got a long way to go."

"Can we finish training now?" Dave groaned, pushing himself back to his feet.

"Very well," said Spidroth, putting her wooden sword back in her belt.

"I'll make us some supper," said Porkins, pulling a smoker out of his bag and placing it down on the ground, where it grew to full size. "How about some delicious mushroom stew?"

"You lot can have mushroom stew if you like," said Carl, "I'm going to have a delicious baked potato."

"Ooo, can I have a baked potato too?" asked Alex.

"How many times do I have to go over this?" said Carl. "We've only got a limited number of baked potatoes, so they're all mine."

After Porkins had finished cooking, the five of them all sat down around a campfire. The sun was starting to go down, making the red sand of the badlands biome look even redder than usual. In the distance, Dave could see tall, narrow spires of rock silhouetted against the setting sun.

"So, how are Dave's magical powers coming along?" asked Carl, taking another bite out of his baked potato.

"I don't have any magic powers," said Dave.

"Well, what else would you call it?" said Carl. "You can see the future. If that was in a comic book, it would be a magic power."

"The Sight is no silly power," said Spidroth. "It is old magic."

"How did Dave end up with it?" asked Alex.

"Is it because he's the chosen one?" asked Porkins. "A legendary hero who was destined to defeat Herobrine and is now destined to slay the ender dragon and bring peace and justice to the world?"

"Of course not, you fool," said Spidroth. "I thought it was obvious why Dave has the Sight."

Everyone looked blankly at her.

"Do none of you know anything about magic?" asked Spidroth, rolling her eyes.

"My uncle used to claim he had a magic pig," said Carl. "According to him, the pig used to poop solid gold blocks. My uncle lived in a big mansion with a swimming pool, but then one day he came downstairs and could smell bacon. One of his maids had accidentally cooked the pig. From that day forward, he never ate pig again."

"Dave has the Sight because he spent most of his life living above an end portal," said Spidroth.

Everyone looked blankly at her.

"Portals are full of magic," said Spidroth. "Don't you fools know anything?"

"Wait," said Dave, "that doesn't make any sense. What about all the other villagers in my village? And my parents? None of them had the Sight."

"And all the villagers in Diamond City," said Porkins. "All those chaps and chapettes lived above an end portal as well."

"Dave, all the people from your village probably *have* the Sight," said Spidroth. "Many people do, and they don't even know it. You didn't even know you had it before Zomba and Zombella told you that you did."

"So all the people in Dave's village could see the future and didn't even know it?" said Carl. "How does that make sense?"

Spidroth sighed.

"No offense, Dave," she said, "but most villagers live very boring lives."

"She's got a good point there," said Carl. "You guys don't even blow yourselves up."

"My point is," said Spidroth, "your typical villager blacksmith or farmer isn't going to have a very exciting future. When a farmer gets visions about his future, all he's going to see is more farming. Yes, he might see some significant events from his future, such as getting married or having children, but he'll just think that these are normal dreams. I bet you never had any exciting dreams before you left your village, did you?"

"Er, not that I can remember," said Dave. "It was only once I set off on my quest that I started to have weird dreams about the

End and Herobrine and dragons."

"Exactly," said Spidroth. "You were destined for a boring life, but once you found that stronghold and made the decision to leave your village, your future changed. Our futures are not set in stone; they change based on the decisions we make and the decisions other people make. That's why even those who are strong with the Sight sometimes make mistakes. Zomba thought she had seen a vision of my father standing triumphant in the ruins of our universe, but, in reality, he ended up trapped in another ruined universe. Premonitions about the future can be misleading, but that doesn't mean that you can't use your powers to be a better warrior."

"So he does have powers," said Carl. "I knew it."

Spidroth rolled her eyes.

"So you're saying that all those chaps in Dave's village and Diamond City were having dreams about the future and just never knew it?" asked Porkins.

"Yes," said Spidroth. "We all have dreams that seem to be telling us things about the future, or making sense of things that have happened to us, so Sight dreams just seemed like normal dreams. Only those who train hard can control the Sight and make it work to their advantage. If Dave can master his powers, he'll be able to see attacks before they're coming, and no one will be able to defeat him in battle."

"I dunno," said Alex, "what if there was a ravager the size of the mountain, and it could shoot other ravagers out of its mouth, and those ravagers were on fire. Would Dave still be able to defeat that?"

"I am not going to answer such a foolish question," said Spidroth. "The point is, even though Dave is a pretty mediocre warrior at the moment, his powers give him the potential to be an amazing fighter."

"I don't want to boast or anything," said Dave, "but I'm pretty good at fighting already. Not as good as you or Alex, but I've defeated a lot of bad guys."

"If you're so good, why did you trap Herobrine in the mirror universe rather than striking him down with the Shadow Blade?" asked Spidroth.

Dave didn't have an answer to that.

"You are a good warrior," Spidroth continued, "but you could be so much better. You couldn't defeat the Ancient and you knew you wouldn't be able to defeat my father, but with practice, maybe one day you'll be able to."

"So, do you have this Sight thing as well?" Carl asked Spidroth.

"I don't," said Spidroth. "I suppose I could spend a few weeks lying under a Nether portal, but I've got better things to do."

"Nether portals?" said Porkins. "I thought it was end portals that gave people the Sight?"

"Any technology designed by the Old People has the potential to give people the Sight," said Spidroth. "Witches in training often spend several weeks or months lying in the middle of Nether portals, with one half of them in the overworld and the other half of them in the Nether, to help them improve their magical abilities. It doesn't always work, of course, but sometimes it does. That's why witches often have such pasty skin — the magical power from the portal does strange things to them. Of course, end portals have far more magic in them than nether portals, but end portals are a lot harder to find."

"Aren't the witches worried about someone breaking one of the portal blocks and chopping them in half?" asked Dave, thinking back to what had happened to King Trotter.

"That does happen," said Spidroth. "It's not uncommon for witches to sneak up, break an obsidian block and chop one of their rivals in two. Or at least it was one thousand years ago. I haven't met a witch since I escaped from the bedrock."

"My grandmother's a witch," said Dave. "She does have pasty skin, so I guess she must have done that portal thing. To be honest, I haven't seen her since I was a kid."

“Great story, Dave,” said Carl.

“Come on,” said Dave, standing up. “I'll build a house, and we can get some sleep,”

As Dave lay in his bed that night, he found himself thinking about the journey ahead of them. It had been weeks since he, Carl, Spidroth, Porkins and Alex had left Spectrite City, and Dave wondered how much longer it would be before they found another end portal. For all they knew, they might be traveling for months. Or even years.

The next day the badlands biome came to an end, and they found themselves in a desert biome. The two biomes were pretty similar, apart from the fact that sand in the desert was yellow instead of red. It was still incredibly hot, and the sweat poured down Dave's forehead as he walked. He was wearing a straw hat to stop himself from getting sunburned. Porkins was still walking naked.

"Us pigmen don't get sunburned," Porkins told them. "It's a good thing too, as I imagine getting sunburned when you walk around naked would get jolly painful."

The desert seemed to go on forever, with nothing to break up the view apart from the occasional cactus and a few rabbits. Alex used her bow to shoot a couple of rabbits, and Alex, Carl, Spidroth and Dave had cooked rabbit for lunch (Porkins had beetroot soup). When Dave had first started traveling with Alex, she had balked at the idea of eating rabbit, but he guessed that she had changed a bit since then. According to Alex, her personality had altered slightly when she'd respawned, so Dave supposed that might have something to do with it as well.

They walked until the sun started to go down, then Dave took some blocks out of his bag to build them a house. But before he could get started, they heard some voices nearby.

Dave and the others crept closer to the voices. They were coming from the other side of a small hill, so they walked to the top of the hill to have a look. When they got to the top, they lay down so that they wouldn't be seen.

Four riders on horseback were looking down at two figures lying on the sand. Dave was amazed to see that the riders were all illagers. They were the first illagers he'd seen since coming to the cowman continent. The two people on the sand both had bags over their heads, and their hands were tied behind their backs.

"Tell us where the Stone of Nuntuck is," said one of the illagers, addressing the two figures on the ground. "Tell us, and we'll let you live."

Another illager jumped down from her horse and pulled the hoods off the two figures on the ground. One of the figures was a cowman with white fur, and the other, Dave was surprised to see, was a yellow creeper.

A creeper with arms and legs? thought Dave, feeling confused. *How can that be?*

The creeper's face was the same as any other creeper: two black eyes and a droopy mouth, but its body seemed to be the same size and shape as a villager or an illager, with normal-sized arms and legs. The creeper was wearing a brown leather jacket, a worn-looking shirt and pants and boots.

"You scoundrels don't scare us," said the yellow creeper. Judging from its voice, it was male.

"The Stone of Nuntuck belongs to Mad Mulligan," said the

illager who had spoken before.

"It belongs in a museum!" shouted the yellow creeper. "Milo and I would rather die than give it up! Isn't that right, Milo?"

"Um..." said the white cowman, who Dave assumed must be Milo.

"Milo!" said the yellow creeper. "Remember who pays your wages!"

"Uh, yes, we'd rather die," said Milo the cowman. Although he didn't sound very enthusiastic about it.

"Enough of this!" barked the illager, pulling out a crossbow and aiming it at the yellow creeper. "Tell us the location of the stone, or die!"

"You want the stone?" said the yellow creeper. "I'll give you the stone!"

For a moment, it looked like the yellow creeper was choking, and weird gargling noises were coming from his throat, then *PHTOOW!* – he spat out a shiny red stone the size of an apple, hitting the illager between the eyes.

"Gah!" The illager yelled, and he fell backward off his horse.

Then something strange happened. The yellow creeper's neck seemed to grow, then his head jumped up, leaving his body behind.

No, that's not his body, Dave realized, *it's some kind of suit with arms and legs, like Carl's golem suits!*

Now that the yellow creeper had jumped out of his fake body, Dave could see what he really looked like. Like Carl, he was a small creeper – half the height of an average creeper – with four little yellow legs. He jumped up, landing on the horse of one of the illagers. Suddenly he crackled with blue electricity, and the illager and his horse were both electrocuted. The horse reared up, and the illager went flying, landing painfully on the ground.

The yellow creeper grabbed the horse's reins with his mouth, tugged at them, and the horse galloped forward, towards one of the other illagers. Before that illager knew what was going on, the yellow creeper jumped off of his horse, landed on the illager's chest and zapped him full of electricity. The illager and the yellow creeper both fell to the ground, and the horse galloped off into the distance.

"ENOUGH!"

The final illager, the only one still on his horse, was aiming his crossbow at the white cowman's head.

"Surrender now," the illager told the yellow creeper, "or your friend gets a crossbow bolt in the brain."

"To be honest, he's really more of an assistant than a friend," shrugged the yellow creeper.

"Master!" whimpered the white cowman.

"Sorry, Milo," said the yellow creeper, grabbing the reins of the last horse with his teeth and swinging himself onto its back. "Sometimes a good adventurer needs to know when to leave his crew behind. Tally ho!"

The yellow creeper tugged at the reigns and then rode off into the distance.

"Master!" the cowman shouted. "Don't leave me!"

The illager on horseback snarled in frustration, then he tugged at his own horse's reins and rode off after the creeper.

The white cowman was left alone, on his knees with his hands tied behind his back. The three remaining illagers, the ones who had lost their horses, walked up to him.

"Looks like you're on your own, cowman," said one of the illagers, pointing her crossbow at the cowman's head.

"Oh dear," said the cowman. "Please don't hurt me."

"We're not gonna hurt you," growled another of the illagers, "we're gonna *kill* you."

"Um... please don't hurt me *or* kill me," said the cowman. "Please?"

"Come on," Dave whispered to the others, "we need to save him."

"I guess so," said Carl.

"Charge!" Dave yelled.

The four illagers looked around in surprise as Dave, Carl, Spidroth, Alex and Porkins jumped out and ran down the hill towards them. One of the illagers fired his crossbow at Carl, but the arrow bounced harmlessly off Carl's netherite golem chest. Another illager raised his bow to fire at Spidroth, but she rushed forward and chopped the crossbow in half with her sword.

"Run!" one of the illagers shouted, and they all scampered off.

"Shall we chase them?" Spidroth asked Dave.

"Nah, let them go," said Dave. He knelt down and untied the cowman's hands.

"Oh, thank you, thank you," said the cowman, getting to his feet. Now come on, we need to save my master!"

"Um, you mean that yellow creeper who left you behind to die?" said Carl. "You really want to save him?"

"He didn't leave me to die," said the cowman. "Master Creepo respects me too much. I'm his invaluable servant."

"Um, I'm pretty sure he left you to die," said Carl.

"Never mind," said the cowman, "we can't waste any more time. Do you have horses?"

"We do," said Dave.

"Then let's get moving," said the cowman. "There's no time to waste!"

CHAPTER TWO
Milo

The cowman —whose name was Milo — insisted that they bring the yellow creeper's robotic body with them.

"This thing is pretty cool," said Carl, picking it up and having a look. "I guess it works the same as my golem body: he just crawls inside and takes control of it."

Porkins strapped the robotic body to the back of his horse. It looked very strange just lying there — as if Porkins had a headless corpse riding behind him. Milo the cowman rode on Dave's horse, sitting behind him.

"Come on, come on!" said Milo, once they were all on their horses. "We need to save my master, or he'll be very angry with me!"

Dave tugged at the reins of his horse and started galloping off across the desert, Porkins, Spidroth, Alex and Carl following him. Carl's golem body was far too big to ride a horse, so as usual, he was running alongside them.

"So, tell me more about your master and that red stone thing," Dave said to the cowman as they rode along. "What's that all about?"

"Master Creepo is an adventurer," said the cowman. "He travels the world in search of treasure, and I'm lucky enough to go with him as his assistant."

"And those illagers want to take that stone off him?" Dave asked. "Is it worth a lot of money?"

"It's not the stone they want," said Milo. "The Stone of Nuntuck just shows the way to the real treasure: The Trident of Emeros."

The Trident of Emeros: Dave was sure he'd heard that name before, but he couldn't remember where.

"What's so special about this trident?" Dave asked.

"It's thousands of years old," said Milo, "it's a priceless treasure, worth a fortune. The Ancients themselves built it."

The Ancients. That was a name that Dave had heard before. It was what Jean-Cowphio had called the Old People.

"Of course, anything built by the Ancients is extremely valuable," continued Milo. "They had technology far beyond anything we have today. They had devices called command blocks that let them alter the fabric of reality, so they could even make things out of bedrock. Using portals, they could move between the overworld, the Nether and the End whenever they liked, and they flew through the air using purple ships. They truly were magnificent people."

"It sounds like you're a big fan of them," said Dave.

"Oh yes," said Milo. "Before I joined Master Creepo on his adventures, I was a professor at Milk City University. I had studied the Ancients all my life, so when Creepo Jones gave me the chance to join him on his quest to find Ancient artifacts, I naturally jumped at the chance. Yes, he can be a bit... unpredictable at times, but he's the greatest adventurer in the world."

"He also left you to die," Dave reminded him. "If we hadn't

come along, those illagers would have given you an arrow in the brain."

"Um, I'm sure he would have come back for me," said Milo. But he didn't sound very convinced. "Besides, I'm an old man. My life is worth far less than that of a priceless artifact."

Suddenly, Dave remembered where he'd heard of the Trident of Emeros before: it had been one of the weapons that Future Dave had owned.

"The Trident of Emeros," Future Dave had said, as he'd shown the weapon to Dave and Carl. *"An ancient weapon created by an ancient civilization of villagers. My troops found it while they were stationed at a desert pyramid."*

Future Dave had then shown them what the trident could do: using it to fire a blast of green energy at a tree, blowing it to pieces.

I guess Future Dave was wrong about the trident being created by villagers, thought Dave. *If Milo's right, it was created by the Old People.*

"There they are!" shouted Spidroth, shaking Dave out of his thoughts.

Up ahead in the distance, two horses were racing across the desert, one chasing the other. When Dave squinted, he could just about make out the illager on one horse and the little yellow creeper on the other.

"Don't worry, Master!" Milo the cowman yelled. "Your loyal assistant is coming to save you!"

"He won't be able to hear you from all the way over here," said Dave. "Come on, we need to catch them up."

Dave tugged at his horse's reins, making it go faster. But even though his horse was going at full speed, the two horses up ahead were going at full speed too, and it would be difficult to catch them up.

"Hurry!" Milo yelled. "We need to save my master!"

"Unless I attach some firework rockets to this horse, I don't think it can go any faster," said Dave.

"Do you have any firework rockets?" asked Milo.

Dave ignored the question.

For the next couple of hours, they chased the two horses across the desert. Sometimes it would look like they were getting closer, but then the horses would speed on ahead, so they could never catch them up. Dave could feel his horse start to lose its energy, and it began to whimper.

The poor thing must be utterly exhausted, thought Dave, *but I guess if our horses are exhausted, their horses must be exhausted too.*

The creeper and the illager would have to stop eventually, Dave knew. They just had to keep on chasing them until that time came.

The sun was starting to get low in the sky now, and it wouldn't be long before it got dark. Riding a horse this fast across the desert would be dangerous then, with all the monsters that would come out once the sun had set.

Suddenly Dave saw something up ahead in the distance.

"Is that... is that a canyon?" Porkins asked.

It was, Dave saw. Up ahead of them, the desert came to an end, and beyond it, the ground dropped down into a vast canyon. It was so big that Dave could barely see the other side.

"That's the Canyon of the Kings," said Milo excitedly. "I never thought I'd see it in person — that's where the ancient Ancients buried their royal families!"

"Ancient Ancients?" said Dave.

"The Ancients were around for tens of thousands of years," said Milo. "The Ancients who built their tombs in this canyon died out long before The Great Fall."

"The Great Fall?" said Dave. "What's that?"

"You've never heard of The Great Fall?" said Milo, sounding amazed.

"Obviously not," said Dave. "Or I wouldn't be asking."

"The Great Fall was when all the Ancients disappeared overnight," Milo explained. "It's said that an evil wizard cursed them, turning them into monsters. Some fled in their ships, and others sealed themselves in the End, destroying all the end portals so that the wizard couldn't follow them. It's said that the Ancients who were trapped in the End gradually lost their minds and their souls and became the endermen. Living beings weren't meant to live in that place for too long, and it corrupted them."

The evil wizard he's talking about is Herobrine, Dave knew. Milo had also confirmed something that Dave had long suspected: that the endermen had once been the Old People. But there had been something else that Milo had said that had piqued Dave's interest.

"You said that Herobrine turned the ancients into monsters," said Dave. "Do you mean he turned them into endermen or something else?"

"Herobrine?" said Milo. "I don't know who that is. I'm talking about Stephen the wizard."

Stephen? thought Dave, feeling confused. He was about to ask a follow-up question, but there wasn't time — the illager and the yellow creeper had both brought their horses to a stop next to the edge of the canyon, and Dave and the others were approaching them fast.

The illager and the yellow creeper were circling each other with their horses, the illager aiming his bow at the creeper.

"You've got nowhere to run," the illager growled. "Give me that stone!"

Then the illager turned and saw Dave and his friends approaching. A look of fear crossed the illager's face as he realized he was outnumbered.

Dave, Carl, Spidroth, Porkins and Alex came to a stop, surrounding the illager and the yellow creeper.

"Lower your crossbow," Dave said the illager.

The illager spat on the ground.

"This isn't over," he snarled, looking at the yellow creeper. Then he tugged at his horse's reins and galloped off, weaving between Porkins and Alex and riding back off across the desert.

"Shall we chase him, Dave?" Alex asked.

"No," said Dave. "Let him go."

Milo jumped off the back of Dave's horse and ran over to the yellow creeper.

"Oh, Master, are you okay?" The cowman asked. "I was so

worried about you."

"Of course I am," said the yellow creeper proudly. "There was no way a scoundrel like that could have defeated the great Creepo Jones!"

"Er, if we hadn't come along, that illager would have shot you with his crossbow," said Carl.

"Nonsense!" said Creepo Jones. "I had the situation in hand."

He gave Carl's golem suit a funny look.

"I don't think much of your robotic body," Creepo Jones said. "It's a bit big, isn't it? And what's the point of having arms and legs unless you're going to wear some nice clothes? Speaking of which, Milo — bring me my body!"

"Yes, Master, of course!" said Milo. The old cowman ran over to Porkins's horse and took the headless robotic body off the back, carrying it over to Creepo Jones. The creeper jumped off his horse, crawled into the body, took control of it and stood up.

"Yes, that's much better," said Creepo Jones, stretching his arms and legs. "Well, it's been nice meeting you all, but I must be off. Adventure awaits!"

Suddenly two gray wings popped up from behind his back.

Dave had seen wings like that once before, worn by a group of witches who had saved his life.

"Master, take me with you!" yelled Milo.

"Sorry, Milo, I've only got one pair of elytra," said Creepo Jones. "Looks like this is where you and I part ways. Tally-ho!"

Then he jumped off the side of the canyon. For a few seconds, Dave feared that he had jumped to his doom, but then he swooped up into the sky, flying off into the distance using the wings.

"Good gravy," gasped Porkins. "I've got to get a pair of those."

CHAPTER THREE
The Confusing Nature of Time Travel

"Well, at least he didn't leave you for dead this time," said Carl, placing a hand on Milo's shoulder. "That's something."

"We need to get after him," said Milo, pushing Carl's hand away. "My master needs me!"

"I must say, old chap," said Porkins, "it does seem that this relationship you have with Creepo Jones is a bit lopsided. He's left you behind twice now, old bean."

"He would have taken me with him, but he only had one pair of elytra," said Milo.

"I dunno," said Alex. "He probably could have carried you. You don't look that heavy."

"What are those elytra things anyway?" asked Dave. "Can we craft some and fly after him?"

Milo laughed.

"Craft elytra?" he scoffed. "You can't craft elytra! They are sophisticated technology beyond our comprehension. They were built by the Ancients, and there are very few pairs left in the world. Of course, there are rumored to be far more of them in the End, but since all the end portals were destroyed, those are lost forever."

"Ooo, they weren't all destroyed," said Alex, "we're actually on a quest to —"

"ALEX!" Dave said quickly. "Milo doesn't want to hear the boring details of our quest."

"No, I do," said Milo, giving Alex a suspicious look, "what were you going to say just then?"

"I'm sure it was nothing," said Dave, "come on, let's all get a move on."

I must have a word with Alex later, thought Dave. Even though Herobrine was gone, Dave was still reluctant to tell anyone about their quest to find an end portal. He didn't know exactly why, but he knew that if the wrong people found the End, it could be dangerous. There was probably some powerful old technology there, and it wouldn't be good if it fell into the wrong hands.

"Right," Dave said to Milo, "this has been fun and everything, but my friends and I really must be continuing our journey. If you want, we can bring you to the nearest town or village. You don't want to be stuck out here in the desert at night."

"I'm not going anywhere!" said Milo. "My master needs me!"

"Give it up, dude," said Carl. "He keeps leaving you behind. You should take that as a hint."

"I will not hear slander against Creepo Jones's name," said Milo. "He is the greatest adventurer the world has ever seen. Once he finds the Trident of Emeros, his name will be known throughout the world!"

"Wait," said Carl, "that crazy creeper is looking for the Trident of Emeros? Dave, that's the Trident that Future Dave had!"

"I know," said Dave.

"Future Dave?" said Milo. "I don't understand."

"This is going to sound a bit strange," said Dave, "but Future Dave was a version of me who came back from the future to change the past. He had all sorts of futuristic weapons, but one of the weapons he had was the Trident of Emeros. He said his troops found it in a pyramid somewhere."

"That's right!" said Milo. "The Trident of Emeros is rumored to be inside the hidden Pyramid of Nuntuck."

"Looks like we have to join Milo on his quest, old bean," Porkins said to Dave. "If the future version of you has this weapon, then I jolly well suppose you have to get it now, in the past."

"Porkins, don't you understand anything about time travel?" said Carl. "Anyone would think you'd never read Seth the Elf issues 222 to 227."

"Oh yeah, the *Lost in Time* saga," said Alex. "Isn't that the one where Seth goes back in time to meet his own grandfather but ends up changing the past, then he goes back to the future again, and all the pigs in the world now have his grandfather's face?"

"That's the one," said Carl.

"What are you two blathering about?" said Spidroth.

"The point I'm making," said Carl, "is that when Future Dave came back to the past, he changed the timeline, so that future will never exist. So Dave will never become Future Dave. Or at least he will, but it will be a different Future Dave to the Future Dave we met. Does that make sense?"

"Um, not really," said Porkins. "But I'll take your word for it, old bean."

"Right," said Milo the cowman, "if you're not going to help me, I need to get going. Creepo Jones needs my help."

Dave climbed off of his horse and passed the reins to Milo.

"Here," Dave said. "I really think you should come with us, but if you insist on going after that creeper, at least take my horse."

"Thank you, Dave," said Milo, climbing onto the horse. Then he pulled at the reins, and the horse galloped off.

"Porkins, do you mind if I ride with you?" Dave asked.

"Don't let him, Porkins," said Carl. "Make him walk."

Dave reached into his bag and took out an eye of ender. He threw it into the air, and it whizzed off across the canyon.

"Well, it looks like we're going to be crossing the canyon anyway," sighed Dave.

"We could just carefully build a bridge across?" said Spidroth.

"I dunno," said Dave, "I think even with all the blocks we have, we might not have enough to build a bridge all the way to the other side. And even if we do, we'll barely have enough to build a bridge one block thick, and that would be far too dangerous to cross."

"Pah," said Spidroth. "When I fought wars in the old days, I would often build bridges one block thick for my troops to cross. Yes, we often lost a fair few of our numbers, but in a war, you have to make sacrifices."

"Um, may I remind you that we are not in a war," said Porkins. "I don't want to make a fuss, but I don't fancy falling down that canyon."

"I wouldn't mind," said Alex. "But then again, I can respawn. You guys need to learn to respawn. It's very useful."

"Yes, I'll bear that in mind," said Carl, rolling his eyes.

“Right,” said Dave, climbing up on the horse behind Porkins. “I guess we’d better get moving.”

CHAPTER FOUR
Finding a Way Down

They rode along the canyon for a short while, looking for a path down, but before long, it began to get dark, so Dave built them a house to stop the night in.

The next morning they rode on again for a few hours until they reached an old mineshaft. There were some rail tracks on the ground, a few minecarts and a tunnel that led underground. Next to the entrance of the tunnel was a small wooden shack.

Dave walked over to the side of the canyon and saw that at the very bottom of the canyon was another entrance to the mine.

"Perfect," said Dave, "we can just follow the passage down through this mineshaft to reach the bottom of the canyon."

"I don't know, old bean," said Porkins, riding his horse up to the entrance. "It looks very dark and spooky in there."

"Aw yeah, maybe they'll be monsters!" said Alex excitedly.

"Of course, there'll be monsters," sighed Carl. "There are always monsters."

"If any foul beasts try to attack us, they will rue the day they met the great Lady Spidroth," said Spidroth.

"I rue the day I met the great Lady Spidroth," said Carl. "I rue that day so bad."

"Then it's settled," said Dave. "We'll take the path through the mineshaft."

Before they entered the mineshaft, Dave decided to have a quick look around the old shack. Inside there wasn't much, apart from a table, some chairs and an old bookshelf full of dusty books. The ceiling was covered in cobwebs, but there was no sign of any spiders.

"I don't think any of these books will be of much use," said

Porkins, looking through the bookshelf. "They're all about mining. Oh, but there is one comic book."

"Give it to me!" Carl demanded, stomping over to the bookshelf in his big golem suit.

"No, I want it!" said Alex, running over as well.

"Gosh, I guess you'll just have to share, chaps," said Porkins.

Alex grabbed the comic book from Porkins and blew the dust off it.

"Oh wow," she said, looking at the cover. "*Diary of a Skateboarding Cowman.*"

Carl grabbed the comic book off of her and read the blurb on the back:

"Timmy Blade, a young cowman, dreams of becoming a skateboarder. There's only one problem: the Mayor of his village has banned wheels. Can Timmy find some wheels, or will he spend the rest of his days walking instead of rolling? You'll have to read this book to find out!"

"Ooo," said Alex, "that sounds fun."

"Well, you're gonna have to read it after me," said Carl.

"No way!" said Alex.

"Knock it off, you two," said Dave. "Porkins is right — you need to share."

"Yes, Dad," said Carl.

"Wait," said Alex, looking confused, "is Dave your dad, Carl? I never knew that."

"Oh brother," said Carl.

"Wait, he's your brother?" said Alex. "Now I'm very confused."

After they'd made sure there was nothing else of value in the shack, they went back outside and tried to lead their horses into the mineshaft. But the horses dug in their feet, and refused to go any further.

"These chaps are scared of the mineshaft," said Porkins, rubbing his horse's nose. "Maybe this is a bad idea."

"Those horses are cowards," snapped Spidroth. "When I was a queen, my horses were so brave that they would even run into lava if I commanded them to."

"Did you ever command them to run into lava?" asked Carl.

"Of course not," said Spidroth. "But if I would have asked them to do it, they would have done it."

"I guess we'll have to leave the horses behind," said Dave. "I don't see what choice we have."

So, with heavy hearts, they all let their horses go. The horses were still spooked from the thought of going down the mineshaft, so they didn't need much encouragement. They quickly galloped off, disappearing towards the horizon.

"Bye, Robo-Horse!" Alex shouted. "Good luck!"

"Wait, you called your horse 'Robo-Horse'?" said Carl. "But it wasn't a robot."

"I named him after Robo-Steve," said Alex sadly.

Dave put an arm around Alex.

"That was very nice, Alex," Dave told her. "I'm sure Robo-Steve would have liked that."

"All right, that's enough of that," said Spidroth, giving Alex a suspicious look, "let's get this over with."

CHAPTER FIVE
The Abandoned Mine

"You know," said Carl, "we could just ride these minecarts down the tracks and see where they take us."

"Fool!" said Spidroth. "Do you really think it's a good idea to ride a minecart into a dark mine when we have no idea what awaits us?"

"It was just an idea," shrugged Carl.

But as they made their way into the mine, they saw that it wouldn't have been possible to ride a cart on the tracks anyway. The tracks were broken in places, with significant sections of rails missing. There was no light in the mine, so Dave put torches down as they went. The tunnels were narrow, with the occasional wooden beam to hold up the ceiling and lots of spiderwebs.

"How long do you reckon this place has been abandoned?" asked Alex. "Maybe this mine was built by those Old People as well."

"I don't think so," said Dave. "This place seems old, but not that old. And those books in the bookshelf weren't that old either."

"Oh yeah," said Alex.

"I wonder why the miners abandoned this mine," said Porkins.

"Maybe something scared them off," said Spidroth. "Maybe they dug up something they did not expect. There are foul beasts that make their home underground, in the darkest places of the world."

"Thanks, Spidroth," said Carl, "that's exactly what I need to hear while going down into a dark, spooky mineshaft. Thanks a lot."

"We'll be fine," said Dave. "With all five of us fighting together, there's nothing that can hurt us."

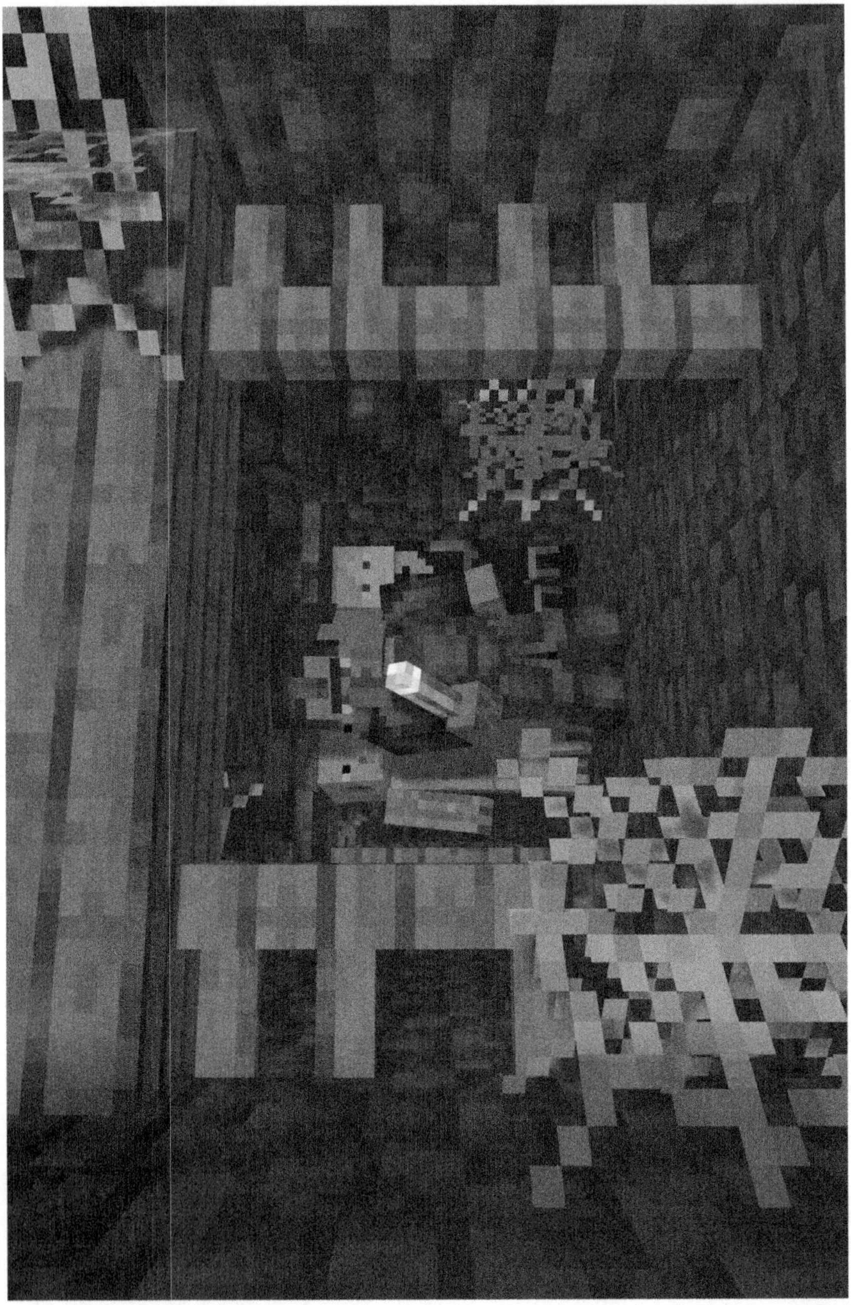

Suddenly an image flashed across Dave's eyes. He saw a vision of a corridor covered in hundreds and hundreds of tiny spiders, their eyes glowing in the darkness. And then, as quickly as it had appeared, the vision was gone.

"Are you all right, Dave?" Spidroth asked. Dave looked up. He realized he was leaning against the wall for support.

"I just had some sort of vision," Dave said. "I'm not sure what it was, but there were lots of spiders."

"It must have been the Sight," said Spidroth. "It must have been a glimpse of our future."

"I hope not," said Dave. "There were so many spiders. They were smaller than regular spiders, and their skin was a very dark blue."

"Cave spiders," said Carl. "Horrible little things. They're smaller than regular spiders, but they can poison you."

"Well, I guess we know where these webs came from," said Porkins, looking up at one of the cobwebs on the top of the corridor.

"Maybe we should go back," said Dave. "Maybe going down this mineshaft was a bad idea."

"We'll be fine," said Spidroth. "You said it yourself, Dave, no foe could stand against all five of us."

Suddenly, they heard a hissing noise up ahead. Dave hadn't placed another torch ahead of them yet, and a green creeper rushed towards them out of the darkness.

"Watch out!" Dave shouted.

With expert speed, Porkins pulled out his bow and *TWANG,* fired an arrow at the creeper. The creeper was pushed back, and Porkins quickly fired another two arrows into it. The creeper screamed and then disappeared with a *POOF,* leaving behind a pile of gunpowder.

"Well done, Porkins," said Alex. "That was cool!"

"You see?" Spidroth said to Dave. "No foe can stand against us. We are all seasoned warriors. Even the creeper isn't too terrible at fighting."

"Wow, Spidroth," said Carl, "I think that's the nicest thing you've ever said about me. And to return the favor, I want to tell you how much I love that bright red skin of yours. It makes you look just like a big, freaky apple."

"Okay, no fighting you two," said Dave, quickly speaking up before Spidroth and Carl started another argument. "Let's keep going."

The mineshaft consisted mostly of corridors, with the occasional set of wooden stairs leading further down. Every so often, they came across some creepers or zombies, but they had their weapons ready and swiftly defeated them. There were also many ores and valuable materials in the mineshaft, so Dave and his friends dug them up and put them in their backpacks.

"I don't know why you're digging up that redstone," Carl said to Dave when he saw Dave using his pickaxe on a block of redstone ore. "I've never seen you make anything with redstone. Not even once."

"Well, I want to learn eventually," said Dave. "So I want to make sure I have plenty of redstone when the time comes."

"Hmm," said Carl, "I'll believe it when I see it."

They also found lapis lazuli, coal, iron, gold, diamond and even some emerald ore, which Dave had never seen before.

"I can see why those chaps built a mine here," said Porkins. "There are so many different ores."

"Which makes it all the more suspicious that they abandoned it," said Carl.

The other strange thing about the mineshaft was that there were loads of spiderwebs, but they hadn't seen one spider.

If cave spiders are smaller than regular spiders, maybe

they're scared of us? thought Dave. But that didn't seem very likely. In the vision he'd had, the cave spiders hadn't seemed scared at all.

They eventually came to a large chamber with stone walls and a dirt floor. In the middle of the room were some sets of abandoned iron armor, and there were lots of arrows stuck in the wall.

"It looks like a battle took place here," said Spidroth.

Dave noticed a scrap of paper lying next to one of the empty sets of iron armor. He leaned down and picked it up.

"To anyone who finds this, please heed my warning," Dave read. "We got too greedy and dug too deep. When we found the cage, we thought it must be some kind of valuable artifact, and we tried to lift it. But no matter how hard we tried, we couldn't make it budge. And then the spiders came — they came from the cage itself, so many of them that we were overwhelmed. We tried to fight back, but they were too quick, and their bite was too venomous. The last of us are holed up in this chamber now, awaiting the final battle. I know the end will come soon: I can hear their feet, scuttling along the walls, the sound echoing down the corridors. The spiders are coming for us. The spiders are coming."

Dave finished reading. None of the others said anything. For once, even Carl didn't make a sarcastic comment.

"The cage they found sounds like a spawner," said Spidroth.

Dave had thought the same thing. He'd come across a spawner once before, at the start of his adventure when he, Porkins and Carl had ventured into the Nether to find blaze rods. They'd come across a blaze spawner in a nether fortress. It was a strange square device that looked like a cage, and blazes had come out of it.

"According to the legends, the Old People built the spawners," said Spidroth. "Using their technology, they could make any mob spawn at will."

"Come on," said Dave, "we need to get out of this mineshaft as soon as possible."

"I think that's a bally good idea, dear boy," said Porkins. "A bally good idea indeed."

"Right," said Carl, "but which way should we go?"

There were five passageways leading off from the chamber: the one they'd come through and four more.

Dave was about to make a decision, but then he heard scuttling: the sound of hundreds of tiny legs echoing down the corridors, getting closer and closer with every second.

"I think the spiders are coming," said Alex.

"I hate spiders," said Carl. "I hate them even more than I hate Spidroth."

That gave Dave an idea.

"Spidroth," he said, "can't you talk to the spiders? You can tell them that we don't mean them any harm."

"I think there are two problems with that plan," said Spidroth. "One, I don't think the spiders care if we mean them harm or not, I think they probably just want to eat us. And two, I've lost all my powers. I tried talking to a spider a couple of weeks back, but I couldn't."

"Well," Dave said, "I guess we'll just have to fight them the old fashion way,"

Dave pulled out his netherite sword. He was already wearing his netherite armor.

"Dave, I wouldn't mind a spare set of armor if you have one," said Spidroth.

"I thought the Lady Spidroth was too tough to wear armor?" Carl mocked.

"Normally, yes," said Spidroth. "But only a fool would fight venomous spiders without protection. All it takes is one bite, and you get poisoned."

"I don't want to get poisoned either," said Alex. "I guess I'd better armor up."

Alex reached into her backpack and pulled out some diamond armor, putting it on over her black ninja robes.

Dave had a spare set of netherite armor, so he gave it to Spidroth.

"Are you sure you don't want to wear anything stronger?" Dave asked Porkins. The pigman was wearing a set of brown leather armor. Porkins always said that leather gave him more freedom of movement for his archery.

"Yes, perhaps I should," said Porkins.

Dave found a set of diamond armor in his bag and gave it to Porkins. The pigman quickly put it on.

"Actually, Dave," said Carl, "I don't suppose you've got a spare helmet? My head will be a bit vulnerable when spiders start dropping from the ceiling."

Dave reached into his bag and pulled out an iron helmet, giving it to Carl. Then he pulled out two shields. Porkins needed both hands for his bow, and Alex used a sword in each hand, but Dave kept one shield for himself and gave the other to Spidroth.

"The lady Spidroth does not normally use a shield," said Spidroth, "but this time, I will make an exception."

Finally, all five of them were ready for battle. Dave and Spidroth had their netherite swords and their shields, Alex was dual-wielding two diamond swords, Porkins had his bow, and Carl had his netherite golem suit. The sound of scuttling spiders was getting louder every second. It was so loud it was almost deafening.

"Brace yourselves," said Dave. "Here they come!"

CHAPTER SIX
Spiders! Not Spiders Again! Why is it Always Spiders?

"Spiders!" whimpered Carl. "Not spiders again! Why is it always spiders?"

"To be fair," said Dave, "it isn't always spiders."

"Well, it seems like it's spiders the vast majority of the time," grumbled Carl.

The scuttling sound of spider legs was all around them now, coming from all five of the passageways that led into the chamber.

Then, all at once, the spiders flooded into the chamber, crawling along the ground and the walls and the ceiling: hundreds and hundreds of them, with small dark blue bodies and glowing red eyes.

As the spiders rushed to attack him, Dave swung his netherite sword in one hand and bashed the spiders with his shield with the other. Out of the corner of his eyes, he could see Porkins rapidly firing arrows at the spiders, Spidroth and Alex slashing at them with their swords, and Carl swinging his massive netherite arms, sending the spiders flying.

Dave felt something heavy land on his head and quickly pushed it off with his sword hand. He looked up to see that the spiders had crawled above them and were now dropping from the ceiling.

"Watch out above!" Dave shouted.

Dave raised his shield above his head to protect himself from falling spiders while using his sword to fight off the spiders on the ground. For every spider he slew, many more came scuttling towards him, hissing and baring their fangs.

If one of those things reaches me, they'll infect me with their poison, Dave thought. He had no idea how potent spider poison was, but he had no desire to find out.

Porkins was starting to struggle now. With only his bow, he didn't have much to defend himself with. He was kicking the spiders away with his diamond boots, but his kicks didn't do much damage.

"Here, Porkins," Dave shouted, reaching into his backpack and throwing Porkins a diamond sword. "Use this instead."

Porkins dropped his bow and grabbed the handle of the diamond sword.

"Much obliged, old chap," said Porkins, nodding his head at Dave. He began swinging the diamond sword, cutting through the spiders, and kicking the ones who managed to get close to him.

Talking of kicking, Alex was doing a lot of it: jumping and spinning through the air like a ninja, using both her diamond swords to cut the spiders down in swathes.

The Ninja Squad would be proud if they could see her now, thought Dave.

Spidroth, as ever, was putting up an incredible fight. Even wearing a full suit of netherite armor, she was swishing and swooping her sword around so fast that it looked like a blur, while defending herself with her shield.

Carl was holding his own as well, sending hordes of spiders flying backward every time he swung his huge arms. The helmet was coming in useful too, as spiders kept dropping down onto his head and his golem suit. Every time that happened, Carl picked them off with his golem hands and threw them against the wall.

Dave had no idea how many spiders he'd slain, but his hands were hurting, and sweat was pouring down his forehead.

"Keep going, everyone!" he shouted. "We can win this!"

And then Dave felt a sharp pain on the back of his neck. He reached around and felt a spider on his back, and quickly shoved it off. But it was too late, the spider had bitten him.

Dave began to feel woozy. His legs felt weak, and he fell to his knees.

"Dave!" yelled Spidroth, running in front of him to defend him from the spiders.

"Poison," Dave gasped, "I've been poisoned..."

He could feel the poison surging through him, burning him up from the inside. He'd never felt pain like it.

"Dave, I know it hurts, but you've got to keep fighting!" shouted Spidroth. "Get up, fool, get up!"

Using all his remaining strength, Dave pushed himself to his feet. He raised his sword and shield, and ran towards the spiders, ignoring the pain searing through his body, and fighting as hard as he could. His limbs hurt every time he swung his sword, but he kept fighting, pushing through the pain.

"Arrrrrrgh!!!!" Dave roared.

The five of them fought on, slaying spider after spider until, finally, the spiders stopped pouring through the passageways, and the battle was won. The ground was covered with bits of string.

Dave tried to say something, to tell the others that they'd done a good job, but instead, he collapsed. He couldn't fight the poison any longer and his vision was starting to blur.

"Dave!" Spidroth shouted, kneeling down next to him.

"He needs a potion," said Carl. "What cures poison?"

"Milk normally does it," said Spidroth. "Does anyone have any milk?"

But no-one had.

"Come on, creeper, pick him up," Spidroth said to Carl. "We need to get him out of here."

The last thing Dave remembered was Carl picking him up in his big netherite golem arms, and then he passed out.

CHAPTER SEVEN
Canyon Town

Dave woke up in bed. He was in an unfamiliar room with sandstone walls.

"Oh, you're awake!" he heard a voice say. A cow-woman in a long white coat appeared, looking down at him.

"Where am I?" Dave asked.

"You're in Canyon Village," said the cow-woman. "Your friends brought you here. It's lucky they did, as that poison had got deep into your system. Thankfully, I managed to cure you with some milk and honey. I'm Gabby, by the way. I'm this village's healer."

Just then, the door to the room swung open and all of Dave's friends entered and rushed over to his bedside.

"You're okay!" said Spidroth, placing her hand on Dave's forehead. "Thank goodness!"

Then, realizing what she was doing, Spidroth quickly took her hand away and looked awkward.

"We thought you were a goner there, for a second," said Carl. "Welcome back to the land of the living."

Dave was feeling much better now, so, with Gabby's permission, he got out of bed and followed his friends out into the village.

Canyon Village was, as its name implied, a village in the middle of the canyon. It was a quiet village, with only a few cowmen and cow-women walking around the small sandstone buildings, and a surprisingly large number of iron golems. Next to the village well, a wandering trader in blue, gold and red robes was selling his wares to some cowmen. But, to Dave's surprise, the trader wasn't a cowman, he was an illager.

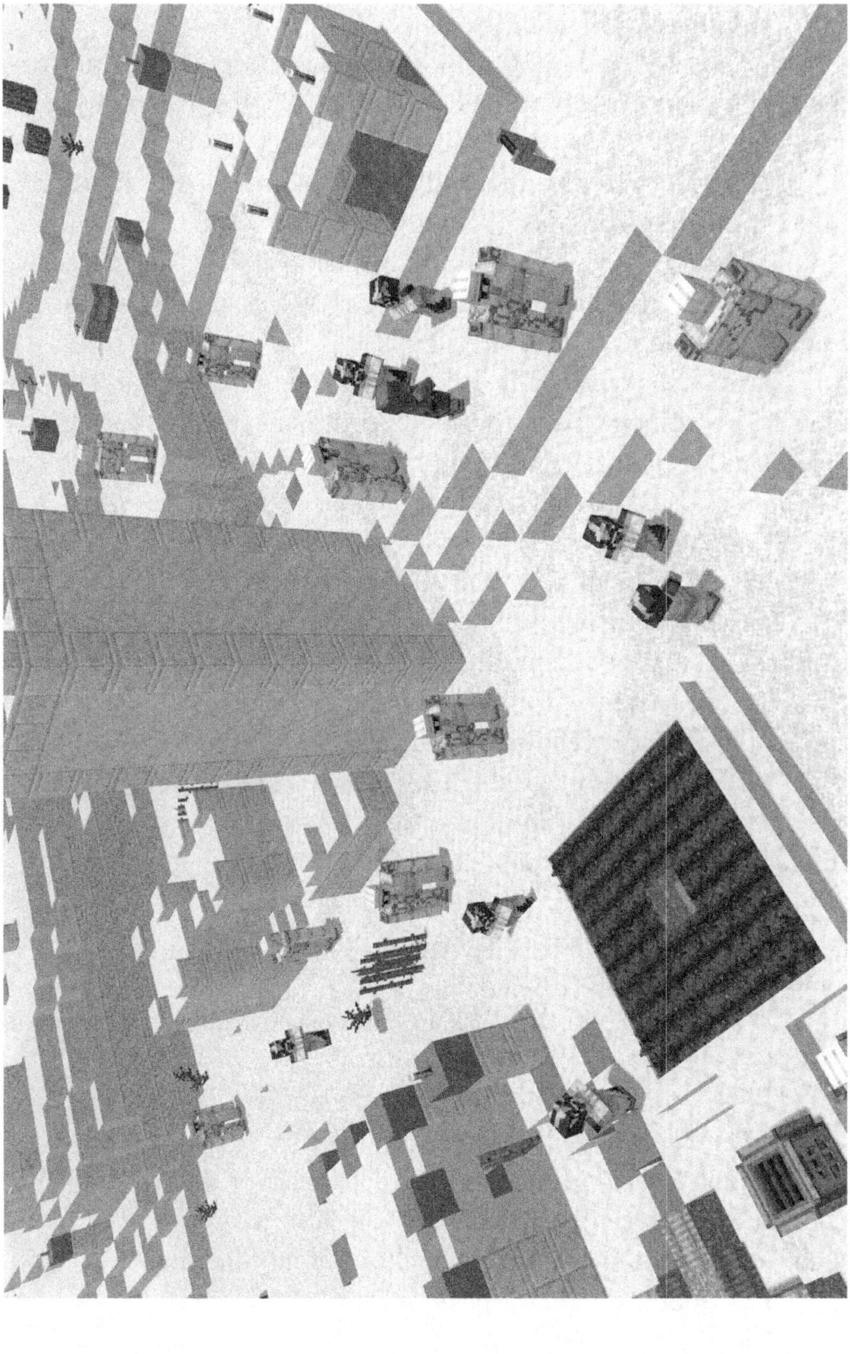

"Do you get many illagers in these parts?" Dave asked Gabby, who had followed them outside.

"A fair few," said Gabby. "Most of them are good folk, but we've been having a lot of trouble with Mad Mulligan and his gang recently."

"Those illagers who attacked the yellow creeper guy mentioned Mad Mulligan," said Alex.

"Mad Mulligan is a local outlaw," said Gabby. "His gang have been causing trouble in these parts for years. That's why we have so many iron golems to protect us."

Dave was surprised to hear that illagers had made it to the cowmen continent. Back on Dave's continent, the villagers didn't even believe that there was any land to the west: but illagers had obviously been traveling to the cowman continent for a while.

"I don't suppose a yellow creeper or an elderly white cowman have passed through here recently?" Carl asked.

"As a matter of fact, we did see a yellow creeper yesterday," said Gabby. "It was the strangest thing: we saw something with wings flying above us, and at first we thought it was a big bat, but it had a normal body and a yellow creeper head."

"Which direction was it flying?" Dave asked.

"That way," said Gabby, pointing. "No idea where it was going, though. It's nothing but desert out there."

Gabby went back inside, leaving Dave and the others alone.

"So, are we gonna see if we can find the Trident of Emeros?" said Carl. "It could be fun."

"Fool," said Spidroth. "We are already on a quest, or have you forgotten?"

"Well, this could be a side quest," said Carl. "Come on, Dave, you remember how cool that trident was."

"I don't know," said Dave." It feels like we've done nothing but side-questing recently. Besides, that yellow creeper already has a head start on us, so we'll probably leave empty-handed."

"Fair enough," said Carl, sounding disappointed.

"Okay, I guess we can put it to a vote," said Dave. "Who votes that we should go on a quest to find the trident?"

Carl and Alex raised their hands.

"Looks like it's three against two, fools," said Spidroth. "Now come on, let's get a move on."

"Actually, um, I'm still not sure," said Porkins. "Going on a quest to find this trident sounds like it might be fun."

"Come on, Porkins," said Carl, "you know you want to."

After a moment's hesitation, Porkins raised his trotter in the air.

"Yes!" said Carl.

"Dave, you're the leader," said Spidroth, "you should order them to stop this foolishness. And if they disobey, you should kill one of them to set an example. That's what a true leader does."

"Um, I'm not going to kill anyone," said Dave. "I guess we've lost the vote. Let's go and try to find the trident."

Dave really wanted to get back on track and find the end portal, but he also didn't want to force his group to do anything that they didn't want to do. They'd been on the road a long time since they'd left Spectrite City, and going on a quest might be good for them.

Dave had been asleep in bed most of the day and the sun was starting to set, but Carl insisted that they head off now, as they had to hurry if they wanted to stand a chance at catching up with Creepo Jones. So they set off by foot, journeying across the dark desert, with only the moon to light their way.

CHAPTER EIGHT
The Pyramid

"Porkins, to your left!" Alex shouted.

Porkins turned around and fired an arrow at the green creeper that was slinking towards him out of the darkness.

Dave heard the clacking of bones and turned around to see three skeletons aiming their bows at him. He quickly dived behind a cactus, avoiding the arrows just in time.

Carl and Spidroth were fighting off a horde of zombies, but they weren't regular zombies, they were husks: zombies with grey-brown skin who wore rags and rotted bandages.

"This is what we get for traveling at night," said Spidroth angrily. "This is all your fault, Carl."

"It's just a few mobs," said Carl. "It's no big deal."

After defeating the mobs, they continued on walking, placing torches down as they went, but even so, they constantly had to fight off attacks from more monsters. Husks, skeletons, creepers and spiders would all come out from the darkness to attack them. By the morning, Dave and his friends were exhausted, and there was still no sign of the pyramid.

"Look," said Porkins, pointing. "How come those brown zombie chaps aren't burning in the sunlight?"

A group of husks was stumbling around one of the nearby sand dunes.

"Husks don't burn in sunlight," said Alex. "I'm not sure how I know that, but I'm pretty sure it's true."

"Wait," said Dave, putting up his hand to indicate that they should stop. "Look up there."

In the distance, standing on the top of a small hill, was Creepo Jones — the yellow creeper — wearing his suit with the arms and legs and holding the Stone of Nuntuck. He was standing on the edge of a vast, empty sand valley, with the stone held above his head. He was chanting in some strange language that Dave didn't understand.

Suddenly, the stone began to crack, and red light shone from the cracks. Then it exploded, leaving behind a small red ruby that floated above Creepo Jones's hands.

"It's working!" he yelled in triumph. "It's working!"

The ruby flew off into the distance, then landed in the middle of the valley, disappearing into the sand. For a moment nothing happened, and then the ground began to shake.

"W-w-what's happening?" said Carl.

Creepo Jones turned around, noticing Dave and the others for the first time.

"Aha!" he said. "I'm glad you're here to witness this historical moment. For the first time in ten thousand years, the tomb of King Nuntuck will be seen by mortal eyes once more!"

Something began to rise up out of the sand in the middle of the valley. At first, there was just a small stone spire, then more and more of it emerged, shaking the ground as it rose.

"It looks like some sort of giant pyramid," said Porkins, in awe.

"It doesn't just look like some sort of giant pyramid," grinned Creepo Jones. "It *is* some sort of giant pyramid."

Finally, the colossal pyramid finished rising up from the sand. It was the largest building that Dave had ever seen: far bigger than any of the buildings in Diamond City had been. It towered over the desert, casting them all in shadow. The pyramid itself looked like it was made from blocks of sandstone and at the bottom of it was a huge entranceway, flanked by two colossal sandstone towers. On the front of the towers were symbols made from some sort of orange material, which Dave guessed must be orange terracotta.

"Behold!" said Creepo Jones excitedly. "The Pyramid of Nuntuck! Inside those walls are treasures beyond imagining."

"What about baked potatoes?" asked Carl. "Will there be baked potatoes in there?"

Creepo Jones gave him a funny look.

"Master! Master!"

They all looked around to see Milo the cowman running towards them. His clothes were torn and covered in sand, and it looked like he hadn't slept.

"Oh, thank goodness I found you, Master," said Milo, falling to his knees and getting his breath back. "And I can't believe you finally found it – the great Pyramid of Nuntuck!"

"Yes, I am pretty amazing," said Creepo Jones.

"Right," said Carl, "are we going in, or not?"

"Well, I'm going in," said Creepo Jones, "but you're not. I'm the one who found this pyramid, so the treasures all mine – including the trident."

"Yes, but we did save your life," said Carl.

"So you keep saying," said Creepo Jones. "But that's not the way I remember it."

Suddenly, there was a rumbling all around them, and husks began to emerge from the sand: hundreds and hundreds of husks.

"It's the Ancients!" whimpered Milo. "They're coming to defend their king's tomb!"

Dave had never seen so many hostile mobs in one place: more

and more husks kept crawling out of the ground, a gigantic army of them.

"Well, lads," said Creepo Jones, "once again, this has been fun, but I must be going."

He pressed a button on his wrist and the elytra opened up behind his back.

"Master, please take me with you!" cried Milo.

"Sorry, Milo," said Creepo Jones, "good luck!"

Then he pulled out a firework rocket from his pocket and attached it to the back of his elytra.

WOOOOM!!!!! The firework exploded, and Creepo Jones rocketed off into the sky, flying towards the top of the pyramid.

"Master!!!" Milo yelled. "Come back!!!"

Dave pulled out his sword and shield, getting ready to fight as the hundreds and hundreds of husks began staggering towards them.

"Everyone stand together," said Dave, "we'll fight them as a unit. It's the only way we'll stand a chance."

"I don't want to die!" whimpered Milo.

"Then get behind us, fool," said Spidroth. "If you are too much of a coward to fight, then don't get in our way."

"I think that's a good idea," said Milo, running behind the others.

Dave took a deep breath, ready to do battle. He had no idea how they were going to defeat this many husks, but it didn't look like they had a choice.

"Look, I know we're all pretty awesome fighters," said Carl, "but there's just too many of them. And these guys aren't like cave spiders — they won't go down so easily."

"But what else can we do?" said Alex.

"Well, first we can buy ourselves some time," said Carl. "Dave, give me your backpack."

Dave handed his backpack to Carl. Carl quickly reached into it and pulled out some blocks, running around as quickly as he could and building a wall three blocks high around them. In a few seconds he'd finished, and the six of them were protected behind the wall.

They could hear the husks trying to bash through outside. Thankfully, Carl had made sure to build the wall out of strong blocks like Cobblestone.

"Well, we're safe for now," said Porkins. "But what do we do next?"

"Um, if I may make a suggestion?" said Milo.

They all looked around at him.

"Come on, fool," snapped Spidroth, "we haven't got time to waste."

"Yes, time really is of the essence, old boy," said Porkins. "That wall won't be able to keep those husk chaps out for long."

"What I was going to say," said Milo, "was that if this pyramid is like other pyramids that my master and I have excavated, then there will be a lot more of it under the surface. Perhaps beneath our very feet."

"You mean that isn't the whole thing?" said Alex, looking up at the huge pyramid.

"I don't think so," said Milo. "I believe if we dig down, we might reach the lower levels of the pyramid."

"Then let's get digging," said Dave, pulling out a diamond spade. He plunged his spade into the sand and began to dig.

CHAPTER NINE
Inside the Pyramid

Dave, Porkins, Spidroth and Alex all began to dig diagonally down with their spades. Carl's golem hands were too big to use a spade and Milo didn't have one.

They dug down, down, down. It was tricky, as every time they dug through a sand block, the other sand blocks above it would fall down. It would have been far easier if they had dug straight down, but Dave knew from bitter experience that that was a bad idea. On the very first night of his adventure, he had dug straight down and almost fallen into a lake of lava.

Finally, they reached some blocks of sandstone.

"This must be the roof of the pyramid," said Milo. "We've found it!"

"How do you know?" said Porkins. "This could just be normal sandstone. You normally find blocks of it under sand."

"But this is chiseled sandstone," said Milo, brushing it with his hoof. "This is it — dig, dig, dig!"

Dave pulled out his pickaxe.

"Be careful, everyone," he said. "We don't want to fall into a bottomless pit or a river of lava."

Suddenly, something blocked the light coming in the tunnel, and they turned around to see the army of husks stumbling down the diagonal slope towards them.

"Looks like those idiots have broken through," said Carl. "Get digging!"

Dave quickly attacked the blocks of sandstone with his diamond pickaxe. He broke through one, only to find another sandstone block beneath it. Then he broke through that one and found another sandstone block.

"If this is the ceiling to the pyramid, it's pretty thick," said Dave.

"Just hurry up!" shouted Carl.

The husks had reached them now, and the others were fighting them off while Dave dug. Spidroth, Porkins and Alex were all firing arrows at the husks, to keep them at bay, but more and more kept pushing their way down the narrow tunnel.

"Here," said Dave, passing Milo a pickaxe, "make yourself useful!"

Milo and Dave got digging, going further and further down, through layer and layer of chiseled sandstone. Finally, Milo cut through a sandstone block, and instead of seeing another sandstone block below it, he saw nothing but darkness.

"We're through!" the cowman said happily, but he was so excited that he accidentally toppled over the edge.

"Waaaaaaaaaa!" Milo screamed, as he fell down into the darkness.

"Milo!" shouted Dave.

For a moment, Dave heard nothing, but then Milo shouted back out of the darkness:

"I'm okay! It's a long fall, but I'm okay."

"Come on, everyone," Dave shouted to the others, "let's go!"

Dave hacked away with his pickaxe to make the hole big enough for all of them.

"You first, Carl," said Dave.

"Why me?" said Carl. "I'm not jumping down into that dark pit."

"It has to be you first as you're the heaviest," said Dave. "We don't want you landing on the rest of us."

"How rude," said Carl, but he jumped down into the darkness nonetheless. "Waaaaaaaa!" Carl screamed, then *THOOM,* there was the sound of something heavy hitting the ground.

"I'm okay!" Carl called up.

"Oww," groaned Milo. "I'm not."

"Carl!" said Dave. "Did you land on Milo?!"

"I didn't mean to," said Carl.

"Dave, dear boy, can we hurry this up a bit?" said Porkins.

Dave turned around and saw Porkins, Alex and Spidroth still fighting off the husks with their bows, but the husks were pushing nearer and nearer.

"Come on, everyone, jump!" said Dave.

Porkins, Alex and Spidroth all put their bows away then ran down towards the hole and jumped into it. Finally, Dave was the last one left. He took a deep breath to steady his nerves, and then he jumped: down into the darkness.

WHAM! Dave landed on the hard ground. His knees hurt from the landing, but he had no time to worry about that. Far above them, he could see the hole that he'd dug, and husks were pouring through it, falling through the air towards them.

"It's raining husks!" said Alex. "That's so cool!"

Dave quickly reached into his bag and placed down some torches. His friends were all gathered around him, but the room they were in was so big that he couldn't even see the walls.

"Run!" shouted Dave.

Dave and the others began running, narrowly avoiding getting crushed by the hundreds falling husks. As they ran through the dark room, Dave placed torches down. He turned around and saw the husks were beginning to get their bearings and were chasing after them.

"Those zombie chaps don't give up do they?" said Porkins.

"Well, they're defending their king's tomb," said Milo. "They won't give up until we're dead."

"Their king's tomb?" said Dave, feeling confused. "I thought you said the Old People built this pyramid?"

"Old People?" said Milo. "Oh, you mean the Ancients! The husks *are* the Ancients."

"Can we continue this history lesson later?" said Carl. "Preferably when we're not running for our lives!"

They reached a solid sandstone wall, but there was no sign of any doorway or any way to leave the room.

"We'll have to make our way around the wall until we find the door," said Milo.

"I've got a better idea," said Dave. He began hacking at the sandstone wall with his pickaxe, building them a hole to fit through. When the hole was big enough, they all ran through, finding themselves in another pitch-black chamber. They began running through this room, Dave placing torches as they ran, and they passed mountains of treasure: huge piles of gold ingots, emeralds and diamonds and lots of strange artifacts and weapons.

"My gosh," gasped Milo, "I could spend a hundred years in here, cataloging all these treasures."

"You do that," said Carl. "The rest of us will keep running from the husks."

Finally, they came to a wide set of stairs. The top of the stairs was so high up that it was covered in darkness, but they ran up anyway. As they ran, Dave looked behind and saw that the husks were getting further and further away.

"I think we're losing them," said Dave. "They can't keep up with us."

The stairs finally came to an end, ending in a huge doorway that led into a corridor. Dave and the others began running through the corridor but suddenly Milo yelled "STOP!"

They all stopped.

"Look," said Milo, pointing.

Dave placed a torch on the wall, and then he could see what Milo was pointing at. The corridor ahead of them was made mostly of sandstone, but every so often, there was a gray stone slab on the floor, and there were gray blocks with holes in them on the walls.

"Pressure plates and dispensers," said Alex.

"That's right," said Milo. "If we accidentally step on one of those plates, those dispensers on the wall will shoot us full of arrows."

"What kind of idiot would build a corridor like this?" asked Carl.

"An idiot who wants to keep people away," said Milo. "When the Ancients built this pyramid, they built it to keep people out."

Dave heard a noise behind them. He looked around and saw the husks were starting to catch up with them, slowly stumbling up the staircase.

"Okay, we'd better get a move on," said Dave.

And so, they began to walk down the corridor. The corridor was only three blocks wide, and there were lots of pressure plates on the floor, scattered about in different places, so they had to weave their way around them. Because he was the biggest, Carl went last, being careful not to put his big golem feet in the wrong place.

The corridor seemed to go on forever. Dave kept putting torches down as they went, but there seem to be no end to the pressure plates and the dispensers on the wall. And soon, he heard the shuffling of hundreds of feet behind them. He turned around to see that the husks had reached the corridor and were starting to follow them.

"Well, at least the pressure plates and the arrows will take those bozos out," said Carl. But he was wrong – when the husks stepped on the pressure plates, nothing happened.

"Oh, come on," said Carl.

"Maybe the pressure plates don't work," suggested Porkins. "Their redstone circuits could have broken over time."

"I doubt it," said Milo. "The Ancients built things to last. If the husks are here to defend this pyramid, maybe there's an enchantment on them and they can't activate the plates."

Dave and the others continued down the corridor, weaving in and out of the pressure plates, but the husks were quickly catching up with them. The husks may have been slower, but they didn't have to avoid the plates, so they were just marching straight down the corridor.

"I can see the end of the corridor!" Alex said excitedly.

Dave looked and saw that she was right: they had nearly reached the end of the pressure plate and dispenser corridor. He only hoped that the room beyond was a bit less dangerous.

Moving as fast as they could, the gang weaved past the final few pressure plates and walked into another huge dark room. However, the husks had almost caught up with them and would soon be in the room as well.

"Are we gonna have to keep running from these idiots forever?"

said Carl, looking back at the husks.

"I've got a better idea," said Spidroth. She walked up to the entrance to the corridor, then quickly slammed her foot down on one of the pressure plates, before moving it out of the way again.

As soon as the pressure plate was pressed, the dispensers along the walls of the corridor began blasting out arrows: hundreds and hundreds of arrows all down the length of the corridor. The husks began *BURR*ing in pain and panic as they were shot full of arrows. It was a husk massacre, with hundreds of the gray-brown zombies dying every second. Before long, all the husks had been slain, leaving piles of rotten flesh all over the floor.

"Wow, Spidroth," said Carl, in awe, "that was... That was pretty ruthless."

"Yes, well, I'm a pretty ruthless person," said Spidroth. "You'd do well to remember that, creeper."

And for once, Carl didn't dare to make a sarcastic comment.

CHAPTER TEN
The Riddle

With the husks now dead, the journey became much easier. They journeyed through dark chambers full of treasure, long staircases and more corridors. Every so often, there would be more traps — pressure plates or tripwires on the floor, deep pits they had to walk around and more — so they walked slowly, taking their time as they journeyed higher and higher in the pyramid. Everywhere they went was pitch black, so Dave had to keep placing torches down, although he tried not to put too many, as he didn't want to run out. The last thing they wanted was to be stuck in this huge dark pyramid without any light.

"My master will be at the top of the pyramid," Milo told them, as they walked over a bridge that led across a dark pit. "According to the legends, King Nuntuck's body is kept there, along with his most priceless treasures. That's where the Trident will be.

"His body?" said Dave. "If he's dead, won't his body have disappeared?"

"The Ancients had ways of preserving the dead," said Milo. "They were obsessed with immortality. That's what led to the creation of the husks: the ancients who built the pyramids were experimenting with ways to keep themselves alive forever."

"So these Ancient chaps turned into husks?" asked Porkins.

"Some of them," said Milo. "Research suggests that the kings and queens of the desert regions experimented on their people, and those experiments became the husks."

"I always thought that husks were just desert versions of zombies," said Alex.

"Well, yes they are," said Milo, "but, of course, zombies came much later. According to all available evidence, the zombies were created by Stephen the wizard. And that was thousands of years after the husks were created."

"Who the heck is Stephen the wizard?" said Carl.

"The wizard who caused The Great Fall," said Milo. "He's the one who brought the civilization of the Ancients to an end. In his rage he cursed them, turning them into the zombies and the skeletons."

"Wait a minute," said Carl, "so zombies and skeletons are the same species?"

"They don't look very similar," said Porkins.

"Shush," said Dave, holding up a hand. "I think I can see something. Carl, look up ahead — can you see anything in the darkness?"

Carl squinted.

"There's definitely something there," whispered the creeper. "It looks like some kind of creature... A really big creature, sleeping in the middle of the bridge."

"Is it a ravager?" whispered Porkins. "I once biffed a ravager in the face, and I can do the same to this chap. Biff, baff, boff!"

"It's bigger than a ravager," Carl whispered back. "It looks more like... an ocelot. A really, really big ocelot."

Suddenly they heard a deep rumbling sound from the darkness ahead of them.

"It's waking up!" Carl whispered. "I think it's purring!"

The bridge began to shake with the sound of huge, heavy footsteps as something big slowly walked towards them.

"Shouldn't we run?" whimpered Milo.

"There's no point," said Carl, "that thing could outrun us in one second." He tensed his netherite arms, getting ready to do battle. Dave and the others all pulled out their weapons.

"Nee shall vo tal," said a deep voice, so loud that it echoed across the chamber. "Ree toh far par!"

And then, a gigantic ocelot, at least ten times the size of a ravager, emerged from the darkness, looking down at them.

"Nee shall vo tal," the ocelot repeated. "Ree toh far par!"

"Um, does anyone speak giant ocelot?" said Carl.

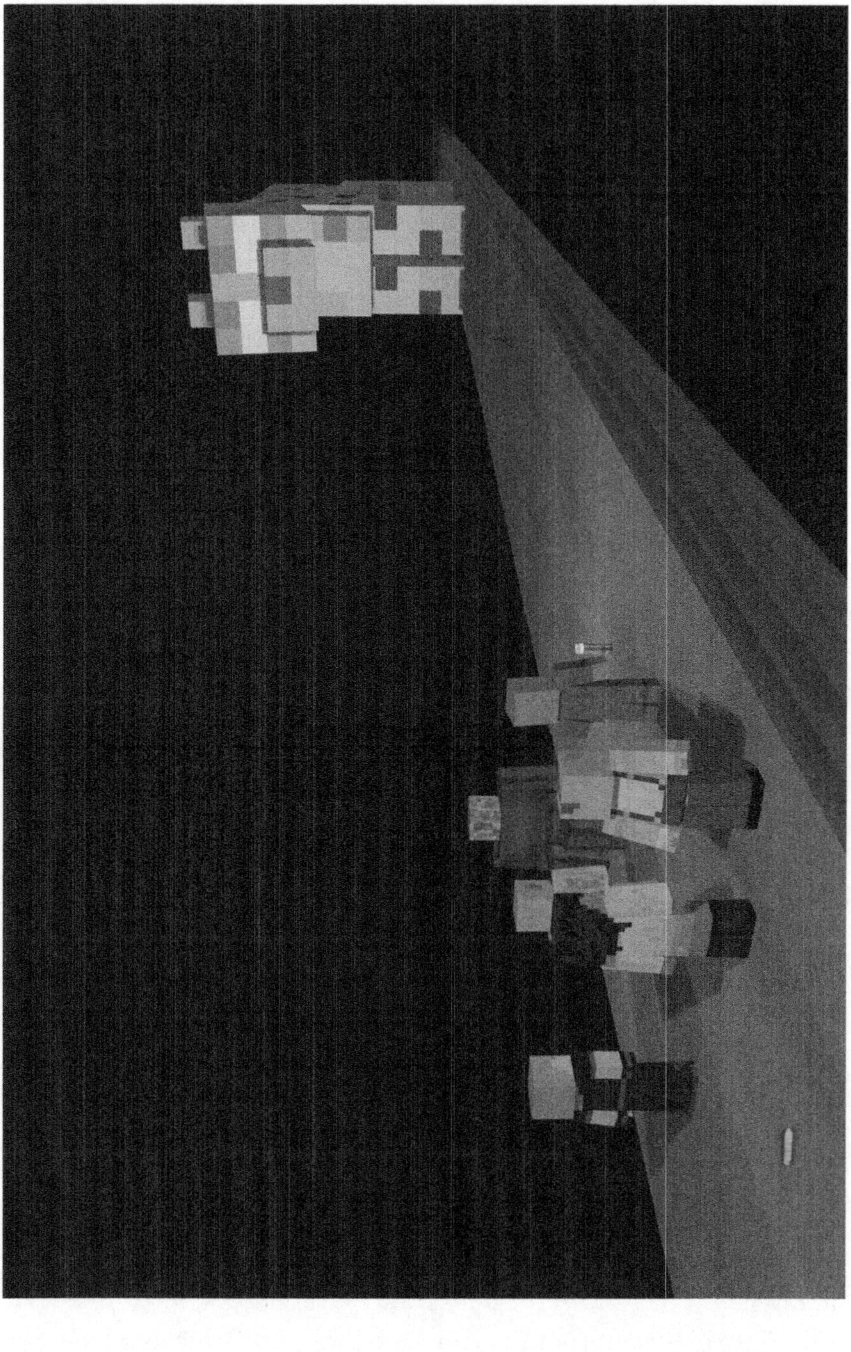

"T-t-that's the language of the old kings of the desert," said Milo, hiding behind Carl's netherite armor and shaking with fear.

"What's it saying?" Dave asked.

"I-i-it says that if we are to pass, we must answer its riddle," said Milo.

"Fine," said Spidroth. "Come on, ocelot, ask us your riddle. Lady Spidrothbrine will solve it in seconds, mark my words!"

"I'm not going to translate any of that," said Milo. "I don't think it's wise to antagonize the giant ocelot."

"For once, I agree with you," said Carl.

"Vorr soo narr la," said the ocelot, in its deep, booming voice, "Doo ra ta nah?"

"Was that the riddle?" Dave asked Milo.

"Y-yes it was," said Milo. "Um, let me see if I can translate it. Um, 'soo' means 'four'... 'la' can mean either 'morning' or 'beginning'..."

"Just hurry up, you nerd!" said Carl.

"Right, okay," said Milo. "If I've translated it correctly, I think the riddle is this: What walks on four feet in the morning, two in the afternoon and three at night?"

"Well, it's obviously a creeper," said Carl. "What else has four legs?"

"Pigs do," said Porkins. "Maybe it's a pig."

"Fools!" said Spidroth. "You're thinking about it too literally. The key to answering riddles is to look beyond the obvious, to the hidden meaning inside."

"So what's the answer then, clever-boots?" asked Carl.

"I don't know yet," said Spidroth. "But I'm sure I'll have it solved in a matter of moments."

"What was the second bit?" Alex asked. "The bit about two legs?"

"Um, I'll just repeat the whole thing again," said Milo. "What walks on four feet in the morning, two in the afternoon and three at night?"

"Two in the afternoon," said Alex, thinking. "Chickens have two legs. Maybe it's a chicken?"

Dave tried to think through the riddle, but he had no idea what the answer was. When he'd been a boy, the other children in the village had often made up riddles for fun, but Dave had never been very good at them.

"So the last bit is about something that has three legs," said Carl, thoughtfully. "What has three legs?"

"A horse that's been in an accident?" suggested Alex.

Once again, Dave thought back to the riddles he'd heard as a child, trying to remember if any of them had been similar to this one. Old Man Johnson had always been fond of riddles as well, telling them to the children and then hobbling off on his walking stick, leaving them to think about what the answer was.

Walking stick... thought Dave. The thought of Old Man Johnson's walking stick sparked an idea in his mind. *Three legs... when an old man uses a walking stick, it's a bit like having three legs.*

But why would an old man only have three legs at night? Why would he have four in the morning and two in the afternoon? It didn't make any sense. And then Dave thought back to how he had played with the other children, and how they'd crawl together when they were babies...

Crawling... thought Dave. *You crawl on four legs...*

And then, like a bolt of lightning, the solution to the riddle appeared fully-formed in Dave's head.

"I've got it!" said Dave excitedly. "It's a villager — when a villager is a baby it crawls around on four legs, when it grows up it walks around on two legs, and then when it gets old, it uses a walking stick! The answer is a villager!"

"Good show, Dave," said Porkins. "By jove, I think you've got it!"

"Yes, impressive," said Spidroth. "Although in a few more moments I would have got it as well."

"Okay, I'll translate," said Milo nervously. "Ood doo farr."

For a moment, the ocelot said nothing. Then it gave its reply:

"Yoh la," it said. "woo no das."

"Ah," said Milo, his white fur turning even more pale than

usual. "I fear there may be a bit of a cultural misunderstanding."

"So is 'villager' not the right answer?" said Dave.

"I'm afraid not," said Milo. "It slipped my mind that in the time of the Ancients, there were no villagers. So this creature has no idea what a villager is. The answer is actually a 'human' — which is what the Ancients called themselves."

"Wor lar tag," the ocelot growled, baring its teeth.

"So what happens now?" asked Alex. "Is it going to give us another riddle?"

"I'm afraid not," said Milo. "It's going to kill us."

"Nice one, Dave," said Carl. "This is what you get for trying to be clever."

CHAPTER ELEVEN
When Ocelots Attack

Porkins put an arrow on his bow and strung it back, aiming at the ocelot.

"Not another step closer, dear boy," said Porkins, "or you're jolly well getting an arrow in the eye."

The ocelot growled and prowled slowly towards them as they began backing away.

"I'll do it!" Porkins warned. "And I assure you, I'm a bally good shot."

But the ocelot kept coming.

"As you wish," said Porkins. He let go of his bowstring and the arrow went flying forward, hitting the ocelot right in the eye... But it just bounced off.

"Ah," said Porkins. "I don't think arrows are going to do the trick, chaps."

"Anyone else got any bright ideas?" asked Spidroth.

"We could try running," suggested Alex.

"We'd never outrun that thing," said Dave.

But what else were they going to do? There was nowhere else to escape to: they were on a bridge above a bottomless pit, with nowhere to go but back.

"I've got an idea," whispered Carl. He reached into his golem suit and pulled out some tiny red blocks. He began passing them to the others as they backed away from the ocelot.

Dave looked down at the blocks that Carl had given him.

"TNT?" said Dave. "Where did you get all this TNT from?"

"Well, I got the gunpowder from all those creepers we had to slay in the mine," said Carl, "and while you were unconscious in bed, back in Canyon Village, I dug up some sand and crafted some

TNT. You never know when you're gonna need some TNT."

"I hate to break it to you, creeper," said Spidroth, "but if an arrow in the eye doesn't hurt this beast, I doubt that an explosion would hurt it either."

"I'm not trying to hurt it," said Carl, "I want to destroy the bridge below it, so it falls into the abyss."

"Hmph," said Spidroth, "for once, that's not a terrible plan."

"Thanks Spidroth," said Carl. "If it works, maybe you can give me a kiss. You gave Dave one, so it's only fair."

"Carl!" snapped Dave, feeling his cheeks glow red. "If we're going to do your plan, we'd better do it now."

The ocelot was starting to walk towards them faster, its teeth bared and a deep growl coming from its mouth. It looked like it was ready to run up and pounce on them at any moment, and once it did, they would have nowhere to escape to.

"Okay," said Carl, "start placing your TNT blocks down now."

"Once that monster sees the TNT, won't it know what we're doing?" asked Porkins.

"I'm hoping that it won't know what TNT is," said Carl. "Milo, what do you think?"

"Um, I've no idea, I'm afraid," said Milo. "I imagine that a magical beast like this has a limited capacity for thought: it can ask its riddle and it knows to kill people if they answer incorrectly, but maybe it doesn't have much intelligence apart from that. although that's just a guess."

"Well, I guess it's the only plan we've got," said Dave. "Let's start laying the TNT."

So as they walked backward, they began placing TNT blocks down along the bridge in a scattered fashion. As they placed the tiny TNT blocks onto the ground, they grew to full-size. Thankfully, the ocelot ignored the TNT blocks, focusing its gaze on Dave and the others. Eventually, the ocelot had walked forward enough that there were TNT blocks underneath its belly.

"Dave, I hope you've got some flint and steel," Carl hissed.

Dave pulled out some flint and steel from his bag.

"Here goes," he said. "When I light the first TNT block,

everyone run."

The others all nodded.

Dave scraped the flint and steel across the nearest TNT block. Instantly it began to flash white. For the first time, the ocelot noticed the TNT, and roared angrily.

"Run!" Dave shouted.

They all ran. Dave heard the pounding of heavy footsteps and turned to see that the ocelot was running after them, it's jaws open and ready to gobble them up.

DOOOOOM!!!!

The first TNT block exploded, creating a chain reaction: all the TNT blocks began flashing, and then they exploded in a chorus of *DOOOOOM*s. The bridge underneath the ocelot was destroyed in the explosion, and the ocelot started to fall.

For a moment, it looked like the ocelot had been defeated, and that Carl's plan had worked, but as it fell, the ocelot grabbed hold of the side of the broken bridge with one of its paws. It roared angrily, trying to pull itself back up.

"Oh no, you don't," said Carl. He ran over to the ocelot's paw and, using all his golem strength, tried to push the paw off the side of the broken bridge. But the ocelots' claws were dug in deep.

"Help me!" Carl shouted.

The others ran over, and they all began pushing the ocelot's paw. The only one who didn't join in was Milo, who just stood behind them looking terrified.

"Milo, we need your help!" Dave shouted. "Please!"

Milo took a deep breath, then ran forward and helped them push the paw. Finally, the ocelot lost its grip, and the paw came loose. With an angry scream, the ocelot fell down, down, down into the dark abyss below.

Dave breathed a big sigh of relief.

"Well done, Carl," he said. "Well done, everyone."

The ocelot was defeated, but now they had a new problem: the bridge was broken. So Dave got some blocks out of his bag, and slowly and carefully, built a three-block wide bridge across the dark abyss, the others following carefully behind him.

When they finally reached the safety of the other side of the bridge, they continued their journey. At the end of the bridge, they came to another set of stairs, but this time they could see light at the top of the stairs: a green light.

"I think we're nearly at the top of the pyramid," said Milo. "Master Creepo must be up there."

"Well, maybe you'll get lucky and he won't run off soon as he sees you this time," said Carl.

Milo ignored him, and they all began to climb the stairs.

CHAPTER TWELVE
King Nuntuck

They climbed up the stairs, the green light getting brighter the further they went. Finally, they reached the top and found themselves inside a colossal chamber. From the way the four triangular walls of the room met at the top, Dave guessed they must be at the top of the pyramid.

The chamber was bathed in green light, which was coming from a glowing green box on the top of a stone altar. Four staircases ran up to the top of the altar, one on each side. The box appeared to be made of some sort of glass, and inside it, Dave could see a figure holding a trident. The figure was standing perfectly still, as if it was asleep.

On one of the staircases below the green box stood Creepo Jones. He was flicking through a huge book and talking to himself.

"Master!" Milo shouted up at him. "Master, you did it – you found King Nuntuck!"

Creepo Jones looked around, noticing them for the first time.

"Ah, you lot," he said. "Well, if you won't stop bothering me, then come up here."

Milo, Dave and the others all climbed the staircase. When they got to the top, Dave could see the figure inside the green glass box more clearly. It looked like a husk, but with more bandages than usual wrapped around it, and it was wearing a gold crown. Clasped in the figure's right hand was the Trident of Emeros – the same one that Carl and Dave had seen Future Dave use, all that time ago.

"So, what now?" Carl asked. "Why haven't you just smashed open the glass box and grabbed the trident?"

"Because I don't want to get crushed by millions of tons of blocks," said Creepo Jones. "If my research is correct — which it always is — King Nuntuck rigged this pyramid to fall apart if anyone tried to steal his trident."

"So what's the plan then?" Porkins asked.

"Well, I spent the last few hours looking through this book," said Creepo Jones, "but I haven't found an answer yet."

"There must be a way of getting the trident," said Dave. "The future version of me said that some of his troops found it in a pyramid."

"If they didn't know what they were doing, maybe they just grabbed it and the pyramid fell apart," said Carl. "Future Dave didn't give us many details: maybe a load of soldiers died to get it."

"Maybe," said Dave.

"By jove, I think I've got it!" said Porkins.

Everyone looked around at him.

"If the pyramid is going to collapse as soon as we grab that trident," said the pigman, "Then we need to make a quick getaway. And what better place to escape to than the Nether!"

"Hmm," said Creepo Jones, "that's not a bad idea."

KA-DOOOOOM!!!!

Suddenly, there was an explosion above them, ripping a massive hole in the roof of the chamber. Daylight shone in, hurting Dave's eyes.

"The pyramid's starting to collapse!" shouted Alex.

"No, it isn't," said Spidroth, pointing, "look!"

Ropes began to unfurl from the hole in the ceiling, then illagers started abseiling down the ropes.

The first illager who landed on the floor of the chamber was the one who had chased Creepo Jones on horseback the day before.

"Mad Mulligan wants that trident," the illager shouted. "And he's going to get it."

More and more illagers abseiled down into the chamber, surrounding the altar. They began to climb up the stairs, with their swords and crossbows ready.

"What do we do?" Milo whimpered. "There are too many of

them."

There was no way they could possibly beat all the illagers in a fight: the illagers were too-well armed, and more and more of them were climbing down the ropes every second.

Then Dave had an idea.

"Prepare yourselves, everyone!" Dave shouted.

Dave took out a diamond pickaxe, then *KRRRAAASSSH*, he smashed it into the green box, shattering the glass.

Instantly, the husk that had been King Nuntuck came to life and staggered towards Dave with the trident. At the same time, the pyramid began to shake, and the ceiling began caving in. Some of the illagers were squashed by the falling debris.

"BURR!" groaned King Nuntuck.

"Burr this," said Creepo Jones, swinging his sword into the husk's head, and snatching the trident out of its hands.

"Porkins, build a portal!" Dave yelled.

Porkins quickly did as he was asked, pulling out some obsidian blocks from his bag and building a portal on the steps of the altar.

"Gosh, I don't have any flint and steel!" He gasped, looking in his backpack.

"I do," said Dave. He pulled out flint and steel from his bag and then struck it across the obsidian frame. The purple portal bubbled into life.

"Go, go, go!" Creepo Jones shouted.

The others didn't need asking twice, and all jumped into the portal. Once they were on the other side, they found themselves in the middle of a crimson forest biome, with dark red trees and lots of confused hoglins looking at them. Creepo Jones immediately started hacking away at the frame of the portal. He broke one of the obsidian frame blocks, and the portal vanished.

They all breathed a big sigh of relief.

"Another splendid victory for Creepo Jones," said Creepo Jones, looking at the Trident of Emeros in his hand.

"Hey, it was Porkins's idea to escape to the Nether," said Carl. "And it was Dave's idea to grab the trident and make the pyramid collapse."

"And I will make sure they are briefly credited in my autobiography," said Creepo Jones. "Now, come on, those pig monsters don't look too friendly."

Dave had to agree: the hoglins were starting to walk towards them, and they did not look happy to suddenly find seven strangers in the middle of their home.

CHAPTER THIRTEEN
The Vision

They walked through the Nether for a short while, then they built another portal. They walked through it, and found themselves back in the overworld, in the middle of the desert.

"Look," said Alex, pointing behind them. "It's the pyramid!"

In the distance behind them, they could see the ruins of the huge pyramid. It had collapsed in on itself, leaving nothing but a giant pile of rubble.

"So much for the Pyramid of Nuntuck," sighed Milo.

"Don't fret, Milo," said Creepo Jones. "At least we managed to rescue its greatest treasure. "

He held up the green trident for them all to see.

"I must say, it is jolly beautiful," said Porkins. "What will you do with it now?"

"I'll bring it back to Spectrite City Museum," said Creepo Jones. "They have a special wing there, dedicated entirely to me and all the treasures that I've found. They have a big statue of me there."

"Yes, but they also have a statue of a kung-fu chicken," said Carl. "So I don't think they're very fussy."

The seven of them made their way back to Canyon Village. By the time they got there, the sun was starting to go down, so they stayed the night at an inn. In the morning they packed their bags and prepared to head their separate ways: Milo and Creepo Jones to Spectrite city, and Dave and his friends heading in the opposite direction to continue their quest for the end portal.

"What is this quest you're on, anyway?" Milo asked them. "You never did say."

"Oh, we're just heading west to see what's out there," said Dave. "We're explorers — we like to explore."

"Hmm," said Milo. "If you say so."

But he didn't sound very convinced.

"Well, at least you also had the honor of meeting the great Creepo Jones," said Creepo Jones. "You can tell your grandchildren about it and watch their faces light up in awe when you mention my name."

"Yeah," said Carl sarcastically, "of course we will."

"By the way, fellow creeper," Creepo Jones said to Carl, "would you like a suit like mine? I made this contraption myself, and, if I do say so myself, it's far less unsightly than the big clumping thing that you wear."

"No thanks," said Carl. "If I had a small body like that, I wouldn't be able to do this."

He reached down and picked up Creepo Jones, lifting him into the air.

"Let me down, you oaf!" Creepo Jones shouted. "Let me down!"

"If you insist," said Carl. And he dropped him. Creepo Jones landed painfully on the ground.

"Oh, and treat Milo nicer from now on," said Carl. "He's a bit of an idiot and a wimp, but he's a nice guy."

And with that, the two groups went their separate ways. Dave, Carl, Spidroth, Alex and Porkins walked across the bottom of the canyon until they reached the cliff edge, then they all used blocks to get to the top: jumping up and placing blocks beneath their feet and doing it again, over and over, getting higher and higher with every jump.

Finally, they reach the top of the canyon. Dave took an eye of ender out of his bag and threw it in the air. It hovered for a moment, then flew off into the distance.

"I guess we just keep walking," said Dave.

"And no more distractions from now on," said Spidroth.

"Oh I'm sure there won't be," said Carl. "From now on I reckon we'll have a nice, peaceful journey to the End, and when we get there, the ender dragon will invite us around for pumpkin pie."

"Talking of pumpkin pie," said Porkins, "we didn't have any breakfast. Why don't we stop and have a nice bite to eat?"

"Sounds like a good idea," said Dave.

So the five of them sat down on the sand and ate some breakfast. Dave, Porkins, Spidroth and Alex all had pumpkin pie, and Carl, as ever, had a baked potato.

"Don't you ever get sick of those things?" Spidroth asked him.

"A creeper who is sick of baked potatoes is sick of life," said Carl. "And besides, don't you ever get sick of being ugly?"

"Okay, that's enough of that," said Dave, interrupting before Spidroth could reply. "We've still got a long journey ahead of us."

"Well, as long as I've got baked potatoes, I'll be fine," said Carl.

Dave laughed, but then suddenly an image flashed in front of his eyes. It was only for a split second, but it was crystal clear: he saw a huge army of blue robots with red eyes — the same type of robots that Robo-Steve had built — marching into a city, with villagers fleeing in terror before them. The image was so brief that

Dave couldn't tell where the city was, or if he'd been there before.

"Are you okay, Dave old bean?" Porkins asked. "You look as white as a ghast."

"It's fine," Dave said, forcing a smile. "Can I have another piece of that pumpkin pie?"

Epilogue

Derek Cool was hoping for a fresh start. As he looked across the ocean, he started to wonder what kind of reception he would get once he returned to Cool City. He was no longer a wanted man there, as his lawyer had got him freed from prison, but he still remembered the look in people's eyes as he left the city.

They looked like they hated me, Derek thought. *But surely that can't be true? The people of Cool City love me. I'm Derek cool – the coolest of them all!*

"Yo, Uncle D," said Derek's nephew Barry, coming over to join him on the prow of the ship. "How's it cheesin'?"

"You think I'm cool, don't you?" Derek asked.

"Yo, Unc, you're the coolest dude on the flippity flop," said Barry.

"Yeah, Unc," said Larry, coming over to join them, "you're the raddest cat around. You're totally cowabunga."

"Yeah, tubular," said Gary, walking over as well. "You're totally gnarly, one-hundred per-cent mondo and outrageously funky."

"Thanks, dudes," said Derek.

They were on a boat, heading towards Cool City. After losing the last of his money in Spectrite City due to an unfortunate incident at a roulette table, Derek was completely broke. He decided that he would go back to the place where everyone had always loved him: Cool City. Using his last few emeralds he had hired the cheapest boat he could, and he and his nephews were sailing across the ocean by themselves. But now Derek was starting to have doubts. Did the people of Cool City really love him as much as he remembered?

The Cool Dude Battle Royale incident wasn't your fault, Derek told himself. As far as Derek had known, all the contestants had been volunteers: warriors who wanted to prove their worth. Derek had had no clue that his assistant Ron had been forcing people to fight against their will.

Now Derek wanted to make amends. He wanted to return home and prove to his people that he was still the cool dude that they remembered. His biggest hope was that they would make him the mayor again. Derek missed living in the big penthouse apartment at the top of the gold skyscraper. He missed people telling him how great he was and having more emeralds than he could spend.

This is my big chance, Derek told himself. *The chance to prove that I'm still the coolest dude in the whole world!*

"Yo Unc," said Larry, shaking Derek out of his thoughts, "there's a ship over there."

Larry was right: coming towards them was a gray ship. As it got nearer, Derek saw that it dwarfed their tiny wooden boat. The ship's hull was painted gray and its sails were black.

"Oh dear, I hope it's not pirates," Derek whimpered to himself.

"Wow, pirates, cool!" said Barry.

"Yo, we've got nothing to fear from pirates, Uncle D," said Gary. "You're a master sword fighter, Uncle. Remember?"

"Um, yes," said Derek. "I may have exaggerated that a bit..."

The big ship was definitely heading towards them; there was no doubt about that. Derek was scared for himself, but he was more scared for his nephews. But what could he do? He had no clue how to fight, and there were only four of them.

You've got to talk your way out of this, Derek, he told himself. *Remember how everyone in Cool City thought you were amazing? You've just got to prove to these pirates that you are amazing as well. Show them what a cool dude you are, and they'll respect you.*

Finally, the big ship dropped anchor and came to a stop next to Derek's tiny boat. Now it was close enough, Derek could see that it was made from wood that was painted gray. A hatch opened on the side of the hull, a wooden gangplank slid down and a group of illagers came running down.

"Please don't hurt us!" Derek whimpered, putting his hands in the air.

"Yo, don't mess with us or our Uncle D is gonna get crazy on you," said Larry. "Crazy like a creeper."

The illagers said nothing and just marched onto Derek's ship. Three of the illagers each picked up one of Derek's nephews, and four illagers picked up Derek, two holding his arms and two holding his legs.

"Do something, Uncle D!" shouted Barry. "Beat them up!"

"Take me, but leave my nephews, please!" said Derek. But the illagers ignored him.

The illagers carried Derek and his nephews onto their ship. Inside the ship were a lot of other illagers, all of them gruff-looking and holding weapons. Finally, the illagers brought the four of them into a fancy cabin. There was a large window on one wall, looking out at the ocean, and there was a red carpet, bookshelves and a bed. Lying on the bed, eating cooked chicken, was an enormously fat villager with a crop of wispy white hair. Derek knew that villager well.

"Dad?" gasped Derek. "How can... I thought you were dead?"

Alexander Wimpy got to his feet, licking the chicken grease off his fingers.

"Hello, son," he grinned. "I've been searching for you."

"Yo, you're Uncle Derek's dad?" said Larry. "You're our granddad?"

"I am," said Alexander Wimpy. "I haven't seen you three since you were toddlers. It looks like you've grown up big and strong, just like your granddad."

"How are you here?" Derek asked his father. "I thought you'd died at sea."

"I had to fake my death," shrugged Alexander Wimpy. "There were some bad stories going around about me. Real bad. So many lies, you know what those journalists are like. They were claiming that I was stealing tax money, and that I hadn't really founded Gold City after all, and that it had all been the work of my business partner."

"Your business partner who was killed by zombies?" said Derek.

"That's the one," said Alexander Wimpy. "They claimed that it was me who released those zombies into his house. A complete lie, of course. I'm a good man. An honest man."

"Dad, I have to tell you something," said Derek nervously, "Cool City... I mean Gold City... I'm not in charge of it anymore. They kicked me out as mayor."

"So I heard," said Alexander Wimpy. "But don't worry, we're going to get the city back."

"Get it back?" said Derek. "How?"

"With a little help from a friend of mine," grinned Alexander Wimpy. "Ah, here he is now."

Derek turned around and saw an illager with a carved pumpkin on his head standing in the doorway.

"This is Pumpkin Head," said Alexander Wimpy. "He used to help me back in the day. If ever there was anyone who owed me money and wouldn't pay up, I just sent Pumpkin Head around to help... persuade them. Anyway, he was in prison for a while, but now he's out. Another good man accused of crimes he didn't commit. He came to see me, and told me all about a new business venture he's got going on."

"Um, how exactly are you going to get Cool City back?" Derek asked. Although he wasn't sure he wanted to know the answer.

Then, to Derek's surprise, two shiny blue robots with glowing red eyes walked through the doorway and stood either side of Pumpkin Head.

"The world is changing, son," grinned Alexander Wimpy. "And when it does, the Wimpy family is gonna be back where we belong: back on top."

To be continued...

BOOK 32

Mad Mulligan

Prologue

Mayor Grady took another swig of milk from his flask to calm his nerves. Then he put the flask away and wiped the sweat off his forehead with his sleeve. It was always hot in the badlands biome, but today was one of the hottest days that Grady could remember.

Even Mayor Grady's horse was getting agitated in the heat. She began to make whimpering noises, but Grady tugged at her reins, making sure she behaved herself.

"It's okay, girl," he told the horse. "We won't be out here much longer." He hoped that that was true. Mulligan's gang were making them wait this time.

“Maybe they’re not coming,” said Tom. “I heard Mulligan lost a load of men in the desert the other day. Something to do with a collapsing pyramid.”

“They’ll be here,” said Grady. “Even if Mad Mulligan lost hundreds of men, he’d still have plenty to spare.”

“From what I hear, it was well over a hundred men,” said Liza. “Daddy, this could be our chance. If Mulligan’s lost a load of his troops, then now is the time to fight back. We can rally the nearby towns and villages, build up an army and — ”

“Hush,” said Mayor Grady. “Here they come.”

Up ahead, five illagers on horseback were riding across the red sand, heading straight towards them.

“Let me do the talking,” Mayor Grady told Liza and Tom. “I don’t want to hear a word out of either of you.”

“But father — ” began Liza.

“Not a word!” snapped Grady.

“As you wish, Mr Mayor,” said Tom. Tom was a cowman, and cowmen by nature were, just like cows, fairly docile and willing to obey orders. Liza was an illager, just like Mayor Grady was, and illagers were always itching for a fight.

But there’s no fighting Mulligan’s gang, Grady thought to himself. Years ago, Grady had always been up for a fight. His headstrong daughter reminded him of himself when he’d been younger, but Grady didn’t have the luxury of being able to go around beating up bad guys anymore. He was a mayor now, and he was responsible for the lives of all the illagers and cowmen in Dead Bush. If he fought back against Mulligan’s gang, like his daughter wanted, Mad Mulligan would burn Dead Bush to the ground. He’d done it before, with plenty of other villages and towns. As much as Grady hated it, there was no fighting back against Mad Mulligan. Not if you wanted to keep your life and the lives of all the people you loved.

As the five illager riders came closer, Grady saw that their leader was Marie, one of Mad Mulligan’s most notorious lieutenants. Grady was a grown man, but some of the stories he’d heard about Marie and the things she'd done had made him feel as scared as a little boy. She was not someone you wanted to mess with.

"Remember," Grady whispered to Liza and Tom, "just hold your horses steady and let me do the talking.

The five illagers came to a stop in front of Grady, Tom and Liza.

"Mayor Grady," grinned Marie, "how good to see you again. I am sorry we're late. We had a bit of trouble with the mayor of Blue Sky Village. She didn't want to pay Mad Mulligan what she owed him, and let's just say... well, Blue Sky Village doesn't exist anymore."

A chill ran down Mayor Grady's spine.

"Well, we have what we owe right there," said Grady, pointing to three sacks on the ground in front of them. "One thousand gold ingots, one thousand diamonds and one thousand emeralds. Just like normal."

Marie put two fingers to her lips and whistled. Immediately, three of the four illagers riding with her jumped off their horses, picked up the sacks, and then climbed back onto their steeds.

"Thank you, Mr Mayor," Marie grinned. "As usual, it's always lovely doing business with Dead Bush."

Marie pulled at the reins of her horse, and it turned around. The four illagers riding with her all did the same, and they began to trot away, back across the red sand desert.

"Oh, by the way," Marie called back to Mayor Grady, "next week we're going to need double."

"Double?!" said Mayor Grady. "That's not possible – we can barely find a thousand of each stone as it is. All the ores around here are nearly completely dug up."

"Well, you'll have to look further afield, won't you?" Marie called back. "Now that Mad Mulligan won't be getting his weekly tribute from Blue Sky Village anymore, he's going to need it from somewhere else, isn't he? We'll see you next week, and you'd better have what you owe. If your people need some inspiration, take them to see what remains of Blue Sky Village. I'm sure that will give them the encouragement they need not to let Mad Mulligan down."

And with that, Marie gave another tug on her horse's reins, and she and the four other members of Mad Mulligan's gang all sped back across the desert, leaving Mayor Grady, Tom and Liza alone once more.

"What do we do now, Mr Mayor?" Tom asked.

"We get digging," said Mayor Grady. "What other choice do we have?"

CHAPTER ONE
Yellow Creepers

"Arrrgh!" yelled Carl, staggering backward. "That thing electrocuted me!"

"It electrocuted me too," said Dave. "I think netherite weapons are out of the question. Let's switch to our bows!"

"That's very offensive to people who can't use bows," said Carl. "Namely, me."

"Will you stop it with your stupid jokes, for once?" snapped Spidroth, pulling out her bow and stringing an arrow.

Dave, Carl, Spidroth, Porkins and Alex had been walking through a badlands biome when suddenly they'd been ambushed by yellow creepers. Dave and Carl had found out the hard way that attacking the creepers with netherite weapons got you electrocuted, and unlike regular green creepers, the creepers didn't even die when they used their electric powers.

"I wonder if any of these chaps know Creepo Jones," said Porkins. "Hello lads, we're friends of Creepo Jones, a yellow creeper just like you! We come in peace!"

The creepers ignored him, just hissing and continuing to head towards them.

"I think these are feral creepers, Porkins," said Spidroth. "They're as brainless as Alex."

"Yeah," said Alex, not noticing the insult, "they're as brainless as me."

Porkins was the first to fire an arrow. As usual, the pigman's aim was true, but when his arrow reached one of the yellow creepers, there was a flash of electricity, and the arrow was burnt to a crisp before it could do any damage. Dave fired an arrow of his own, but the same thing happened.

“Okay,” said Dave, “using netherite weapons gets us electrocuted, and we can’t use arrows either. Anyone got any bright ideas?”

“Maybe a diamond blade will teach these fools a lesson,” said Spidroth, reaching into her backpack and pulling out her old diamond sword.

She slashed at one of the yellow creepers, *SWOOSH, SWOOSH, SWOOSH,* and it exploded with a *POOF.*

“Oh yes,” said Alex, “I forgot – diamond doesn’t conduct electricity. Good job, Spidroth!”

Alex, who had recently replaced her two diamond swords with two netherite swords, reached into her backpack and pulled out her old diamond blades. Dave and Porkins did the same, both taking out their old diamond sword as well.

“So, if I just had my old diamond armor, I could have clobbered these guys no problem,” said Carl. “Remind me to give Boggo a beating the next time I see him.”

Dave, Alex, Spidroth and Porkins all began attacking the yellow creepers with their diamond swords. The battle was going well, but suddenly Dave had a vision.

"Everyone, move!" he shouted. "We need to get out of here now!"

"Get out of here?" said Carl. "Dave, we're in the middle of the desert."

"I saw something with the Sight," said Dave. "Something's coming... Something's coming from underground – we need to run!"

Suddenly the red sand beneath their feet began to rumble and the ground began to shake.

"Okay, maybe running is a good idea," said Carl.

The five of them all scattered, running off in different directions, pushing past the yellow creepers.

FWAAAKOOOOOMMMM!!!!!!

Something gigantic burst from the sand where they'd just been standing. It shook the ground, and they all fell over. Dave turned around and saw a giant yellow monster sticking out of the sand: a huge, long yellow neck – thicker than any tree trunk – with a yellow creeper head as big as a house on the top of it.

"RRRRAAAAGGGHHH!!!!" the yellow creeper monster roared.

"I'm going to assume that's a yellow creeper queen," said Dave.

"I think that would be a safe assumption," said Carl.

Suddenly, the yellow creeper queen slid back into the sand, disappearing.

"Maybe it's given up?" suggested Porkins.

"I don't think so," said Alex, "can you feel that rumbling?"

FWAAAKOOOOOMMMM!!!!!!

Suddenly the sand beneath Porkins's feet exploded, the yellow creeper queen bursting out of it. The force sent Porkins flying high up into the air.

"Chaaaaaaaaaaaaaaaaaaaaaaps!" Porkins screamed. "I'm in the soooooooooooooooooooooooooup!"

The yellow creeper queen opened her mouth wide, looking up at Porkins. Porkins stopped flying upwards and began to fall:

heading straight towards the yellow creeper queen's open mouth.

"Waaaaa!" Porkins screamed. "Heeeeeelp!"

Dave was about to run forward to attack the yellow creeper queen with his sword, but suddenly he heard a hissing behind him, and he was blasted with electricity, sending him falling forwards. He turned around and saw that some of the yellow creepers had caught up with him and were slithering towards him across the sand.

Nooooooooo!" Dave heard Porkins yell. He turned and watched as the pigman fell straight into the yellow creeper queen's mouth.

"Porkins!" Dave shouted. He pushed himself to his feet and attacked the yellow creepers behind him with his diamond sword – *SWOOSH, SWOOSH, SWOOSH.*

Meanwhile, Carl ran forward towards the yellow creeper queen in his netherite golem armor, with Alex and Spidroth running alongside him.

"We'll save you Porkins!" Alex shouted. "Try not to get digested before we rescue you!"

Carl, with his netherite golem legs, was the first one to reach the yellow creeper queen. He pulled his arm back and *WHAM,* punched the yellow monster right in the neck, but then he went flying backward, skidding across the red sand.

"Oww, looks like the queen is full of electricity as well," Carl groaned as Spidroth and Alex ran up to him.

"Fool," said Spidroth, rolling her eyes. "Looks like it is up to Lady Spidrothbrine to save the day once again."

"And the Lady Alexrothbrine as well!" said Alex.

"Pah," said Spidroth. "Just don't get in my way, fool."

Spidroth ran forward towards the yellow creeper queen, her diamond sword clasped in her hand.

"Carl, do you think Spidroth likes me?" Alex asked.

"I don't think Spidroth likes anyone," said Carl. "Apart from Dave, of course. But I think that's only because she's got a thing for bald heads."

"Well, I'm going to make sure she likes me," said Alex, "I think

Spidroth and I could be really good friends."

"You're going to be really dead friends if we don't defeat that yellow monster," said Carl. "Stop blabbing and go and save Porkins!"

"Oh, right," said Alex, nodding. "Here goes!" And with that, she ran towards the yellow creeper queen as well.

With Dave fighting off the yellow creepers, Carl unable to help due to his netherite golem suit and Porkins eaten, Alex and Spidroth were the only ones left to fight the yellow creeper queen. Spidroth was the first to reach the queen. She began hacking its neck with her diamond sword, but her blows didn't seem to do anything.

"Maybe we need to get up to the head," said Alex, rushing over to join Spidroth.

"Well, why don't you try climbing up the neck and see how you get on?" said Spidroth.

"Ooo, good idea," said Alex.

Alex ran and jumped towards the neck of the yellow creeper queen, intending to run up the side of it like a ninja, but as soon as her boots touched the yellow skin, she was blasted with electricity and went flying backward, rolling across the sand.

"Fool," said Spidroth, looking down at Alex with a nasty grin.

"But you were the one who told me to do it," said Alex, rubbing her head.

"I said nothing of the sort," said Spidroth. "You must be hearing things."

The yellow creeper queen finally spotted Spidroth and Alex and let out another mighty roar. It leaned its head forward, opening its mouth wide as it lunged towards them.

"Now is our chance," said Spidroth. "When it tries to eat us, we'll jump up and plunge our swords into its eyes."

"Ah, cool," said Alex. "Like how they defeated the Dragon Queen in the *Seth the Elf* and *Captain Cowman* crossover."

"This is no time for your foolishness!" Spidroth snapped. "Just get ready to jump!"

The yellow creeper queen lunged its head towards them, and when it came near enough, Alex and Spidroth both jumped up, swinging their swords back, ready to plunge them into the creature's eyes. But the yellow creeper queen, realizing what they were doing, quickly darted its head back again, straightening its neck and looking down at them.

"Bah!" Spidroth scowled at Alex. "Foolish girl, you jumped too early — you gave the game away!"

"But I jumped at the same time as you," said Alex.

Spidroth was about to respond, but then the yellow creeper queen opened its mouth and fired a blast of blue flames down at them. Alex and Spidroth both jumped out of the way just in time as the blue fire scorched the red sand where they'd just been standing.

"I've got an idea," said Alex. "Follow me!"

"Whatever foolish idea you have, I want no part of it," said Spidroth.

Alex pulled out both of her diamond swords and ran towards the yellow creeper queen.

"Hacking at its neck does nothing!" Spidroth called after her.

"I'm not going to hack at its neck," Alex called back, "I'm going to climb up it!"

"Fool!" Spidroth snapped. "Don't you remember what happened when you tried that before?"

But Alex kept running, heading straight towards the yellow creeper queen's neck. When she got there, she jumped up, plunging one of her swords into the neck. Then she used all her ninja skill and strength to spring herself upwards with that sword, then she plunged her second sword into the neck at a higher point. Then she used that sword to spring herself up and plunge the other sword into the neck: climbing higher and higher up the neck with every swing. Spidroth watched in awe from the ground.

"Wow," Spidroth gasped. Then she shook herself out of her amazement and ran over towards the yellow creeper queen's neck to join Alex. Spidroth only had one diamond sword, but she had an old stone sword in her backpack. She jumped up and plunged her stone sword into the creature's neck, then used it to push herself up, flipping into the air and then plunging her diamond sword into the neck higher up. She used both her swords to swing higher and higher up the creeper queen's neck.

By now, Dave had slain all the yellow creepers. He was standing next to Carl, both of them watching in amazement as Alex and Spidroth swung up the yellow creeper queen's enormous neck using their swords.

"Okay, that is pretty impressive," said Carl. "Those two have some serious ninja skills. I mean, I'd probably be able to do that too if I had arms and legs, but it's still pretty awesome."

"Yeah," said Dave, "it is."

The yellow creeper queen was squirming in frustration, trying to get Alex and Spidroth off its neck. Since it was just a long neck with a head, it had no arms, so couldn't just grab them off. They had almost reached its head now and only needed to do a couple more swings with their swords.

The creeper queen, realizing that its attempts to get Alex and Spidroth off were futile, tried a different tact. In one swift movement, it withdrew its neck back into the sand, disappearing from view along with Alex and Spidroth: all three of them disappearing beneath the red sand.

"No!" Dave shouted.

For a moment, the sand rumbled from the impact of the yellow creeper queen withdrawing underground, but then the rumbling stopped, and everything was still. Dave and Carl stood alone in the middle of the red desert, with no sign of the yellow creeper queen and no sign of Spidroth, Alex and Porkins.

CHAPTER TWO
The Legend of Carl the Creeper

"No," Dave repeated, falling to his knees on the red sand. In the space of a few minutes, he'd lost three of his closest friends.

"I'm sure those idiots are okay," said Carl, putting a hand on Dave's shoulder. However, he didn't sound very sure.

"That yellow creeper queen," said Dave, gritting his teeth, "if I ever see it again, I'll — "

FWAAAKOOOOOMMMM!!!!!!

Suddenly the sand near them erupted, and the yellow creeper queen burst from the ground once more.

"RRRRRAAAAAAGGGGHHHHHH!!!!!" it screamed. Alex and Spidroth were standing on its head, Alex with two swords in one of the creature's eyes and Spidroth with two swords in the creature's other eye. Both of them were balancing on their swords, with their legs in the air so that they wouldn't be electrocuted by the creeper queen's yellow skin. How they were managing to keep their balance while the creeper queen moved, Dave had no idea.

This time the yellow creeper queen emerged completely from the sand. Its body was long and thin, like one big tail, and it wriggled across the ground, screeching in pain.

The yellow creeper queen was slithering across the ground at an incredible pace, heading straight towards Dave and Carl.

"Um, we should probably get out of the way," said Carl.

"Wait," said Dave, "do you still have any of that TNT left?"

"Yeah," said Carl, grinning. "Let's give the creeper queen a surprise."

Carl quickly placed some of the TNT in his backpack down on the red sand, and then Dave lit one of the blocks with his flint and steel. Carl picked Dave up and ran, as the TNT block began to flash white. The yellow creeper queen was slithering straight towards the TNT, too distracted by Spidroth and Alex to notice.

The yellow creeper queen reached the TNT. The flashing TNT block exploded, causing all the other blocks to explode, and there was a massive explosion underneath the creeper queen's head. The creeper queen reared its neck up, screeching in pain, and Alex and Spidroth went flying. They landed on the sand next to Dave and Carl.

The yellow creeper queen let out one more roar, then *POOOOOOOF*, it exploded. On the red sand lay a pigman with one metal arm.

"Porkins!" Dave shouted.

Dave, Carl, Spidroth and Alex all ran over to Porkins. The pigman raised his head, looking very dazed.

"Hello... chaps..." he said. "Thanks for saving me. I was in a bit of a spot of bother."

"Are you okay, Porkins?" Alex asked.

"Yes, thank you, dear girl," said Porkins, pushing himself to his feet.

"You two were amazing back there," Dave said to Alex and Spidroth. "That thing you did, using your swords to flip up in the air – even if I trained for a hundred years, I'd never be able to do anything like that."

"Well, Alex deserves the credit for that one," said Spidroth reluctantly. "She is far less of a fool than I'd first thought her to be."

"Thanks, Spidroth," grinned Alex, giving her a hug. Spidroth looked very awkward.

"Yes, that's quite enough of that," said Spidroth, pushing Alex away.

"The sun is starting to set," said Dave, looking up at the sky. "I think we all deserve some rest. I'll build a house, and we can have an early night."

Once Dave had finished building the house, the five of them all sat around the netherrack fireplace, eating some beetroot soup that Porkins had made them. For once, Carl didn't have a baked potato: A few days earlier, he'd noticed that his supply was starting to get low, so he was trying to eat one every two days, rather than one every day.

"So, Carl," said Alex, taking a sip of her beetroot soup, "is your mum one of those big creeper queens as well?"

"I don't want to talk about it," said Carl. "Now come on, let's get back to our comic."

Alex pulled out some sheets of paper from her backpack, and she and Carl began to look through them.

"You two are writing a comic?" said Dave, looking at the drawings on the sheets of paper.

"Yeah," said Alex excitedly. "We've read all the *Seth the Elf* and *Captain Cowman* comics that we have, and we finished *Diary of a Skateboarding Cowman*, so we thought we'd write a comic of our own."

"Gosh, how fun," said Porkins, "what's it called?"

"*The Legend of Carl the Creeper,*" said Carl. "It's the true story of all my awesome adventures."

Dave picked up one of the pages. On the page was a crudely drawn picture of Carl fighting a big green squid. Above the picture of Carl was a speech bubble:

Taek that craken! Itz creepa tiem!

And above the picture of the squid was another speech bubble:

O no Carl the creepa, u hav defeeted me!

"Um, there are a few spelling errors," said Dave.

"No one cares about spelling errors," said Carl, "it's all about the epic story."

"Wait a minute," said Dave, looking at the picture again, "is this meant to be you defeating the kraken? Are you punching it in the face?"

"I've changed some of the stories to make them a bit more exciting," shrugged Carl.

Dave picked up another page. This one showed Carl and Alex both beating up a big black monster with tentacles. There was a speech bubble above Alex's head:

Taek that endabrin! Did sumbuddy orda the Alex?

"Um, and I suppose this is you two defeating Enderbrine?" said Dave. "And what is this thing you're saying Alex — 'did somebody order the Alex?'"

"Yeah," grinned Alex. "Captain cowman's catchphrase is 'did somebody order the beef?'. So, my catchphrase is 'did somebody order the Alex?'"

"These are all early drafts," said Carl. "Once we bring it to a publisher and they pay us a load of emeralds, we'll get our secretary to rewrite it all."

Dave picked up another page. This one showed Carl punching Herobrine and Herobrine's head exploding.

"Right," said Dave, putting the page back down, "um, it looks great so far."

"Don't forget us when you're both rich and famous, chaps," said Porkins.

"I can't promise that," said Carl. "If I get rich and famous, I'm going to live in a big diamond house with lots of guard wolves, so I can just sit around eating baked potatoes all day. If anyone tries to disturb me, the wolves will slay them on sight. So, you'd best be careful."

"Crikey," said Porkins, his cheeks turning pale.

"Idiots," said Spidroth, rolling her eyes.

That night, Dave's dreams were full of strange images. He dreamed of blue robots with red eyes marching in front of a building with a blue-green prismarine dome. He was sure the building was familiar, but he couldn't place where it was, and when he woke up the next morning, the dream quickly faded away.

The next day, Dave and the others ate some more beetroot soup for breakfast and then headed on their way. As he did every morning, Dave threw an eye of ender into the sky to check they were still following the route to the end portal. The eye of ender floated in the sky for a moment before zooming off towards the west. Dave felt like he'd been traveling west forever.

We must be getting near to an end portal by now, he thought, as they walked across the red sand. *How much further can it be?*

When Dave had begun his journey, all that time ago, he'd never imagined that his quest would take him so far and would last so long. Sometimes he felt as if his adventure was going to last forever, and he didn't know whether to feel happy or sad about that. Dave knew that once his quest was over, he would have to fulfill his debt to the meeps. He'd promised them that after Herobrine was defeated and he'd slain the Ender Dragon, he would become their new Farmer — guarding their heard of magical mooblooms until the end of his life.

Maybe I won't have to be the Farmer if I don't slay the dragon, Dave thought to himself. But he knew that probably wasn't the case. The meeps were unlikely to accept that as an excuse: he'd made a promise to be their Farmer, and he doubted that was a promise he'd be able to break. No, eventually, Dave would have to pay his debt to the meeps and be the new guardian of the mooblooms.

Dave looked over at Spidroth. He would have never told anyone this, but sometimes he dreamt of what his life would be like if he and Spidroth could get married and live together. He didn't know if Spidroth still felt the same about him, but Dave knew it would be pointless anyway. After his adventure was done, Dave wouldn't be able to get married or have children — he was going to have to be the Farmer. It wasn't something he thought about very often, but it made him sad every time he did.

Come on, stop being so miserable, Dave told himself. *You've got good friends, and you're on the adventure that you always dreamt of going on. What more could you ask for?*

Dave had seen and done more things in a few short months than most villagers had in a lifetime. He knew he should be grateful, so he tried to push thoughts of the meeps and his future out of his mind.

Around midday, they all sat down in the shade of some tall cacti and had lunch. While the others were relaxing, Spidroth forced Dave to have another sword-fighting lesson.

"Use the Sight," Spidroth barked at Dave, as she slapped him across the legs with her wooden sword for the fourth time. "Try to see where my attacks are coming before I make them."

"I'm trying," said Dave. "The trouble is it's difficult to see what's happening at the moment and what's going to happen in the future at the same time; my brain gets all muddled."

"Stop making excuses," said Spidroth, whacking Dave on his netherite chest plate with her wooden sword. "There are no excuses in a battle."

"You should tie some cloth around your eyes when you fight," suggested Carl. "That's what Seth the Elf did when he was trying to get in touch with the Elven Force. It allowed him to concentrate on his powers rather than what was going on around him."

"Fool," barked Spidroth. "This is real life, not some stupid comic book."

"It was just a suggestion," Carl shrugged.

After a bit more sword practice, Dave was battered and bruised, so he suggested that they start walking again. They'd been walking for about an hour when they saw a town up ahead of them.

The buildings of the town were made from red sandstone. It stood in the middle of a wide-open badlands plateau, with no hills or cliffs around it: only endless red sand.

"Shall we see if they've got an inn?" Dave asked the others. It had been a while since they'd stayed in a village or town.

"Good idea," said Carl. "Maybe there'll be some traders in town with more potatoes."

"Can you give this ridiculous obsession with potatoes a rest?" said Spidroth.

"Hey," said Carl, "don't insult potatoes."

"I wasn't insulting potatoes," said Spidroth, "I was insulting you."

"Oh," said Carl. "That's not so bad then."

They made their way into the town. Before they reached the first buildings, they saw a red acacia-wood sign that said:

DEAD BUSH

"I guess that's an appropriate name for this town," said Carl, looking at the scraps of dead bush that were scattered across the plateau.

They entered the town, but there was no one to be seen. All the doors were closed, and nobody was walking the streets.

"Maybe these chaps go to bed really early," said Porkins, looking at the setting sun.

"Or maybe they're just hiding from us," said Spidroth. "Haven't you noticed those faces at the windows?"

Dave looked harder. At first, he thought all the buildings were empty, but then he caught the occasional glimpse of someone looking at them from one of the windows. Whenever Dave spotted anyone, they quickly moved away and hid.

"I guess they don't know if we're friendly or not," said Dave. He put his hands to his mouth: "Hello! We're just looking for a room at an inn!"

A door creaked open and an illager in a cowboy hat and dusty brown clothes walked out of a building.

"I'm afraid we don't take kindly to strangers in this town," said the illager. "You folks are gonna have to keep on moving."

"Okay, but before we do, do you have any potatoes?" asked Carl. "It's a question of utmost importance."

"I said, you're gonna have to keep on moving," said the illager, touching the hilt of the iron sword on his belt. "I'm the mayor of this here town, and I'm ordering you to leave."

"Okay, we're leaving," said Dave. "We don't want any trouble."

"Well, if you leave nice and quickly, you won't get any," said the illager.

“Come on,” Dave said to the others, “there’s no point staying here if we’re not welcome.”

The five of them started to walk back the way they’d come, but suddenly a bell rang out across the town: *CLANG-A-LANG A-LANG-A-LANG!*

“Husks!” someone shouted from one of the rooftops. Dave looked up and was surprised to see that it was a cowman. “Husks are attacking!”

CHAPTER THREE
Husks

Dave, Carl, Spidroth, Porkins and Alex all ran to the edge of town, following the illager mayor. Other people had come out of their houses now, and Dave was surprised to see that there were both illagers and cowmen, all living side-by-side.

When they reached the edge of town, they saw that the lookout on the roof had been correct: hundreds of husks were staggering across the red sand towards the village. The sun had almost set now, and the plateau around the village was mostly hidden in darkness, making it hard to tell exactly how many husks there were.

"Why don't you fools have a town wall or a moat?" Spidroth asked the mayor.

"That's none of your business," said the mayor.

A group of illagers and cowmen and cow women ran over to the mayor. There were about twenty of them, and they were all wearing iron armor and had iron weapons.

"We are ready to fight," said one of the cowmen.

"Okay, Tom," said the mayor, "but use your bows first. You don't want to get bitten by one of those things."

"As you say, Mr Mayor," said the cowman, pulling out his bow. He and the others in iron armor climbed up some nearby ladders, climbing on top of two buildings either side of the town's main street and aiming their bows down at the husks.

"Are those all your soldiers?" Spidroth demanded. "You'll need more warriors than that to defeat those husks. Why are the rest of your townsfolk not coming out to join the fight?"

"Listen, red," said the mayor, pointing a finger in Spidroth's face, "I don't know who you are, but no one tells me how to run my town."

"We can help you fight," said Dave.

"No," snapped the mayor. "If any of you try to get involved, I'll cut you down where you stand."

"I'd like to see you try," said Carl, looking down at the mayor.

"Stop it, Carl," said Dave.

"Those men and women up on those rooftops are the Dead Bush volunteer army," said the mayor. "They're the best fighters in this town, and I won't hear a word against them."

"But why are there so few of them?" asked Porkins.

"Fifteen soldiers are all we're allowed, so fifteen soldiers is all we have," said the mayor.

"Allowed?" said Alex. "Why are you only allowed to have fifteen soldiers? I thought you were the mayor?"

"That's enough talk," said the mayor. "I have a town to defend."

The mayor pushed past them, climbing a ladder and joining one of the groups of iron-armored soldiers on a rooftop. The mayor and his fifteen soldiers were aiming their bows down at the husks, waiting for them to get near enough to hit.

"Why wouldn't they accept our help?" said Alex.

"I don't know," said Dave, "but something is going on here. There's more to this than meets the eye."

"So, are we just going to stand here and watch as those fools get slaughtered?" Spidroth asked.

"We'll respect the mayor's wishes for as long as we can," said Dave. "But if the battle starts to go wrong, there's no way I'm standing by and watching this town get destroyed by husks." He pulled out his netherite sword.

Finally, the husks got within firing range. The illagers and cowmen and cow women on the roofs all began firing their bows. Their finger work was clumsy, Dave couldn't help but notice, and they kept dropping arrows or fumbling their shots.

"Good gravy," Dave heard Porkins mutter. "These chaps have no idea what they're doing."

The illager mayor was fighting alongside his soldiers, firing down at the husks with his bow. In fact, the mayor appeared to be the only one of them that knew how to fire a bow properly. He was no Porkins, but his fingers were quickly loading and firing arrows, much quicker than the other soldiers could. Even so, the archers on the rooftops had barely made a dent in the number of husks. The husks had reached the town and had started to walk down the main street, heading straight towards Dave and his friends. All the other illagers and cowmen were safely locked in their houses, but the husks began to climb the ladders where the archers were.

The archers realized they were in trouble and started firing arrows at the husks on the ladders, but for every husk they slew, another took its place. In a few more seconds, the husks would have breached the rooftops, and the soldiers would be in big trouble.

"Right," said Dave, "that's enough standing by and watching. Everyone, attack!"

Dave and his friends ran forward towards the husks. Carl, who could run as fast as a horse, was the first one to get there. He smashed through the husks with his huge netherite arms, sending groups of husks flying with every punch. He cleared a path over to one of the ladders, then reached up and pulled the husks off of it. Then he barged his way over to the other building and pulled the husks off of that ladder as well.

Meanwhile, Dave, Alex and Spidroth ran into the crowd of husks, slashing at them with their netherite swords. As usual, Alex was using two swords and was flipping all over the place like a ninja, cutting the husks down in droves.

Porkins was good with a sword, but he was much better with a bow and arrow. He stood in the middle of the main street, firing arrows at the husks as fast as his fingers could move – which was very fast indeed.

The soldiers on the two rooftops had stopped fighting and were just watching Dave and the others in awe until, finally, the mayor came to his senses.

"Keep firing!" He told his soldiers. "Don't just watch, help them!"

The iron-armored soldiers on the two rooftops started firing their bows again. They managed to hit a few husks, but it was nothing compared to the number of husks that Dave and his friends were slaying.

Before long, all the husks were slain, leaving nothing but piles of rotten flesh all over the ground. Someone began ringing a bell on one of the rooftops again, but this time it wasn't to signal danger, it was to signal victory — the town had been saved.

CHAPTER FOUR
The Dream

Suddenly the town was full of grateful illagers and cowmen, all rushing out of their houses to come and thank Dave and his friends.

"That was amazing!" one cowman said, slapping Dave on the back.

"I've never seen husks taken out so quickly," said a female illager, "you five are amazing warriors!"

"We are pretty amazing, that's true," said Carl. "And just like true warriors, we don't want any reward – apart from all the potatoes you can spare."

"What's a potato?" asked a cow girl.

Carl sighed. "I hate this continent."

The mayor and his fifteen iron-armored soldiers walked over then.

"We owe you our lives," the mayor said, shaking Dave by the hand. "Thank you. I'm sorry I was so harsh to you five before. I'm Mayor Grady, by the way."

"Dave," said Dave. "And this is Spidroth, Alex, Carl and Porkins."

"We don't get many strangers around here," said Mayor Grady, "but I'm glad you five were passing through. I wish I could offer you some rooms for the night, but... things are complicated here. I'm sorry."

"Oh, come on, Daddy," said an illager girl who was about Dave's age. "You can't send these heroes away after they've just saved our town."

All the other illagers and cowmen muttered in agreement.

"I'm sorry," Mayor Grady told his people, "but Mad Mulligan's gang is coming back tomorrow and – "

"All the more reason to keep these five heroes here," said the illager girl. "Mulligan's goons won't stand a chance against them."

"Mad Mulligan," said Dave, "we've heard that name before. We teamed up with a creeper named Creepo Jones, and some illagers from Mad Mulligan's gang were trying to stop him. They were very keen to get their hands on this artifact called the Trident of Emeros."

"That makes sense," said the illager girl. "Mulligan is obsessed with ancient weapons and stuff like that."

"Did you five have anything to do with that pyramid collapsing?" asked Tom, one of the cowmen in iron armor.

"Yep, that was us," said Alex proudly. "Dave made it collapse and squished all those bad illagers."

The townsfolk all muttered in approval.

"This is a big thing to ask, but will you help us defeat Mad Mulligan's gang tomorrow?" the illager girl asked. "Every week, five illagers come, and we have to give them one thousand emeralds, one thousand diamonds and one thousand gold ingots."

"Two thousand of each this time," muttered a cowman. "We've been working our hooves to the bone all week."

"You want us to defeat five illagers?" said Carl. "Easy. We could do that in our sleep."

The townsfolk all cheered.

"You hear that, Daddy?" the illager girl asked.

"I do, Liza," sighed Mayor Grady, "but even if we defeat the five who come tomorrow, Mulligan will send more."

"No, he won't," said Liza. "That nutter Marie is his best lieutenant. If we defeat her and her four goons, Mad Mulligan will know that he can't mess with Dead Bush anymore. He'll know that this town is off-limits."

The townsfolk cheered again. It was clear that they all agreed with Liza rather than her father.

"I don't like this," said Mayor Grady, "but I can see that I'm outnumbered. Very well, strangers, you may stay the night in our town. And if you're willing, we'd be grateful for your help tomorrow to defeat Marie and her soldiers."

"We accept," said Dave, but in reality, he had the same reservations that Mayor Grady seemed to have. If Mad Mulligan had an endless supply of illagers in his gang, would defeating five of his troops really convince him to leave Dead Bush alone? Dave didn't know the answer, but he knew he couldn't turn down a request for help.

The sun had fully set now, and the moon was in the sky, so Dave and his friends were brought straight to the local inn, where they were given the biggest room. The landlady set up five beds for them and told them to tell her if they needed anything.

"Just a big plate of baked potatoes, please," said Carl.

"Baked po-what-o's?" said the landlady.

"Never mind," sighed Carl.

The five of them sat talking for a while — and Carl and Alex did some more work on their comic.

"I was thinking," said Alex, "maybe instead of the title being *The Legend of Carl the Creeper*, what if it was *The Legend of Carl the Creeper and also Alex*?"

"It's not quite so catchy," said Carl. "Let's just stick with *The Legend of Carl the Creeper*. If you want, we could add an extra word in there, like *The Legend of Carl the Awesome Creeper*. What do you think?"

"Er, yeah, I guess that's pretty good," said Alex.

"*The Legend of Carl the Awesome Creeper* it is," said Carl.

After talking for a bit longer, they all crawled into bed. Dave fell asleep fairly quickly, but again, he had strange dreams. His dreams weren't about blue robots this time, but instead, he dreamt he was back in his childhood home. He could smell his dad's cooking wafting from the kitchen, but when he walked through the door, it wasn't his dad by the smoker; it was an illager.

"Howdy," said the illager, giving Dave a big grin. There was something about that grin that Dave didn't trust.

"Who are you?" Dave asked the illager.

The illager laughed.

"That's funny," he said, "I was just about to ask you the same question. Wait... I'm getting it now... It's on the tip of my tongue..."

"What are you —" Dave began.

"Dave," the illager interrupted. "Your name's Dave, isn't it? Nice to meet you, Dave. Now, the more important question is, why are you here? And why are you interfering in my business?"

"Why am I here?" asked Dave, feeling confused. "This is my home."

"No, it isn't," said the illager, the grin disappearing from his face. "This is my home, and you'd do well to remember that. Because if you don't remember that, things are gonna go very badly for you. Now, what are villager, a creeper, a pigman and two of the strangest women I ever saw doing out here at the end of the world?"

Dave realized that he wasn't in his home village anymore; he was standing on the main street of Dead Bush. The street was empty, and all the buildings were in ruins. The illager was standing in the middle of it, holding a sword as red as blood.

"Actually, I know what you're doing this far west," the illager grinned. "I mean, it's not hard to figure out. Why else would you be here unless there's something really, really special? Something that you just can't find anywhere else."

The illager strolled towards Dave, then leaned down and whispered in his ear:

"We both want the same thing, Davey boy. The only difference is, I'm going to get it, and you're going to be dead."

The illager began to laugh, and all around him, the buildings began to crumble and burn.

"I'll see you soon, Dave," the illager said, pointing his red sword at him. "Mad Mulligan's coming for you, and you're gonna regret getting involved in my business."

Dave woke up, sitting up in bed and gasping for breath. His whole body was covered in sweat. He jumped out of bed, ran to the window and pulled open the curtains. The town of Dead Bush was still there, all its buildings intact and lit by the blue light of the moon. He turned and saw that his friends were still safe in their beds, all of them asleep.

"It was just a bad dream," Dave told himself as he climbed back into bed.

But he knew that it wasn't.

CHAPTER FIVE
Marie

The next morning, Liza, the mayor's daughter, and Tom the cowman showed Dave and his friends around the village.

"I've never seen a town like this before," said Porkins, looking around at the red sandstone buildings, "two different groups of people, cowmen and illagers, just living in harmony. It's marvelous."

"Yeah, Dead Bush is pretty unique," said Liza. "As you know, back on your continent, there's a lot of distrust of illagers. My great grandpappy and some of his friends were fed up with villagers persecuting them, so they came over to this continent. He was one of the founders of Dead Bush."

All the illagers and cowmen they passed by waved and said hello to them. In the space of one day, Dave and his friends had become local heroes, it seemed. Carl, Porkins, Spidroth and Alex seemed to be enjoying it, but Dave couldn't stop thinking about the dream he'd had the previous night.

No, thought Dave, *it wasn't a dream; it was some sort of vision. That was the Sight.*

But he'd never had a Sight dream like that before. It had almost been like Mad Mulligan had been inside his dream, but Dave knew that couldn't be possible.

Liza and Tom led Dave and the others to a big hole in the middle of the village. Minecart tracks were going into the hole, and from inside it, they could hear the sound of pickaxes.

"This is our mine," said Liza. She and Tom led them down into the mine. To Dave's surprise, the mine was massive, with tall, wide passageways and caverns in every direction. It was all lit by torches and seemed to be much, much bigger than the village above it.

"We have to keep making the mine bigger to find all the gold, diamonds and emeralds to pay Mad Mulligan's gang," said Tom sadly. "Of course, every time we expand the mine, we run the risk of running into creepers and zombies and other monsters. Er, no offense, mister," he said, looking up at Carl.

"None taken," said Carl. "I like being called a monster. Monsters are cool."

All the illagers and cowmen working in the mine looked exhausted. They were hacking away at the walls with iron pickaxes, but there seem to be no ore to be found anywhere.

"Wouldn't they be better off using diamond pickaxes?" said Alex.

"Mad Mulligan has forbidden us from using any tools and weapons stronger than iron," Liza said bitterly. "As you saw yesterday, he doesn't even let us have more than fifteen people in the town using weapons, so every time there's a husk attack, we take heavy losses."

"This Mad Mulligan idiot sounds like a bully," said Carl, smashing his netherite fists together.

"What time are Mulligan's men coming for their payment today?" Dave asked.

"Noon," said Tom. "There's always five of them, and they're normally led by an illager called Marie. She looks skinny, but according to the stories we've heard about her, she's a vicious fighter."

"I don't care how vicious she is," said Spidroth, "she won't stand a chance against the Lady Spidrothbrine."

"That's right," said Carl. "As soon as those bad guys see Spidroth's face, they'll flee in the opposite direction."

"CREEPER!" Spidroth roared, pulling out her netherite sword. Dave quickly rushed to stand in front of her.

"Come on," he said, "save all that rage for Mad Mulligan's gang."

"Pah," said Spidroth, putting her sword away. "You got lucky this time, creeper."

"Not that lucky," said Carl, "I still have to look at your face."

Spidroth scowled, but she said nothing.

"What can you tell us about Mad Mulligan himself?" Dave asked Liza and Tom.

"Well, he's never come to the village in person," said Tom, "but everyone in this region knows his name. His gang has been demanding money off us for years. Any settlements that don't make their payments, or try to fight back, get wiped off the map."

"How awful," gasped Alex.

"That was why my father was so reluctant to ask for your help," said Liza sadly. "He means well, but if we don't fight back now, our town will be terrorized by Mulligan forever. He's asked us for double the usual amount of gold, diamonds and emeralds this week, but what's to stop him from asking for even more in the future? We have to fight back."

"Well, at noon we'll give this Marie character the beating of a lifetime," said Spidroth. "Then Mulligan will know that your town is under our protection."

"Does Mad Mulligan... does he use a red sword?" Dave asked.

Liza and Tom both looked at Dave in surprise.

"Oh, yes," said Liza, "or at least he does according to the stories. How did you know that?"

"Was it the Sight?" Spidroth asked. "Have you seen a vision, Dave?"

"It was probably nothing," said Dave. "I just had a weird dream last night. There was an illager with a red sword, and he was talking to me — telling me to keep out of his business."

"That doesn't sound like a Sight dream to me," said Spidroth. "Maybe it was just a normal dream. You properly heard someone talking about Mad Mulligan having a red sword and forgot all about it."

"Yeah, probably," said Dave.

"We should go to the edge of town," said Liza. "It'll be noon soon, and Marie will be coming."

"And we'll be ready and waiting when she does," said Porkins. "That scoundrel will rue the day she messed with your town."

So, Tom and Liza led Dave and his friends out of the mine. Liza brought out some horses from a nearby stable for Dave, Spidroth, Porkins and Alex, and then all seven of them rode out of the town, with Carl running in his golem suit alongside the horses.

They rode out into the red sand desert until the town was only a faint spec behind them. Tom and Liza brought their horses to a standstill next to an exceptionally tall cactus. Mayor Grady was already there on his horse, waiting for them.

"Daddy," said Liza, "I didn't know you'd be here."

"I may not like this plan, but this is still my town, and I need to make sure everything goes okay," said Mayor Grady, taking a swig from a hip flask.

"We won't let you down," said Dave.

"Yes, we've faced far tougher foes before then a bunch of criminals," said Spidroth. "These fools will be no match for us."

"Yeah, we're gonna kick their butts," said Alex. "It will be like a real-life version of *The Legend of Carl the Creeper*."

"Um, what's *The Legend of Carl the Creeper*?" asked Mayor Grady.

"It's an award-winning comic book that's hitting shelves soon," said Carl. "Look out for it in your nearest comic book shop."

"What's a comic book shop?" Tom asked. "And what's a comic book?"

"And what awards has it won?" asked Dave.

"Well, it's going to win awards one day," said Carl, "so we're going to write 'award-winning' on the cover now, so we don't have to add it later."

"Riiiiiight," said Dave.

"Quiet, fools," said Spidroth. "Here they come."

Spidroth was right, Dave saw: there was a cloud of dust coming towards them from the east, kicked up by five horses. On each of the horses was an illager.

"It's Marie," said Mayor Grady darkly. "We need to be careful. She won't be easy to take down."

"She will be for us," said Spidroth confidently.

The five illagers brought their horses to a stop. The illager at the front of the group was a female illager who Dave assumed must be Marie.

"Who are your new friends, Mayor Grady?" Marie asked, eyeing Dave and the others suspiciously. "And where are the gold ingots, diamonds and emeralds that you owe Mad Mulligan?"

"Let me do the talking," Mayor Grady whispered to the others. He trotted his horse forward towards Marie.

"That's close enough," said Marie. The four other illagers all pulled out crossbows, aiming them at Mayor Grady.

"Dead Bush doesn't belong to Mad Mulligan anymore," said Mayor Grady. "Our town is now under the protection of these gentlemen and ladies."

"Is that so?" Marie said. "Mad Mulligan will be very disappointed to hear that. Very disappointed indeed."

"Then maybe Mad Mulligan needs a demonstration of what our friends can do," said Liza. "Everyone, attack!"

Dave was caught a bit off-guard. He wished they'd talked through this plan in more detail, but there was no more time to think — only time to act. He pulled at the reins of his horse and charged forward towards the illagers. Alex and Spidroth did the same, riding their horses forward as well, and Porkins pulled out his bow and started firing arrows. Carl charged forward in his golem armor and was the first to reach the illagers. He smashed the first illager he reached with a netherite fist, sending the illager flying off of his horse. Another illager fired a crossbow bolt at Carl, but it just bounced harmlessly off his netherite golem suit.

Alex and Spidroth both jumped off their horses, kicking two of the other illagers off their horses. The illagers landed painfully on the ground. Dave rode his horse straight at Marie, but to his surprise, she pulled out a trident — not a magical trident, like the Trident of Emeros, but just a regular blue-green trident. She threw it at Dave, but he swerved his head out of the way, and it soared past him.

"You missed me," said Dave.

"Did I?" grinned Marie. Suddenly the trident reappeared back in her hand.

That trident's got a loyalty enchantment, thought Dave. He'd heard about that enchantment — it allowed a thrown trident to reappear back in the user's hand, so they could use it over and over again.

Marie threw her trident once more, and this time it hit Dave in the chest. He was wearing his netherite armor vest, but the force of the trident hitting him sent him flying backward off his horse, and he landed on the red sand. Marie jumped off of her horse, pulling out a diamond sword in midair and preparing to slice it down on Dave's head. Dave looked up from the red sand, unable to react quick enough to stop her.

CLANG! Suddenly another sword blocked Marie's sword, saving Dave's life. It was a netherite blade, and Alex was holding it.

"Did somebody order the Alex?" Alex asked.

"What?" said Marie, looking confused.

WHAM! Alex kicked Marie's legs out from under her, and the illager fell to the ground. Dave looked over and saw that Alex and Spidroth had knocked out the two illagers they'd pushed off their horses. Carl had knocked out the other two illagers, and Marie was the only one left conscious.

"Surrender," said Spidroth, pointing her netherite sword down at Marie. Alex did the same, both of them pointing their swords at the illager.

"You did it!" Dave heard Tom the cowman squeal excitedly. "You defeated them!"

"Defeated me?" scowled Marie. "You think you've defeated me?"

Suddenly Marie flipped to her feet. She did a spinning kick, hitting Spidroth and Alex and sending them flying. Carl ran over and tried to grab her with his netherite arms, but Marie flipped over his head, landing on the sand behind him. Dave ran at Marie with his netherite sword, but she pulled out an ender pearl from her pocket and threw it through his legs. *ZAP!* Marie teleported behind Dave and kicked him in the back, sending him flying down onto the red sand.

Carl charged at Marie once again, but she threw her trident straight at his creeper head. Carl had no choice but to duck down into his golem suit, and that was the chance Marie needed — she jumped up and dived into the neck hole of the golem suit. A second later, Carl went flying out of the neck hole.

"Not cool!" the tiny creeper shouted as he flew through the air. Dave quickly stood up and caught him.

Suddenly Marie's illager head popped out of the top of the golem suit. The golem suit's netherite fists smashed together, and Marie grinned down at them.

"I've taken control of your suit, creeper," said Marie.

"Well, I'm going to take control of your face," said Carl.

"What does that even mean?" said Marie.

"I'm not sure," said Carl. "It sounded a lot cooler in my head."

Marie charged forward in the golem suit, heading straight

towards Dave and Carl. Dave picked Carl up and jumped out of the way, narrowly avoiding getting trampled. Marie turned around for another attack, but Alex and Spidroth were running towards her now, with their netherite swords at the ready. They jumped up, ready to strike her down, but Marie was too quick for them — she swung both her netherite arms at the same time, hitting Spidroth and Alex and sending them flying.

"Take this, you scoundrel!" Porkins shouted, firing arrows at Marie's exposed head. But she simply raised one of her golem arms, blocking the arrows.

"I love this suit," Marie grinned, "I'm gonna have so much fun with this once I'm done with you lot."

"If you touch any of the baked potatoes in there, I'll hunt you down to the ends of the earth," said Carl.

"Don't worry, creeper," said Marie, "in a few seconds, you'll never have to worry about baked potatoes ever again."

Marie charged forward, heading straight towards Dave and Carl once more, but this time something big bashed into her from the side — it was a horse, ridden by Mayor Grady.

The impact of the horse sent Marie staggering to the side, almost toppling over. Before she could get her balance again, Mayor Grady grabbed her by the head and started to pull.

"Get off!" Marie screamed.

POP! Mayor Grady pulled Marie out of the netherite golem suit. She fell, landing unceremoniously on the hard red sand. Dave ran forward and threw Carl up into the air. The tiny creeper landed back in his golem suit, taking control of it once more. He immediately reached down and picked up Marie by her collar using one of his netherite arms.

"Not so tough now, are you?" Carl grinned.

"Pah," Marie scowled.

The other four illagers had started to wake up now, after being knocked out. Carl threw Marie down in the middle of them.

"Tell Mad Mulligan what happened here today," said Mayor Grady, looking down at the five criminals from his horse. "Tell him that Dead Bush is now off-limits."

Marie scowled, then she got to her feet and started running back across the desert, followed by the other four illagers. Mayor Grady breathed a big sigh of relief.

"You did it!" Liza shouted. "You all defeated them! And Daddy, that was amazing!"

"Hopefully, that will scare those scoundrels off for good," said Porkins.

"There's no chance they'll come back after that," Tom grinned.

"I hope you're right," said Mayor Grady, but he didn't sound very sure.

"Come on," said Tom, turning his horse back around to face the town. "When everyone else hears what happened here today, there will be the biggest celebration that Dead Bush has ever seen."

CHAPTER SIX
The Celebration

As Tom had promised, that night there was a huge celebration. The people of Dead Bush had lived under the tyranny of Mad Mulligan for so long that they could barely believe that they were now free. A long table had been set out down the town's main street, and all the townsfolk were sitting around it, eating a gigantic feast. There was music and dancing too, and everyone was having a fantastic time.

The only person who looked like he wasn't having a good time was Mayor Grady. Dave noticed that the mayor smiled when people spoke to him and said all the right things, but whenever he thought no one was looking, his face fell. The mayor obviously thought that the threat from Mad Mulligan was far from over, and Dave had to agree with him. He kept remembering the strange dream he'd had the night before and the warnings that Mad Mulligan had given him.

You're gonna regret getting involved in my business, Mad Mulligan had told him. Perhaps it had just been a dream, but Dave had learned by now that his dreams were never as simple as they seemed.

Dave and his friends were seated at the head table, along with Mayor Grady, Liza, Tom and a few other important illagers and cowmen. Porkins was chatting away to Tom, the two of them getting along like a forest on fire. At the end of the table, Carl and Alex were chatting away while flicking through bits of paper. Dave went over to see what they were up to.

"Netherothbrine is far cooler than Ghastrothbrine," said Carl. "It's not even a question."

"No way!" said Alex. "Ghastrothbrine can shoot ghasts from her mouth! And she's Herobrine's long-lost sister!"

"What are you two arguing about?" asked Dave.

"We're trying to come up with more names for Herobrine's kids," said Carl.

"Um, why?" Dave asked.

"We want to make the battle of Jeb's Peak even more epic than it was in real life," said Alex, "so we're giving Herobrine loads more kids in our comic book. They've all got awesome powers and cool names."

"Yes, but why does Herobrine need to have a long-lost sister as well?" said Carl.

"Long lost siblings are awesome," said Alex. "Haven't you read the issue where Seth the Elf discovers he's got five twin brothers?"

"Of course, I have," said Carl. "Anyway, Dave, here's the list of Herobrine's kids we've come up with so far. Tell us what you think."

"Er..." said Dave.

"Thunderothbrine," said Carl. "He's Herobrine's youngest son, who escaped from Herobrine's lava castle by turning himself into a bolt of lightning. He dedicated his life to the ninja arts, and now he can throw shurikens made of electricity."

"Why would Herobrine have a lava castle?" Dave asked.

"Because it's cool," said Alex.

"Okay, here's another one," said Carl. "Alex came up with this one. *Reverserothbrine.* She looks just like Herobrine, but everything about her is reversed. Her head faces the other way, and she wears shoes on her hands and eats her dinner with her feet."

"Um..." said Dave.

"I told you that one was rubbish," Carl said to Alex. "Now what about this one, Dave: *Fishrothbrine.* He can summon krakens and can breathe underwater for up to three hours. Or this one: *Deathrothbrine.* He dies every issue, but then comes back alive in the next issue."

"Tell him my other one," said Alex.

"All right," said Carl, rolling his eyes. "Alex came up with *Cakerothbrine.* She can summon cakes and is Herobrine's long lost wife, who left him after he never helped to clean the house. She has triplet daughters who are all ninjas: Firerothbrine, who has the power of fire, Waterothbrine, who has the power of water, and Porkchoprothbrine, who has the power of porkchops."

"What's going on here?" said a voice. The three of them turned around to see Spidroth standing behind them.

"Er, nothing," said Carl, quickly hiding the bits of paper.

"We were just coming up with more brothers and sisters for you," said Alex happily. "I know you've got two brothers and a sister already, but we thought it would be more epic if you had more of them, all with cool powers."

"Shush," said Carl, nudging Alex in the ribs.

Spidroth snatched one of the pieces of paper out of Carl's hands.

"Horserothbrine," said Spidroth, reading the caption over an image of a horse's head on a person's body.

"He can summon exploding horses," said Alex.

"Yeah, um, that one needs a bit of work," said Carl.

Spidroth looked angrier than Dave had ever seen her – which was pretty angry.

"You realize..." said Spidroth, barely able to get her words out, "that I had ninety-six other siblings, all of whom perished? And now you want to make up more of them ... for a comic book?"

"Yeah, maybe that wasn't such a great idea," said Carl, looking sheepish.

For a moment, Spidroth looked like she was going to pull out her sword and strike Carl and Alex down, but instead, she stormed off, chucking the piece of paper with Horserothbrine onto the floor.

"I think you two need to abandon the idea of Herobrine having more long-lost children," Dave said to Carl and Alex.

"Good idea," said Carl.

Dave ran off after Spidroth. She was sitting alone outside one of the red sandstone buildings.

"Hey," he said.

"Hey," said Spidroth, looking down at her feet.

Dave sat next to her.

"Those two didn't mean any harm," said Dave, "they were just being idiots."

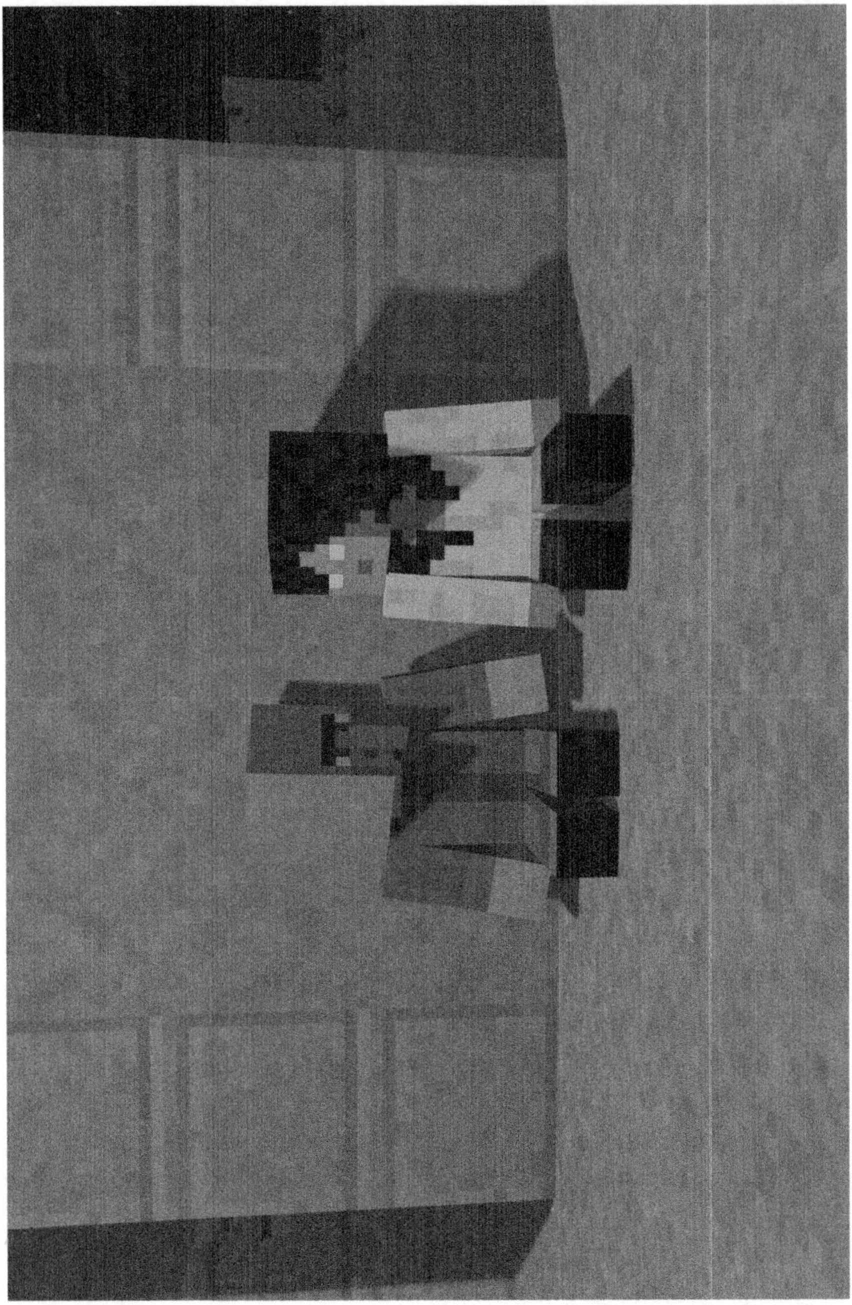

"I know," said Spidroth, "but those fools and their stupid ideas just brought it all back to me. All those horrible memories of when Herobrine and his witches pitted my siblings and I against each other. Only the ones of us who survived — Vioroth, Necroth, Slimoth and me — were given names. The other ones all perished nameless. I'm ashamed to say it, but I've forgotten all of their faces."

"It was over a thousand years ago," said Dave.

"It still makes me ashamed," said Spidroth. "And now I've found out that Herobrine had another son as well — Enderbrine. He was a monster, but only because my father made him that way."

"The only person who should feel ashamed is Herobrine," said Dave. "He treated you all terribly. But he's gone now, and no one will harm you ever again. I'll make sure of it."

Spidroth looked up at him. Her white eyes were all glossy from crying, Dave noticed.

"Dave," she said softly. Dave found his head moving towards Spidroth's, the two of them getting closer and closer and —

CLANG-A-LANG-A-LANG-A-LANG!!!!

A bell rang out from one of the rooftops. Dave and Spidroth jumped to their feet, pulling out their netherite swords.

"An army is coming!" someone yelled. "There's an army approaching the town!"

Dave and Spidroth ran as fast as their legs would take them. In a couple of seconds, Alex, Carl and Porkins had joined them, all of them running towards the edge of town. When they got there, they saw that a gigantic army of illagers with flaming torches was gathered in the darkness just outside of the town. Some of the illagers were on horseback, but some, Dave was horrified to see, were riding ravagers.

"Oh no," gasped Porkins.

Mayor Grady, Liza and Tom all ran forward to join Dave and the others. The illager and cowmen soldiers who had fought the husks the night before ran to join them as well, wearing their iron armor.

"There's so many of them," said Tom in disbelief. He was wearing his iron armor too.

One of the illagers in the enemy army rode her horse forward. It was Marie, and she was grinning.

"Mad Mulligan is not happy with you!" Marie shouted. "He thought the people of Dead Bush were his loyal friends, and you've betrayed him!"

"Mad Mulligan is no friend of ours!" Liza called back.

Marie laughed.

"I'm feeling generous tonight," she said, "so I won't destroy your town. But I am going to teach you all a lesson. A lesson you'll never forget. Attack!"

At Marie's command, the illager army charged forward: ravagers, horses and foot soldiers all rushing towards the town.

Dave had no idea what to do. He'd never been one to back down from a fight, but they were completely outnumbered.

"Everyone, get back to your houses!" Mayor Grady shouted to the illagers and cowmen who'd gathered at the edge of the town to see what was going on. "Get in your houses and lock the doors!"

The townsfolk didn't need telling twice. They all ran off, shouting and panicking and scrabbling to get as far away from the illager army as they could.

Now the only ones gathered at the edge of the village were Dave and his friends, Mayor Grady, Liza, Tom the cowman and the fourteen other volunteer soldiers in their iron armor.

"You should all go and lock yourselves in your houses as well," Dave told Mayor Grady and the others.

"No chance," said Liza, pulling out an iron sword, "we're going to fight."

Mayor Grady looked like he was about to argue with his daughter, but they were out of time: in a few seconds, the horses and the ravagers would be at the edge of the town.

"Battle stations," Dave shouted, quickly putting on his netherite armor and pulling out his netherite sword.

One ravager was charging ahead of the others. Its rider was an illager woman in diamond armor.

"Stand back, chaps," said Porkins, walking forward, "this one's mine."

"Porkins, what are you doing?" said Dave. "You're going to get trampled!"

The ravager's rider grinned and charged straight towards Porkins. If the pigman was afraid, it wasn't showing on his face.

"Take this, you scoundrel!" Porkins shouted, then *WHAM*, he punched the ravager in the face with his iron arm. To Dave's amazement, the ravager went flying backward, its rider landing on the ground.

"Wow," said Alex.

"That's definitely going in the comic book," said Carl.

The other ravagers and the illagers on horseback had reached the edge of the town now, and a ferocious battle began. Carl ran around punching ravagers and pulling riders off their horses, while Porkins attacked more ravagers with his iron arm and Dave, Spidroth and Alex used their swords. Mayor Grady was fighting alongside his daughter Liza and Tom the cowman, all three of them using iron swords. It was clear that the mayor's priority was protecting his daughter, and he never left her side. The other soldiers in iron armor were doing their best, but it was clear that they were inexperienced at hand-to-hand combat, and their iron swords were outmatched, as many of the soldiers in the invading army had diamond swords.

"Stop!" a voice screeched from above them. Dave looked up and saw Marie on one of the nearby rooftops, along with a load of illagers with crossbows. The illagers all had their bows pointed down at Dave and the others. Dave looked around at the other nearby rooftops and saw that they had illagers with crossbows on them as well.

"Stop or we'll fill you all full of arrows!" Marie screeched.

"Stand down, everyone!" Mayor Grady shouted.

Dave and the others all stopped fighting.

"Put down your weapons," Marie shouted.

They did as she asked. They didn't have a choice.

Marie climbed down a ladder, then walked over to Mayor

Grady.

"Good to see you again, Mr Mayor," she grinned. She turned to one of her soldiers. "Go house-to-house and smash down the doors. Bring all the townsfolk here – I want to speak to them."

The illagers did as she asked, going through the town and forcing the townsfolk to leave their homes. They all gathered on the main street, shivering and afraid.

"People of Dead Bush," Marie shouted, addressing the crowd, "this is your last chance. There will be no more warnings. Next week you will provide my soldiers and I with *three* thousand gold ingots, *three* thousand diamonds and *three* thousand emeralds. If you don't, I will personally see to it that every block of this village is wiped from the face of the earth. Do I make myself clear?"

"You don't scare us!" one elderly cowman shouted.

Marie laughed.

"That's exactly what the people of Blue Sky Village said to me," she grinned. "Why don't you go and ask them how that worked out for them? Oh, wait, you can't, because Blue Sky Village doesn't exist anymore. Now, if I come back next week and you try any sort of stupid plan, or you don't have the treasure I've asked for, I will destroy your town. And to show you I'm serious, I'm taking a hostage. You, come here."

Marie was pointing at Liza.

"No," said Mayor Grady, stepping in front of his daughter, "take me instead. Please don't take my daughter."

"I won't ask again," said Marie. "Come here, girl. *Now.*"

"It's okay, Daddy," said Liza, putting a hand on her father's shoulder. "It's all gonna be okay."

Liza walked over to Marie. Marie pulled out some rope from a pouch on the side of her horse and tied Liza's hands together. Then she tied Liza's hands to her horse.

"We'll see you all next week," grinned Marie. "And in case you're thinking of trying anything, just know that I'll be bringing an army – an army even bigger than this one."

She turned her horse around and began trotting away, Liza walking behind her. Liza took one last look at her father and the rest of the townsfolk, then she turned back around and kept walking.

The illagers on the rooftops all climbed down, and then the illager army, along with all the horses and ravagers, left the town, walking back across the dark desert.

"What now?" an elderly cow woman said.

"Now we fight," said Mayor Grady. "Now we put an end to Mad Mulligan and his gang once and for all."

CHAPTER SEVEN
Training

The next day, the training began. Mayor Grady had asked Dave and his friends to train the people of Dead Bush to fight, and they'd agreed. Few of the illagers and cowmen who lived in the town had ever used a sword before, let alone a bow, but they were all eager to learn. They'd finally had enough of being pushed around by Mad Mulligan's gang, and Liza being taken as a hostage had been the final straw. They had a week until Marie and her army returned, so they had to be ready by then. It wasn't long, but Dave believed that he and his friends could train the town to fight in time. He thought back to when he, Carl and Porkins had trained the villagers of Greenleaf, all that time ago. They'd all been complete noobs, but with a bit of training, they had become proper fighters. Dave was sure that the same thing could happen with the townsfolk of Dead Bush.

To defeat Mad Mulligan's forces, they'd need archers as well as swordsmen, so a quarter of the townsfolk went with Porkins to train at archery. The pigman set up some targets around the town market, and his recruits spent their days practicing their aim. At first, they were all hopeless and could barely even string their bows, but before long, they started to get the hang of it.

One problem the townsfolk had was that they didn't have much armor or weapons, so Tom supervised a new digging effort down the mine. Normally, the miners didn't bother much with iron ore, as they had been concentrating on finding gold, diamonds and emeralds for Mad Mulligan, so there was still a lot of iron left in the walls. The townsfolk got to work digging all that iron up and then turned it into armor and swords. They also dug up gravel to get flint for their arrows and hunted spiders to get more strings for their bows.

One of the things that the town was lacking was a wall. Mad Mulligan had forbidden the people of Dead Bush from building a wall, but since they were now planning on fighting against him, there was nothing to stop them from finally building one. Carl supervised the building effort, shouting orders at the poor illagers and cowmen and making sarcastic jokes at their expense. When Dave suggested that the creeper be nicer to them, Carl insisted that his methods produced the best results.

"If you're rude to people, they're more productive," Carl insisted. "It's a well-known fact."

Dave wasn't quite so sure about that, but he let Carl get on with it. As well as building a three-block high wall around the village, made from red sandstone, cobblestone and whatever other blocks they could find, the townspeople also built a moat around the wall. Carl's original plan had been to fill the moat full of lava, but when it became clear that they'd never be able to get enough lava in time, he'd settled for water. Water would at least slow the enemy forces down before they reached the wall, he reasoned.

As they were by far the best hand-to-hand fighters in the group, Alex and Spidroth trained the townsfolk to use swords. At first, there weren't many iron swords, so many of the townsfolk had to make do with wood, but as the week went on, and the illagers and cowmen in the mine dug up more materials, eventually all the townsfolk had at least a stone sword, and many of them had iron swords and a few even had diamond.

At one point, Dave had the idea to lead a mining expedition into the Nether to get some netherite ingots. Mad Mulligan's gang seemed to have no netherite, which hardly surprised Dave as it was a very new material. Dave reasoned that if the townsfolk could have netherite swords and armor, they would easily be able to outclass Mad Mulligan's gang in battle. However, Dave soon learned that netherite wasn't easy to come by. He led a group of ten illagers and ten cowmen into the Nether, but after a whole day of digging, all they had to show for their troubles was one netherite scrap. Plus, several of their number had all almost fallen into lava. Eventually,

Dave decided that they'd have to do without netherite after all.

Carl also supervised the building of some iron golems. Unfortunately, they needed most of the iron they found for weapons and armor, but Mayor Grady agreed that they could spare some ingots to build golems. Golems took lots of iron ingots to build, so they only built four of them, but that was better than nothing. Dave had seen firsthand how strong iron golems were, although he had no clue whether they'd be strong enough to fight off ravagers.

If only we all had iron arms like Porkins, Dave thought. *They'd really come in useful right now.*

Dave also wanted to set a trap for Mad Mulligan's gang. Carl still had a few TNT blocks left, but Dave wanted more, so he set off alone into the mine to find some feral creepers. It didn't take him long, and soon creepers were crawling out of the darkness to attack him. Dave slew them, getting some more gunpowder in the process.

On the night before Mad Mulligan's gang was due to return, Mayor Grady took Dave, Carl, Spidroth, Alex and Porkins aside.

"I hate to ask this," said the mayor, "but my daughter... If we defeat Marie and her forces, Mad Mulligan might harm Liza."

"Then we will rescue her," said Spidroth. "Tomorrow, Marie will be bringing her army to Dead Bush, so that will be the perfect time to sneak into Mad Mulligan's base when he doesn't have as many troops there as usual. Alex and I will sneak in and rescue your daughter."

"Oh, wow, thanks for choosing me, Spidroth!" said Alex.

"You and I may not always see eye to eye," said Spidroth, "but I cannot deny your ability as a warrior and a ninja. We will need all your ninja skills tomorrow to sneak into Mad Mulligan's base and rescue Liza."

"Thank you, both of you," said Mayor Grady.

"And who knows," grinned Spidroth, "we may even get the chance to take out Mad Mulligan himself and put an end to him once and for all."

"Now that would be something," smiled Mayor Grady. "The whole region would owe you a huge debt."

"I do not promise anything," said Spidroth, "we don't know how many guards Mulligan will have around him, but if we have the opportunity to take him out, we will."

That night, no one in town slept very well. The townsfolk were all nervous, knowing that they may lose their lives in the battle ahead. Dave was nervous too. He knew that he and his friends had trained the people of Dead Bush well, but it may all count for nothing against Marie and her army.

When the sun rose the next day, Alex and Spidroth rode off on their horses, heading north to where Mayor Grady had told them Mad Mulligan's camp was. Everyone else ate as much breakfast as their nervous stomachs could take, then they got their armor on and prepared themselves for the battle ahead. As usual, Marie was due to come at noon. The illagers and cowmen all took their places, the archers going onto the rooftops and the town wall, and the swordsmen standing in formation inside the town. The plan was that the archers would try to keep out the enemy forces as long as possible, but when the walls were finally breached, the swordsmen would go into action. Dave hoped that the archers would whittle down Marie's forces quite a bit because none of the townsfolk were still that brilliant with swords.

Porkins was on the wall, and his job would be to command the archers. Dave and Carl were with the foot soldiers, ready to command them once the walls were breached. Mayor Grady was on the wall with Porkins, and he wore a full set of diamond armor with a diamond sword.

"I never thought I'd be wearing this again," said Mayor Grady, looking down at his armor.

"You've fought in it before?" Dave asked him.

"Let's just say I had ... an interesting past," said Mayor Grady. "If we all survive today, I'll tell you about it over a glass of milk."

"You've got yourself a deal," said Dave.

For Dave and the others in the town, the worst part was the waiting. At least the archers on the walls and the rooftops could see what was going on, but the swordsmen inside the village couldn't see anything. They just had to stand in their rows, sweating in their armor as the sun beat down on them.

"How are you feeling?" Dave asked Carl.

"Let's just say that this golem suit is gonna need a good clean," said Carl. "I've never sweated so much in my life."

Dave knew what Carl meant. Not only did they have the prospect of the terrifying battle ahead of them, but it was midday, and the sun was blazing down. It was the perfect recipe for a set of very sweaty armor.

Finally, when Dave was starting to think that Marie and her forces would never arrive, he heard the sound of a bell ringing on one of the rooftops.

"They're here!" a cowman on the rooftops shouted.

Dave could just about see one of the town walls from where he was standing. He saw the archers all tensing up, preparing their bows.

The battle's about to begin, Dave thought, wiping the sweat off his forehead with his sleeve. *Let's hope that luck is on our side today.*

CHAPTER EIGHT
The Base

Mad Mulligan's base was exactly where Mayor Grady had said it would be: right in the middle of an eroded badlands biome, nestled next to a small mountain. The biome was full of natural rock spires, made from layers of different color terracotta. It made the whole biome seem like the mouth of some gigantic beast, with the stone spires being the beast's teeth.

On the outskirts of the base were four outpost towers, made from dark oak wood and cobblestone. There were illagers inside the towers, keeping a lookout. Underneath the towers were tents made from white wool, with illagers sitting outside sharpening their weapons or practicing with their crossbows, shooting at scarecrows made from carved pumpkins and hay bales.

The base itself was a collection of short red sandstone buildings, with illagers with crossbows standing on the roofs. Even though Marie had taken a whole army of illagers to Dead Bush, there were still plenty more left to guard the base.

"So, what's the plan?" Alex whispered. She and Spidroth were lying on top of a nearby hill, scoping out the base from afar.

"One of those sandstone buildings has bars on the windows," said Spidroth. "That must be where they're keeping Liza. It looks like a prison."

"Wow, Spidroth," said Alex, "you're pretty smart."

"Of course, I am, child," said Spidroth. "I am the Lady Spidrothbrine."

Spidroth found it hard to know what to make of Alex. In many ways, the girl was completely immature and seemed to have a child's mind, even though she looked like an adult. But then Alex would come up with a piece of wisdom or knowledge far beyond her years, or she would perform some extraordinary feat in battle. Alex was a clone of Steve, Spidroth knew, and somewhere in that head of hers were Steve's memories and skills.

Steve had been a disappointment to Spidroth as well. She had heard countless stories about his adventures and exploits, but when she had finally met him in person, when they'd been captured together by the Empress back in the Nether, Spidroth had seen that Steve was nothing but a fool. Alex was the same – a fantastic warrior with the brain of a moron. But every time that Spidroth thought that she had Alex figured out, the girl would do something surprising. Spidroth had been amazed at the technique that Alex had used to climb the yellow creeper queen's neck. Spidroth would never have thought of a technique like that, but it had come to Alex easily.

"We want to avoid being seen," said Spidroth, "so we will only attack any guards we come across if we have to. The plan is to sneak over to the prison, break Liza out, and get out of there."

"I thought we were gonna try and kick Mad Mulligan's butt as well?" Alex asked.

"Only if the chance presents itself," said Spidroth. After seeing how many guards there were in the base, Spidroth had slightly gone off the idea of taking out Mad Mulligan. Even if they managed to sneak up and defeat him, there were so many illagers on the base that they might not make it out alive. No, they would concentrate on rescuing the mayor's daughter first and only go after Mad Mulligan if it was easy enough to do so.

Alex and Spidroth began sneaking towards the base, using the shadows from the rock spires to hide themselves. They kept as far away from the lookout towers as they could, sneaking past outcrops of rock and using whatever they could find for cover.

As they passed the tents made from white wool, Spidroth heard some snippets of conversation between a group of illagers.

"Mulligan was real mad about that trident," said one of the illagers. "I dread to think what he's gonna do to that yellow creeper when he catches him."

"Well, whatever he does, I hope I get to watch," said another illager. "Getting electrocuted by that little thing was no joke, let me tell you."

Spidroth and Alex kept creeping forward, sneaking past another outpost tower and some more tents, until finally, they reached the cluster of red sandstone buildings. There were more guards standing around the buildings than Spidroth had first thought, but most of them were chatting or sharpening their weapons, so Alex and Spidroth easily sneak past them.

Finally, they reached the building with the iron bars on the windows. Spidroth peered through the bars and saw that the building was one big room, with a single prisoner sitting in the corner.

"Liza," Spidroth hissed, whispering as loud as she dared, "over here."

Liza looked up. When she saw Spidroth, she grinned. She ran straight over to the window.

"It's so good to see a friendly face," Liza whispered.

"That's the first time anyone's ever called my face friendly," grinned Spidroth. "Now stand back. I'm going to break you out."

Spidroth took out her netherite pickaxe and began picking away at the bars, taking it slowly and trying to make as little noise as possible. Finally, the bars broke.

"Come on," said Spidroth.

Liza squeezed through the window, then landed next to Spidroth and Alex.

"Hi Liza," Alex whispered.

"Hi," Liza whispered back. "Now, which way do we go?"

"Follow me," said Spidroth. She began tiptoeing between the buildings, with Alex and Liza following behind her. They'd almost cleared the sandstone buildings when they heard some voices ahead of them.

"Jones and his squad are on the way to the coordinates you gave them, boss," an illager was saying. "Hopefully, they'll find the yellow creeper there."

"Oh, they'll find him, don't you worry about that," said a deep voice. The voice was gruff, but there was a tinge of laughter in it as well, as if the speaker didn't have a care in the world.

"Of course, boss," said the other illager.

Then they heard the sound of footsteps disappearing into the distance.

Spidroth, Alex and Liza crept forward, peering around the side of one of the buildings. An illager in a black leather jacket with a red scarf around his neck was leaning against a barrel. The other illager who'd been speaking had gone now, leaving the illager with the red scarf all alone.

"That's him," Liza whispered nervously, "that's Mad Mulligan."

"You're sure?" Spidroth whispered back.

"Positive," said Liza. "I've seen him through the bars of my cell."

Spidroth gave Alex a nod, and the two of them pulled out their swords. This was a better chance than they could have ever asked for: they'd come across Mad Mulligan, and he was all alone.

It's time to put an end to this once and for all, thought Spidroth, then she rushed around the corner, running towards Mad Mulligan with her sword held high.

CHAPTER NINE
The Battle

"Don't fire until I tell you to, chaps!" Porkins shouted. "Hold your bows steady!"

The illagers and cowmen archers on the wall were all getting nervous, and Porkins couldn't blame them. A huge army of illagers and ravagers marched slowly towards the town across the red sand of the badlands plateau. It was hard for Porkins to get an idea of exactly how big their army was, but there were a lot of them. Far more than Porkins had hoped there would be.

"I don't know if I can do this," a cow woman said, lowering her bow, "I need to get out of here."

Porkins put a trotter on the cow woman's shoulder.

"Just remember your training, dear girl," Porkins told her. "I've seen you hit the center of a target from thirty blocks away. Now you need to use those skills on those blaggards outside. They want to destroy your village, and you're not going to let them."

"Yes, sir," said the cow woman, a new look of determination crossing her face.

"That goes for the rest of you as well," Porkins shouted. "Are you going to let these scoundrels destroy your village?"

"No, sir!" all the illagers and cowmen shouted back.

"Jolly good," said Porkins. In reality, Porkins was a bundle of nerves, but he knew that he couldn't show fear in front of the troops.

The illager army came to a stop, just outside of arrow range. Then one female illager on horseback rode forward. It was Marie.

"I'm here for Mad Mulligan's payment," Marie shouted, a nasty grin on her face. "Three thousand gold ingots, three thousand diamonds and three thousand emeralds, as agreed."

Mayor Grady was standing on the town wall a short way to the right of Porkins.

"We never agreed to anything," Mayor Grady called back. "Dead Bush no longer belongs to Mad Mulligan, and he won't get so much as an emerald from us anymore."

"Very well," grinned Marie. "I can see you've made your decision, Mayor Grady."

Marie turned her horse around to face her troops. Then she raised her sword to the sky and blew a wooden horn.

AWWWOOOOOOOOOOOOO!!!!!

The sound of the horn rang out across the desert, then, all at once, the army of illagers started marching forward.

"Get ready," Porkins shouted to his archers.

A group of ravagers ran forward, ahead of the rest of Marie's troops. These ravagers didn't have riders, and they were charging at full speed straight towards the town wall.

"Fire!" Porkins shouted. The illagers and cowmen on the wall unleashed a volley of arrows against the ravagers.

"What about the trap, sir? An illager archer asked Porkins.

"We're saving that for the ground troops," Porkins told him. "Now start firing, man, chop, chop!"

The first ravager reached the edge of the town, but when it tried to charge into the wall, it fell into the moat instead, splashing about in the water. The moat was deep, and the water in it was three blocks down, so the ravager couldn't get out. Two more ravagers fell into the moat, but then the rest of them managed to stop in time. The ravagers ran around aimlessly, trying to find a way across the moat, all the while being shot at by the archers. Some of the ravagers were slain by the arrows and the ones that weren't panicked and ran away. The archers on the walls all cheered.

"Jolly good show, chaps!" Porkins shouted.

They'd thwarted the ravagers, but the rest of the invading army kept coming. The next ones to arrive within arrow-firing distance were illager ground troops with shields. The archers on the walls unleashed another volley of arrows, but the illagers on the ground all raised their shields to protect themselves.

"Keep firing, chaps!" Porkins shouted. "Aim at the gaps between the shields!"

The archers did as Porkins commanded, but the illagers on the ground kept in formation, with their shields close to each other, so it was very hard to find any gaps. The archers managed to take a few of the ground troops out, but before long, the ground troops had reached the moat. The troops at the front began placing down cobblestone blocks, building a bridge across the water.

"Oh crumbs," muttered Porkins.

Now they had the bridge, the ground troops could get right up to the town wall. While being protected by the shields, the troops at the front pulled out diamond pickaxes and began hacking at the wall.

"Tell our swordsmen to get ready," Porkins told a nearby cowman. "Those blaggards are about to breach the wall."

*

"This is boring," sighed Carl. "I like beating people up, but I don't like having to wait to beat people up."

"You may not have to wait much longer," said Dave. A cowman with a bow was rushing towards them down the main street.

"Mad Mulligan's forces are about to break through the wall," the cowman panted.

"Everyone, get ready," said Dave, pulling out his sword. Behind him, all the other illager and cowman troops pulled out their swords as well. Dave took a look behind him. The Dead Bush townsfolk looked like a proper army now, with full sets of armor and swords, but they all looked terrified. This would be the first battle most of them had ever fought in.

"We can do this," Dave shouted, addressing the troops. "Remember your training, and remember that these people are trying to destroy your town."

"And remember to give them a bashing," said Carl. "Repeat after me — Bashing! Bashing! Bashing!"

To Dave surprise, all the illagers and cowmen joined in:

"BASHING!" They began to chant. "BASHING! BASHING! BASHING!"

"Er, right," said Dave.

Up ahead, Dave saw that the wall had finally been breached, and Marie's army of illagers was pouring through, into the town. The archers on the wall were still firing arrows at the invading army, but there were too many of them, and the illagers who'd got through were charging down the main street, straight towards Dave and his forces.

"Charge!" Dave shouted. He and Carl ran forward, and the people of Dead Bush ran behind him, all of them shouting at the top of their lungs.

Carl was the first to reach Marie's forces, and he immediately began swinging his netherite arms, sending the illagers flying. Seeing Carl make easy work of the invading army gave the rest of the townspeople the inspiration they needed, and they charged into battle, swinging their swords at the invading foes.

*

Back on the wall, Porkins and his archers were still firing endless arrows at the invading forces. They couldn't stop Marie's soldiers from breaching the hole in the wall, but they were able to thin their numbers down. Some riders on ravagers tried to charge at the wall, but the archers were quickly able to take out the riders, and without their riders, the ravagers just ran off in random directions.

Far behind the army, Porkins could see Marie, sitting on her horse and watching the battle unfold.

The coward won't even fight in her own battle, Porkins thought bitterly.

Porkins turned around and saw that a fierce battle was taking place inside the town, with Dave's troops fighting with their swords against the invading illagers. Porkins couldn't see Dave, but he could see Carl: the creeper was rushing around and sending the illagers flying with his huge netherite arms.

"Good show, old chap," Porkins grinned.

There were still many more illagers outside, pouring into the town, but Porkins was confident. The people of Dead Bush were fighting a good fight, and if they kept fighting the way that they were, Porkins had every confidence that they could win this battle.

"Is it time for the trap, sir?" a cowman asked Porkins.

"Yes," said Porkins. "I believe it is."

Porkins ran over to a lever on the wall and pulled it. For a split second, nothing happened, then *KAAAAADOOOOOOOOOM,* an explosion burst from the ground underneath the feet of the enemy illagers outside the town, as the TNT trap that Dave had laid went off. The explosion took out a load of Marie's forces and created a huge crater, but there were still plenty more of them left.

"Keep firing, everyone," Porkins heard Mayor Grady shout. The mayor and Tom the cowman were on the wall a short way away from Porkins, firing their bows at the invading troops. Some of the invading illagers started placing ladders and climbing up the wall, but Mayor Grady pulled out a diamond sword and swung his blade at them, sending them flying. It was clear to Porkins that Mayor Grady, unlike the rest of the people in the town, had been in battles before.

"Keep going, chaps!" Porkins shouted to his archers. "We can do this!"

*

Dave was in the thick of things, with the invading illagers all around him. Somehow, he'd got separated from Carl and the rest of the troops and was now in a narrow back alley, surrounded by illagers in diamond armor with diamond swords.

"You're in trouble now," one of the illagers hissed at him. "I don't know what that fancy armor of yours is, but I reckon Mad Mulligan will be real pleased when we bring it to him."

"You'll have to kill me first," said Dave.

"That's the idea," the illager grinned.

The illagers charged at Dave. Dave swung his netherite sword, blocking one blow, then swiveling around and blocking another, then another, then another. One of the diamond swords whacked into his head, but thankfully his netherite helmet took the impact. More swords were whacking into his netherite vest plate.

My armor is holding up, for now, Dave thought, as he blocked another blow with his sword, *but how much more can it take?*

Suddenly, one of the illagers managed to slice their sword down into the gap where Dave's vest plate met his shoulder plate, cutting through Dave's robes and hitting his skin.

"Arrrrggghh!!!!" Dave yelled, falling to his knees.

"Now it's time to say goodnight, villager," one of the illagers grinned. All the illagers raised their diamond swords, ready to strike Dave down. There was no way he could take them all on, even with his netherite sword. Unless...

I've got to use the Sight, Dave thought. Spidroth had told Dave that he could become a fantastic warrior with the Sight — maybe even better than her. If he was ever going to put that to the test, now was the time. Dave tried to clear his mind and concentrate, trying to predict where the blows from the illagers would come from.

Allowing the Sight to guide him, Dave raised his blade, blocking one sword blow, then he swiveled and blocked another, chopping one of the illager's diamond swords in two. He could sense that another illager was about to strike him down with their sword, so Dave quickly turned around and blocked that blow. Then he sensed another blow coming from behind, so he moved his sword around and blocked that blow without even looking.

This is amazing, Dave thought. It was like there was a hand guiding his movements. But then things began to go wrong: an illager charged at Dave from the front but at the same time Dave had a vision of the same illager attacking him from the side. In his confusion, Dave was unable to block the blow. And the illager smashed his sword down on Dave's helmet, making Dave's ears ring.

I'm getting what's happening now mixed up with what's about to happen, Dave knew. Then he remembered the joke that

Carl had made before – *"You should tie some cloth around your eyes when you fight."*

Against his better judgment, Dave closed his eyes. Now, the only thing guiding him was the Sight, not what he could see with his own eyes.

I hope this works, Dave thought.

Letting the Sight guide him, Dave raised his sword and blocked a sword blow. Then he turned around and blocked another blow.

"This moron is fighting with his eyes closed," Dave heard one of the illagers say. "Kill him!"

Keeping his eyes closed and letting the Sight guide him, Dave swooped his sword down in an arc, blocking another sword blow. Then he brought his sword quickly up, chopping one of the illager's diamond swords in half. Then he turned and kicked one of the illagers in the chest with his netherite boot, sending the illager tumbling backward into a wall.

Before long, Dave had defeated all the illagers: chopping their diamond swords in half and making them useless. He opened his eyes and saw all the illagers looking at him in terror.

"Let's get out of here," said one of the illagers, and they all scampered off out of the alley, leaving Dave alone.

That was awesome, thought Dave, grinning.

CLANG-A-LANG-A-LANG-A-LANG!!!

Someone was ringing the bell on one of the rooftops.

"The battle is won!" Dave heard someone shout. "The town is saved!"

Dave staggered out of the alley, still clutching his shoulder, and saw that it was true: the townsfolk of Dead Bush were triumphant. The members of Mad Mulligan's gang who hadn't fled or been slain had all been captured, with groups of Dead Bush illagers and cowmen standing around them, guarding them. Carl spotted Dave and ran over to him.

"Another successful battle," the creeper grinned.

"How were our losses?" Dave asked.

Carl's face fell. "We didn't lose too many," the creeper said, "but we still lost some good soldiers."

Dave and Carl walked down the main street, congratulating the townsfolk as they went. Finally, they climbed the town wall and joined Porkins, Mayor Grady and Tom. Most of the wall was nothing but a ruin now, full of holes where the illagers had broken through.

"I can never thank you all enough for what you've done for this town," said Mayor Grady.

"We were glad to help," said Dave. "Hopefully, this is the end of Mad Mulligan terrorizing Dead Bush. I'm sure that Spidroth and Alex are bringing your daughter back even as we speak."

"I hope so," smiled Mayor Grady.

Dave looked out across the desert. The sun was starting to set now, but all the illagers were gone.

"That coward Marie fled as soon as the battle started to go our way," said Porkins bitterly.

"Good riddance," scowled Tom. "Let's hope we never see her face here ever again."

"Wait," said Carl, squinting as he looked across the red sand, "someone's coming."

"Is it Spidroth and Alex?" asked Dave.

"Do they have Liza?" asked Mayor Grady.

"It's Marie again," said Carl. "And she's with another rider. A rider on a ravager."

Marie rode her horse to the edge of the town, followed by the rider on the ravager. The rider was another illager — a male illager. Marie and the other rider pulled their steeds to a stop, and then the male illager jumped off the ravager and looked up at Dave and the others with a big grin. Dave had seen this illager before — it was the illager who had been in his dream.

"Davey-boy!" The illager shouted. "It's so good to see you again!"

"How do you know my name?" Dave asked. "I've never met you before."

"Sure you have," the illager grinned. "We met in your dream, although I didn't introduce myself properly. Very rude of me. I'm Mad Mulligan."

CHAPTER TEN
Mad Mulligan

Dave finally got his first proper look at Mad Mulligan. Mulligan was a tall illager who wore heavy-looking black boots, a black leather jacket and a red scarf around his neck, tucked into the jacket. He seemed to have a permanent grin on his face as if everything was amusing to him. The red sword that Dave had seen in his dream was attached to the illager's belt. Dave had never seen a sword like that before, and he had no idea what it was made of.

"Mayor Grady," said Mad Mulligan, looking up at the mayor, "it's nice to meet you face-to-face at last. Now I know you and my associate Marie have had some disagreements over the past couple of weeks, so let's come to a compromise."

Mad Mulligan went over to his ravager and took something off the back of it. Dave saw that it was Liza — her arms and legs were tied up with rope, and she had a piece of cloth wrapped around her mouth.

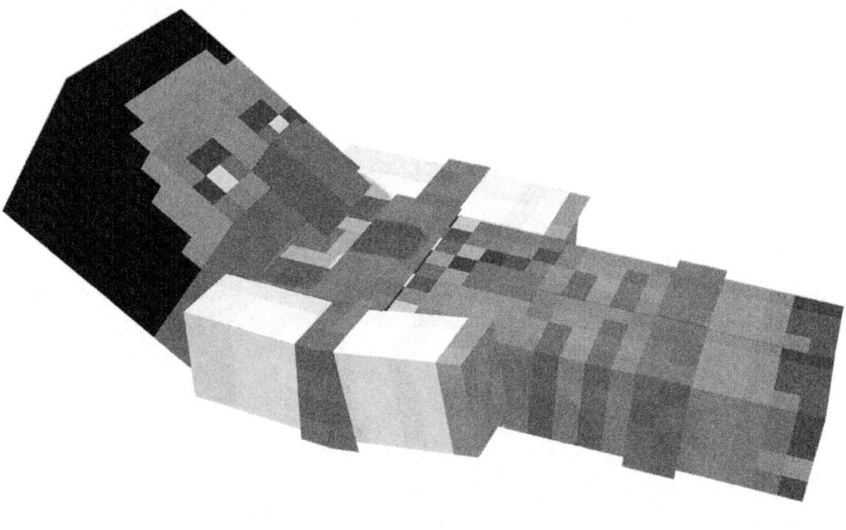

"Maybe three thousand gold ingots, diamonds and emeralds every week was a bit of a big ask," said Mad Mulligan. "So, from now on, let's go back to two thousand. Every week, Marie will come and see you, and you'll provide her with two thousand gold ingots, two thousand diamonds and two thousand emeralds. If you don't, Marie is going to test out whether or not your daughter can swim in lava."

Marie grinned evilly. Liza looked terrified.

"Anyway, that was the boring bit," said Mad Mulligan. "The person I've really come here to see today is Dave. Hi Dave!"

"What do you want with him, you bozo?" asked Carl.

"Ah, Carl the creeper," Mad Mulligan grinned. "You're the funny one, aren't you? Man, some of those jokes you tell have me in stitches. Spidroth says something aggressive, and you make a funny comment, then the two of you argue, then Dave tells you both to behave yourselves. It's funny stuff."

"How do you know so much about us?" Dave demanded.

"That's a good question," said Mad Mulligan. "I must admit, when I first heard about you guys, I was very confused. Some of my troops came back from that collapsed pyramid, talking about a villager, a pigman, a creeper in a strange suit, a woman with orange hair and this weird woman with red skin and white eyes. When I first heard about you guys, you know what it reminded me of? It reminded me of a group of heroes, the kind you get in comic books. Man, I used to love comic books when I was a kid, especially the ones about teams of heroes. So, when I heard about you guys, I wondered: what are a group of heroes doing out here at the end of the world? And then I reasoned, you must be on a quest. But a quest for what?"

"Maybe we're on a quest to kick your butt," said Carl.

"Maybe," grinned Mad Mulligan, "but the more I thought about it, the more I realized that there could only be one thing that you could be after. One thing that is so rare that you travelled all the way here, to the end of the world, to find it."

"Listen, dear chap," said Porkins, "we've defeated your army, so you can bally well go away now. You're not welcome here anymore."

"Oh, Porkins the pigman," said Mad Mulligan, "the last of his kind. Have you seen those new pig creatures they've got in the Nether now? *Piglins,* I think they call themselves. They're okay, but they're nothing compared to the classic pigmen. The originals are always the best."

"Hand Liza over, then leave this town alone," said Dave. "As Porkins says, your army's been defeated."

"Okay, Dave, I'll do you a deal," grinned Mad Mulligan, "you and I fight in single combat, and if you win, I'll give you Liza and your friends back."

"What friends?" asked Dave, but he thought that he already knew the answer.

Mad Mulligan went over to his ravager and took something else off the back of it. At first, Dave thought it was a sack, but then he saw the orange hair and the pale skin and realized it was Alex. Like Liza, her hands and legs had been tied up, and there was a piece of cloth around her mouth. Mad Mulligan dumped her on the ground next to Liza, then he returned to his ravager and took Spidroth off the back of it. She was tied up too. Mulligan dumped her next to Alex.

"Man, you should have seen the epic fight we all had," Mad Mulligan grinned. "Spidroth came at me with her sword, and Alex joined in, using two swords — it was crazy. Alex was doing all these ninja flips in the air, Spidroth was calling me a fool and trying to cut my head off. It was pretty epic stuff. I have to say, these two are probably the greatest warriors I've ever fought in my life. And then even Liza joined in. She's not much of a fighter, and she didn't have a sword, but she tried to help Alex and Spidroth out nonetheless. Anyway, long story short, they all put up a good fight, but I managed to beat them. One against three — pretty impressive, huh?"

"I don't believe you," said Dave. No matter how good a fighter Mad Mulligan was, there was no way that he would have been able to take on both Alex and Spidroth at the same time.

“Well, come and fight me then,” Mad Mulligan shrugged. “As I said, if you win, you can have all three of your friends back.”

“And what happens if you win?” Dave asked.

Mad Mulligan grinned.

“If I win,” he said, “there’s something I need you to help me with. It’s a surprise, but I think it’s one you’re gonna like.”

CHAPTER ELEVEN
Dave Steps Up

"Are you crazy?" Carl whispered. "If that idiot defeated Alex and Spidroth in hand-to-hand combat, you don't stand a chance."

"Carl is right, old bean," said Porkins. "This Mulligan chap means business."

"Listen, Dave," said Mayor Grady, "let's order our forces to march out of the town and capture Mulligan and Marie. I don't care how good they are at fighting; they won't stand a chance against all of us."

"If we do that, they may harm your daughter or Alex and Spidroth," said Dave. "If Mad Mulligan wants to fight; I'll give him a fight."

"But if he could defeat Alex and Spidroth — " Porkins began.

"For all we know, he's lying about that," said Dave. "A whole army of illagers could have ambushed Alex and Spidroth, and Mad Mulligan is just taking all the credit. Besides, I have a power that Mad Mulligan doesn't know about."

"You'd better not be talking about that stupid Sight thing," said Carl.

"During the battle, I was surrounded by soldiers," said Dave. "I thought that there was no way that I could win against them, but I closed my eyes and let the Sight take over. At that moment, I fought better than I ever had before. If I can use those same abilities against Mad Mulligan, I'll be able to defeat him, no matter how strong he is."

"I still think it's a pretty stupid plan," said Carl.

"I have to agree, old boy," said Porkins.

"I know," said Dave, "but this could be our only chance to save Spidroth, Alex and Liza."

The rest of them fell silent. They knew that Dave was right.

So, Dave walked out, leaving the town via the hole that the illager army had made in the wall, walking out across the red sand to meet Mad Mulligan. Mulligan was waiting with a big grin on his face.

"Nice one, Dave," Mad Mulligan grinned. "Isn't this so much more fun this way? An epic one-on-one fight — these are the things that make life worth living."

Dave looked over at Spidroth, Alex and Liza. They were all lying on the ground next to the ravager. Apart from the fact that they were tied up, they all looked fine, Dave was pleased to see, and they were eagerly watching the battle.

Everything is going to be okay, Dave tried to tell them with his eyes. *I'm going to save you.*

Mad Mulligan took out his red sword, the setting sun making the blade seem even redder than before. Dave took out his netherite sword.

"Netherite," said Mad Mulligan, nodding at Dave's sword. "I've heard good things about netherite. Some people are saying that it's even better than diamond."

"You'll see just how good it is in a minute," said Dave.

"Fighting talk, I like it," Mad Mulligan grinned.

Dave closed his eyes and tried to let the Sight guide his actions.

"You're really going to fight me with your eyes closed?" he heard Mad Mulligan ask.

Dave said nothing.

"Fair enough," said Mad Mulligan.

Dave sensed Mad Mulligan rushing towards him. It was the strangest sensation: it was like Dave could detect Mulligan's movements before he even made them. Even though Dave couldn't see Mulligan with his eyes, he could feel exactly where the illager was. Dave sensed Mad Mulligan swinging his red blade at him, and Dave raised his netherite sword to block the blow.

But no blow came — at least not from the direction that Dave had thought it was going to come. Instead, he felt a hard sword blow on the back of his helmet. Dave staggered forward, feeling dazed.

He opened his eyes and turned around, just in time to see Mad Mulligan hit him in the nose with an elbow.

Dave fell to the floor. He reached for his netherite blade, which he had dropped, but Mad Mulligan kicked the sword away with his big black boots. Then Mad Mulligan pointed his red sword at Dave, grinning down at him.

"Sorry, Davey-boy," said Mad Mulligan, "but there's something I didn't tell you before. You know that Sight thing you've got? Well,

I've got it too."

Dave tried to push himself to his feet, but Mad Mulligan put a boot on his chest, pushing him back down. Then the illager raised a hand to his lips and whistled. For a moment, nothing happened, and then Dave saw dust clouds in the distance. He heard the sound of hooves — hundreds of hooves — and saw more riders on horseback and ravagers galloping across the desert towards the town. There were hundreds and hundreds of them — far more than there had been during the first attack.

"Marie," said Mad Mulligan, turning to the illager woman on horseback, "I want you to destroy the town. No survivors."

"As you say, boss," grinned Marie.

"Now, Dave," said Mad Mulligan, looking down at him, "you and me are gonna go open an end portal."

To be continued...

BOOK 33

Mad Mulligan Strikes Back

CHAPTER ONE
No Survivors

"No survivors?" said Dave. "But I thought you were going to give the town one last chance?"

"I was," grinned Mad Mulligan, "but I changed my mind. That's the good thing about being the boss — you can change your mind. No, I've decided that Dead Bush is too much trouble. In my experience, once a town starts to rebel, they find it difficult to go back to doing what they're told. Dead Bush will serve far better as a lesson to all the other towns and villages I control — to let them know what happens to rebels."

Dave could see the huge army of illagers, some on horseback, some on ravagers and some on foot, all of them charging across the desert towards Dead Bush. The town's walls were in ruins, and her soldiers had been fighting for hours — there was no way they'd be able to survive another assault. Dave tried to push himself to his feet once more, but Mad Mulligan pushed him down with his boot.

"Right, Dave," said Mad Mulligan, "it's time for you and me to make a move."

The illager took some rope from his backpack and turned Dave over, tying his hands together. Dave tried to struggle, but Mad Mulligan was too strong. Mulligan tied Dave's legs together as well, so he couldn't move. Then the illager lifted Dave up and put him on the back of his ravager.

"You won't get away with this," Dave told him. "My friends and I have defeated bigger bullies than you."

Mad Mulligan laughed. Then he tied a piece of cloth around Dave's mouth.

"Right," said Mad Mulligan, "now it's time to make sure you behave."

Mad Mulligan walked across the red sand to where Alex, Liza and Spidroth lay on the ground. All of them were tied up. Spidroth and Alex were desperately trying to break free of their bonds, but the ropes were tied too tight.

No, don't hurt them! Dave thought. He tried to struggle free, but the ropes around him wouldn't budge. Mad Mulligan took a block out of his pocket and placed it on the ground, where it grew to full-size. It was an ender chest, but the chest's black wood had a slight red tint to it, rather than the green tint that ender chests normally had. Mad Mulligan opened the red ender chest, then picked up Spidroth, throwing her over his shoulder. Mulligan looked at Dave and grinned, then threw Spidroth into the ender chest. Then he slammed the lid shut, punched the ender chest to turn it back into a tiny block again, then put it back in his pocket.

Mad Mulligan walked over to Dave.

"I'm sure you know how ender chests work, Davey Boy, but in case you don't – only I can access that chest's contents. If anything happens to me, your girlfriend is gonna be trapped in that chest for a long time."

Dave looked at Mad Mulligan with pure hatred in his eyes. Dave had never been one to hate people or want revenge, but he knew that if he had the chance, he would strike Mad Mulligan down with no hesitation.

"Boss, what do you want me to do with the other two?" Marie asked, nodding her head at Liza and Alex.

"Kill the illager," said Mad Mulligan, "but watch out for the one with orange hair – she can respawn. Lock her up and surround her with guards night and day."

"As you wish, boss," said Marie.

Mad Mulligan secured Dave's ropes and attached him to the back of the ravager's saddle. Then he jumped onto the ravager's back and gave it a kick in the side with one of his boots. Immediately the ravager began galloping off. Dave watched helplessly from the back of the ravager as Alex, Liza and the town of Dead Bush got further and further away. Suddenly the gigantic illager army passed by them, heading in the other direction: ravagers, hundreds of horses and countless numbers of illagers on foot, all charging straight towards the town.

The situation seemed hopeless, but Dave knew that Carl and Porkins were still in the town. If anyone could save the people of Dead Bush, it was those two.

Good luck, Carl, good luck, Porkins, Dave thought. *It's up to you now.*

CHAPTER TWO
They're Here to Destroy Us

Carl didn't like this. He didn't like this one bit.

Dave and Mad Mulligan faced each other across the red sand, Dave with his netherite sword and Mulligan with his red sword. Carl had no idea what that red sword was made of, but he knew it was probably some sort of stupid magical thing.

Carl, Porkins, Mayor Grady and the soldiers on the wall were too far away to hear what Mad Mulligan and Dave were talking about, but it looked like they were about to start fighting.

Wait, thought Carl, *is Dave closing his eyes? Surely, he can't be closing his eyes? What kind of idiot would fight with his eyes closed?*

Mad Mulligan charged towards Dave. Dave raised his sword, but Mad Mulligan dashed to the side and whacked Dave in the helmet with his red sword. Then he bashed Dave in the nose with his elbow. Dave fell on his back, and Mulligan put a boot on Dave's chest, stopping him from getting up.

"We have to go save him!" shouted Porkins.

"Agreed," said Carl, getting ready to jump down from the town wall and go and save his friend.

"Wait," said Tom the cowman, "look!"

Tom was pointing into the distance. A huge cloud of sand had appeared on the horizon and was rushing towards the town.

"Is that a sandstorm?" asked Porkins.

"It's no sandstorm," said Carl, "it's an army."

Carl had the best eyes of any of them, and he could see that a gigantic army of illagers, horses and ravagers was charging towards the town, kicking up the sand as they went.

"It's another army," gasped Mayor Grady. "How many troops

does Mad Mulligan have?"

"Too many," said Carl.

"Well, we fought off the first army, and we can fight off this second one as well," said Tom.

"No, we can't," said Carl. "Our walls are destroyed, our forces are weak, and there are far too many of them."

"But they can't be coming to destroy us," said Tom, a note of panic in his voice. "Mad Mulligan said he wanted us to pay two thousand gold ingots, diamonds and emeralds per week. Maybe he's just showing us his army to show how strong he is."

"You don't bring an army that big to a battlefield just to show off," said Mayor Grady darkly. "They're here to destroy us."

Carl noticed that Mad Mulligan was tying Dave up with rope. He had to save his friend, but he also had to help the people of Dead Bush escape, or they'd all be destroyed.

"Porkins," Carl said, putting one of his netherite hands on the pigman's shoulder, "you need to get everyone – everyone in the town – into the mine. Follow whatever caves you can find, and get them out of here."

"But what about you, old bean?" Porkins asked.

"And what about my daughter?" asked Mayor Grady, looking over at Liza, who was still lying on the red sand next to Spidroth and Alex.

"I'll save her," said Carl, "I promise. Now all of you need to get out of here before Mad Mulligan's forces arrive. Go!"

"Everyone to the mine!" Mayor Grady shouted. "Go, go, go!"

"You're going to save our friends, aren't you?" Porkins asked Carl.

"I'm gonna try my best," said Carl. "But if I die horribly, plant a potato tree in my honor."

"Um, I don't think potatoes grow on trees, old bean," said Porkins.

"Well, plant a tree and stick some potatoes in the branches," said Carl. "Come on, use your imagination."

Porkins smiled.

"Good luck, dear chap."

Carl had already wasted enough time, so he gave Porkins a nod, then jumped down from the town wall, landing with a thud on the red sand of the badlands plateau. In the distance, the huge army of illagers was getting nearer every second, and Mad Mulligan was riding off on his ravager, with Dave tied to its back.

"Oh no you don't," Carl muttered, and he began running forward as fast as his golem legs would take him. Alex and Liza were still tied up on the sand, but there was no sign of Spidroth. Marie, Mad Mulligan's ruthless lieutenant, had jumped off of her horse and was approaching Alex and Liza with her sword out. Marie lifted her sword, preparing to bring it down on Liza.

Carl put in an extra burst of speed, rushing towards Marie. Marie looked up, spotting him, and as he went to charge into her, she jumped up into the air, flipping over his back.

"You again, creeper," Marie grinned as she landed gracefully on the sand. "Are you back for a rematch?"

I don't have time for this, Carl thought. The huge army was getting closer to them every second. He needed to take Marie out quickly, but he'd already seen what a good fighter she was. Either way, Carl didn't have a choice.

Carl charged towards Marie. She pulled out her diamond sword and ran towards him as well. Carl swung one of his huge netherite arms, trying to hit her, but Marie ducked out of the way, then swung her diamond sword at Carl's legs: *THWACK, THWACK, THWACK!*

Carl fell over backward, and Marie jumped on top of him, raising her diamond sword over his creeper head.

"Any last words, creeper?" she said.

"Yes," said Carl, "you're a big idiot, and I hate you."

Carl jumped out of the neck of his golem suit, tackling Marie in the stomach. Marie toppled backward, falling off the golem suit, and Carl quickly crawled back into the neck hole. He got to his feet, then *POW,* biffed Marie before she could get her bearings, sending her flying.

Carl quickly ran over to Alex and Liza. He pulled off the piece of cloth around Alex's mouth.

"Where's Spidroth?" Carl asked Alex.

"Mad Mulligan put her into an ender chest and then rode off with Dave," said Alex. "We have to rescue them!"

Carl looked around at the huge illager army rushing towards them.

"I think Dave and Spidroth are going to have to be on their own for now," he said. "But if anyone can handle themselves, it's those two."

The huge army of illagers had almost reached them now, so there was no time to untie Alex and Liza. Carl threw Liza over one shoulder and Alex over the other then started to run back towards the town. He could hear the ravagers behind him, so close that he could hear their snorts and grunts.

Come on, Carl, come on, he told himself, pushing his golem legs as fast as they would go. He headed towards one of the holes in the town wall that Mad Mulligan's forces had opened up during the first attack. He ran through the hole, emerging on the town's main street. He was pleased to see that all the townsfolk were gone: hopefully, Porkins and Mayor Grady had got them all down into the mine.

FADOOOOM!!!! Carl looked behind him and saw that two ravagers with riders had broken through the town wall, and Mad Mulligan's army was beginning to pour through.

I have to buy Porkins and the others some time, Carl thought. He put Alex and Liza down and quickly untied their ropes.

"You two get out of here," Carl told them. "I've told Porkins and Mayor Grady to bring everyone down into the mine to try and escape through the cave system. You both go and join them."

"No, Carl," said Alex, "I'll hold them off. I can respawn, and you can't. Plus, no offense, but I'm a much better fighter than you are."

"Um, offense taken," said Carl.

"Just go!" Alex shouted, picking up a diamond sword lying on the ground from the aftermath of the previous battle.

As much as Carl hated to leave Alex there, he knew that she was right. She would be able to keep the illagers back for much longer than he would, and she wouldn't have to give her life to do so: she would just respawn as soon as she was slain.

"Good luck," Carl told her.

"Go!" Alex shouted. "There are some bad guys here who ordered a large Alex with extra Alex, and I'm going to give it to them."

Carl thought that Alex was stretching her catchphrase to the limit, but this wasn't the time to say it. Instead, he picked Liza up and threw her over his shoulder.

"Hey!" said Liza. "I do have legs, you know — I don't need you to carry me!"

"Yes, but can your legs run as fast as a horse?" said Carl.

"Good point," said Liza.

Carl began to run, heading towards the mine at the center of the town. As he ran, he turned around and saw Alex standing in the middle of the main street, the diamond sword in her hand as the illager army rushed towards her.

Good luck, Alex, Carl thought. *Hopefully, I'll see you soon.*

CHAPTER THREE
Did Somebody Order the Alex?

The illager army came to a halt in front of Alex. At the front of the army was an illager in diamond armor riding a ravager. The illager looked down at Alex with a nasty grin.

"Are you the only one in this pathetic town brave enough to face us?" the illager mocked. "What good do you think you can do against all of us?"

"Well, if you don't all leave immediately, I'm going to bash your butts," said Alex, gripping her diamond sword. "This is your last warning."

The illager laughed.

"Kill her," he said, "then destroy the town."

The illager on the ravager pulled at the reins, and the enormous beast charged forward. At the same time, all the other illagers charged as well, all of them heading down the main street straight towards Alex.

The ravager's rider was the first to reach her, charging straight towards her as if he meant to squash her flat.

Not today, Alex thought. She sprang up into the air, then *WHAM,* she kicked the illager in diamond armor off of the ravager and landed on its back.

Alex had never ridden a ravager before, but as far as she could tell, it seemed to be a lot like riding a horse. She sat down and tugged at the beast's reins, making it turn around and charge towards the rest of the illagers.

"Watch out!" an illager shouted.

KATHAAAM!!!! Alex's ravager charged straight into the illagers, sending them flying. The illagers began to flee in terror, pushing and shoving to get out of the path of the ravager. It was all looking good for Alex, but then she saw three other ravager riders charging towards her from up ahead.

"Uh-oh," said Alex.

The three ravagers reached Alex at the same time, all of them charging straight towards her. Using all of her ninja training, Alex jumped high up into the air just in time, as the three ravagers bashed into her ravager, making it explode with a *POOF*.

Alex landed on the back of one of the other ravagers. The ravager rider looked around at her with a mixture of surprise and terror on his face.

"Off you get," Alex said, grabbing the illager by the shoulders and throwing him off the ravager. Then she jumped onto the back of one of the other ravagers, kicking its illager rider off the saddle as well. Now there was only one ravager left with a rider. The illager rider tugged at the reins of his ravager and began charging towards her. Alex jumped up and landed behind him on the ravager's back. She pulled out her diamond sword, but before she could strike him down, the illager turned around and fired his crossbow at her: *BLAM, BLAM, BLAM!*

Alex looked down at the three arrows sticking out of her belly.

"Oh," she gasped. Then *POOF,* she disappeared.

Immediately, Alex woke up in bed. For a moment, she was confused about who she was and what was going on, but then it all came flooding back. She was lying under the covers in the bed she'd stayed at the previous night in the Dead Bush inn. She jumped out of bed and ran over to the window. Outside, the illager army was still marching down the street, the ravager rider who just killed her leading the charge.

Alex didn't have a weapon, but she was a ninja now: her body *was* a weapon.

Alex kicked the window, smashing the glass, then, with a running start, she jumped out of the window.

"Did somebody order the Alex?!" she shouted as she soared through the air. The illagers all looked up at her in amazement. She landed on the back of the front ravager. The illager who'd just killed her looked around at her in terror.

"I slew you!" he gasped. "I just slew you right now!"

"Well, now I have something else you can slay," said Alex. "The ground!"

POW! She kicked the illager, sending him flying off the ravager's back and rolling across the dusty sand. Alex grabbed hold of the ravager's reins, turning it around and charging into the illager army once more. The ravager swung its horns this way and that, sending illagers flying.

Hopefully, I'm buying Carl and the others some time, Alex thought. She was putting up a good fight against Mad Mulligan's army, but hundreds more illagers kept pouring into the town through the gap in the wall, and she wouldn't be able to keep them back much longer. She just had to delay them long enough so that Carl, Porkins and the people of Dead Bush could make their escape through the mine.

The illagers on the ground were firing arrows at Alex's ravager and hitting it with their swords. Finally, the ravager exploded with a *POOF,* and Alex landed on the ground. She didn't have a weapon, and the illagers were closing in from every side, aiming at her with crossbows or getting ready to cut her down with their swords.

"Fire!" one of the illagers shouted. All at once, the illagers began firing their crossbows. Alex jumped up into the air as high as she could, and all the arrows that had been fired hit other illagers instead. An illager with a diamond sword went *POOF,* and Alex landed and picked up the blade. More illagers tried to fire arrows at her, but Alex jumped and ducked out of the way of them and began fighting off the illagers with her sword. There were hundreds of them, and they kept coming and coming, but Alex kept on fighting. She managed to pick up a shield from somewhere and used that to block arrows with one hand as she swung her sword with the other, cutting through the illagers who were trying to attack her. She was exhausted, but she kept fighting — knowing that every second she kept fighting was an extra second that Carl and the others could use to escape.

Come on, Alex, she told herself, *you can do this.*

There were so many illagers around her that she could barely tell what was going on. She was just swinging her sword at anything she could hit and trying her best to dodge arrows, but finally, one arrow struck her — plunging into her right thigh.

"YAAAAAH!!!" Alex screamed.

"Kill her!" one of the illagers shouted.

"No, you idiot," said another illager, "she can respawn. Capture her!"

Before Alex knew what was happening, the illagers snatched her sword and shield and pinned her to the ground. She tried to move, but an illager had tied her wrists together with some rope.

"We've got her!" a female illager said triumphantly.

Using all her strength, Alex pushed the illagers off her and jumped to her feet. Her hands were tied together behind her back and she had no weapon, but she still had her legs.

"Come on then," Alex snarled at the illagers surrounding her. "Let's see what you've got."

"Don't kill her," said the female illager who'd spoken before. "Take her alive."

As the illagers began rushing towards her, Alex jumped up, performing a spinning kick that sent a whole horde of illagers flying backward. Some more illagers tried to grab her from behind, but Alex spun around and kicked them as well. Another illager tried to dive into her, but Alex jumped over him, landing behind the illager and then kicking him in the butt, sending him flying.

"She's making us look like fools!" one illager shouted. "Kill her!"

An illager with a diamond sword swung it at Alex, but Alex jumped up and landed on the blade. The illager looked up at her in amazement, then *POW,* Alex booted him in the face, sending him flying backward.

Alex landed gracefully on the ground, just in time to hit three more illagers who were charging towards her with another spinning kick. She landed, but this time she wasn't quick enough, and an illager charged into her from behind, grabbing her legs and making her fall to the ground. Other illagers piled on top of her, and this time there were too many of them to escape from. They all held her down, and she couldn't move.

"Well, well, well," said a female voice. Alex looked up to see Marie looking down at her.

"What shall we do with her, boss?" an illager asked.

"Tie up her legs and take her back to the base," said Marie. "And bring enough soldiers so that she doesn't escape. Now come on, we've wasted enough time — let's destroy this town and everyone in it. The people of Dead Bush are going to regret ever messing with Mad Mulligan."

"When this is all over, you're going to be the one regretting," said Alex. "You're going to be regretting you messed with my friends and me!"

Marie grinned nastily.

"We'll see," she said. "We'll see."

CHAPTER FOUR
Exodus

"Come along, chaps!" Porkins shouted. "We need to pick up the pace a bit!"

"How much further?" asked an elderly cowman. "My hooves are killing me."

"Mad Mulligan and his chaps will kill you if you don't get a move on," said Porkins. "Chop chop!"

Porkins and Mayor Grady were leading the people of Dead Bush through the mines and caves that lay underneath the town. They'd come to the end of the mine now and were making their way through a dark, unexplored cave, with Porkins placing torches down as they went. Every so often, zombies, creepers, skeletons or spiders would appear from the darkness to try to attack them, but Porkins kept them away with his bow and arrows, slaying any mobs who came too near.

The cave network underneath the town was vast, so the plan was to keep going until they were so far that Mad Mulligan's forces wouldn't be able to find them. Tom the cowman was at the end of the procession, picking up the torches that Porkins had put down, to make sure they didn't leave a trail that Mad Mulligan's army could follow. It was slow going, because there were so many illagers and cowmen, many of them very old or very young, but they all knew that it was far too dangerous to stop.

Somewhere behind him, Porkins could hear sobbing. It was just one person at first, and then others began sobbing too. Porkins felt his heart break: he knew that the people of Dead Bush must be terrified, but if they didn't keep quiet, they would be caught.

"Quiet!" hissed Mayor Grady, turning around to face his people. "I know this is tough, but if we don't all keep quiet we'll get caught!"

Mayor Grady's words seem to work, as, after that, Porkins no longer heard any sobbing. They carried on through the dark caves in solemn silence.

"How long do you think we should keep going?" Mayor Grady whispered to Porkins.

"We'll keep walking until we can't walk anymore," said Porkins. He knew that Mad Mulligan's forces wouldn't give up looking for them easily, so they had to get as far away as possible.

After walking for a while longer — it was hard to keep track of time in the darkness — they came to a huge cavern. Their path led them along a narrow ledge, with a sheer stone wall on one side and a huge drop on the other. Far, far below them, they could see the orange glow of lava. One wrong step would mean certain death, so Porkins told them all to walk single file. With so many illagers and cowmen, it took forever for them all to walk along the ledge. Porkins and Mayor Grady waited at the end of the ledge, where their path led back inside another stone corridor. Finally, when they had all crossed the cavern, they resumed walking normally, all of them huddled together as they walked through the dark cave.

Porkins had been tempted to build a nether portal, as distance was different in the Nether, and they would be able to get further away from Mad Mulligan's forces more quickly, but he knew from experience how dangerous the Nether could be. He might have been confident in leading the people of Dead Bush through the old Nether, but the Nether that he had known as a child had changed, and he was no longer so familiar with it. That thought made Porkins feel strangely sad. He had not only lost his people but his home as well. The Nether that he and his tribe had known was gone, replaced by another one full of strange biomes and new creatures.

I guess the people of Dead Bush are like me now, thought Porkins. *They've lost their home too.*

After walking for what seemed like hours, they found themselves in another large cavern. Porkins placed torches down, but the cavern was so vast that its roof and sides were hidden in darkness. He didn't like crossing such a vast space without knowing what was around him, but what choice did they have?

"We'll need to guard our flanks," Porkins told Mayor Grady, "to make sure we're not attacked from the side."

"Agreed," said Mayor Grady. He commanded Tom and his other best warriors – the fifteen of them who had been Dead Bush's only soldiers until recently – to form a perimeter around the rest of the townsfolk. They all slowly made their way across the huge cavern, with Porkins and Mayor Grady at the front, placing down torches. Tom was at the back, picking up the torches so that they wouldn't leave a trail, and the other soldiers were walking along the outside of the group to fend off any attacks from the side.

"This cavern seems jolly quiet," Porkins whispered to Mayor Grady. "I thought we would at least have seen a few zombie and creeper blaggards by now."

Before Mayor Grady could answer, they heard a hiss from somewhere up ahead.

"A creeper," Mayor Grady whispered, pulling out his diamond sword and holding up a hand to tell everyone to stop.

For a moment, there was silence; then they heard more hissing noises coming from all around them. Porkins pulled out his bow and notched an arrow. Behind him, he could hear the illagers and cowmen of Dead Bush whimpering in terror. Some of them had started sobbing.

"Come on, my friends and I trained you chaps to be warriors," Porkins shouted at the townsfolk. "Pull out your weapons!"

The illagers and cowmen who had swords and bows took them out. Porkins had no idea how many creepers were surrounding them, but it sounded like a lot.

Then, up ahead of them, they could suddenly see a blue, glowing thing. Porkins squinted and saw that it was a creeper: a yellow creeper crackling with blue electricity.

Suddenly more blue glowing things began appearing around them, hundreds and hundreds of them. Porkins realized, to his horror, that they were all yellow creepers. There were yellow creepers surrounding them on the ground and more yellow creepers standing on ledges all around the outside of the cavern, looking down at them.

"There must be thousands of them," a cowman behind Porkins whimpered. "We don't stand a chance!"

"I hate to say it, but he's right," Mayor Grady whispered to Porkins. "How are we going to get out of this one?"

Before Porkins could answer, the yellow creepers began rushing towards them, hissing and crackling with electricity.

"Archers to the front!" Porkins shouted. "Hold them back!"

As the cowman and illagers with bows stepped forward and began firing at the creepers who were rushing towards them from all sides, Porkins reached into his backpack and pulled out some obsidian.

"What are you doing?" Mayor Grady asked him.

"Hatching an escape plan," said Porkins. He placed a tiny obsidian block down on the ground. It stuck to the ground with a *THUNK*, growing immediately to full-size. Then Porkins ran along, placing more obsidian blocks down, building the widest Nether portal frame that he could. When he finally finished, he lit the frame with some flint and steel, and the purple liquid of the portal bubbled into life.

"Everyone into the portal!" Porkins shouted. "Move it, move it!"

Most of the townsfolk didn't need telling twice and began running towards the purple portal. Thankfully Porkins had built it wide enough so that lots of them could enter at a time. The archers were still firing at the yellow creepers, who were closing in on them from all sides, and Porkins pulled out his bow and began firing at the yellow creepers as well.

"Come on, chaps!" Porkins shouted. "We need to get out of here!"

The archers began to back towards the portal, firing arrows to keep the yellow creepers at bay. More and more of them entered the Nether portal until finally, Porkins and Mayor Grady were the last ones left. They both jumped through the portal.

As he entered the Nether, Porkins had a brief moment to register his surroundings: they were inside one of the new biomes with blue-green grass and giant cyan mushrooms.

Porkins quickly pulled out his diamond pickaxe and hacked away at one of the blocks of the portal. The block broke, and the purple forcefield vanished. They were safe – at least from the yellow creepers.

"Is this the Nether?" said Mayor Grady, looking around. "It's changed a lot since I was last here, although that was many years ago. It used to be nothing but red rocks and lava."

"These changes are fairly recent," said Porkins. "We need to be on our guard, chaps. I've no idea what kind of monsters we might encounter here."

The townsfolk had huddled together under the huge mushrooms, all looking scared. Porkins doubted that many of them had ever left the town before, let alone been to a place as strange as this.

"What do we do now?" an illager woman asked.

"We need to keep walking," said Porkins. "If we build another Nether portal too close to this one, it will just take us back to the same place. We need to travel through the Nether, and when we've gone far enough, we can build another portal, and hopefully, it will take us somewhere less dangerous."

"Can we please rest?" an elderly cowman pleaded. "My legs are so tired."

Many of the other townsfolk muttered in agreement.

Porkins and Mayor Grady looked at each other. They both knew that it was best to keep moving, especially in a strange place like this, but it was clear that many of the illagers and cowmen were too exhausted to go on.

"What do you think, Porkins?" Mayor Grady asked. "I'm sure you know the Nether much better than I do. Will it be safe to stop here?"

"I don't know," Porkins admitted, "but I do know that many of these chaps and chapettes need some food and a rest."

As strange as the cyan biome was, there were plenty of mushrooms on the ground, so at least they would have food to eat. The stalks of the giant mushrooms looked like they were made of wood as well, so they'd be able to build a shelter for everyone to stay in.

"We'll stop here for some rest," Mayor Grady announced to the group. "If you are fit and able, please collect mushrooms and gather as much wood as you can. We'll eat, then we'll sleep, and then we'll be on our way again."

The younger townsfolk all went off to do what Mayor Grady had asked, while the old folk sat down and rested their weary legs.

"Are you all right, Mr Mayor?" Porkins asked. Mayor Grady was looking at the broken Nether portal frame with a frustrated look on his face.

"I was just thinking," said Mayor Grady, "if Mad Mulligan's forces find that portal frame on the other side, they'll know exactly where we've gone to."

"I had the same thought," said Porkins. "But with all those yellow creeper chaps on the other side, there's not much we can do."

Porkins had thought about going back through the portal into the cavern and destroying the frame to hide all evidence of where they'd gone, but even if the yellow creepers didn't slay him, he would have to build another portal somewhere to come back to the Nether. Mayor Grady was a good leader, but Porkins knew that the mayor and his people would have a hard time navigating the Nether without his help.

"Well, let's just hope that those yellow creepers keep Mad Mulligan's soldiers away from the cavern," said Mayor Grady.

"Yes," said Porkins, "let's hope that they do."

CHAPTER FIVE
Carl Lost

Carl was lost. He and Liza had been wandering through the caves for what seemed like hours and had seen no sign of Porkins and the Dead Bush townsfolk. When they'd first entered the mine, they'd found a group of illagers all tied up on the ground, who they quickly realized were members of Mad Mulligan's gang who had been taken prisoner after the first battle. Porkins and Mayor Grady must have realized that bringing the prisoners along with them would be more trouble than it was worth, so they'd left them all behind. Carl and Liza had done the same thing, ignoring the prisoners and heading into the caves. No doubt Marie and her soldiers would free the prisoners when they came down into the mine, but it couldn't be helped.

"This is hopeless," sighed Liza. "We haven't found a single torch. For all we know, they could have gone off in a completely different direction."

"Or escaped into the Nether," said Carl. He supposed that if the townsfolk had escaped into the Nether, there would be a Nether portal left behind, but the cave system was so vast that it could have been anywhere.

"I just hope my father and the others are okay," said Liza, sitting down and leaning against the cave wall.

"Porkins will take care of them," said Carl. "I know he sounds a bit of an idiot, with all his strange phrases, but he knows what he's doing."

Carl sat down next to Liza in his netherite golem suit.

"So, what now?" asked Liza.

Carl wasn't sure. Porkins and the townsfolk had done such a good job of covering their tracks that Carl had no idea which way they'd gone. Dave had been captured by Mad Mulligan and brought off to who knew where, and Alex...

"I know I'm going to regret this," said Carl, "but I'm going to go back and save my friend Alex. Porkins and your dad are gone, hopefully to a safe place, and I've no idea where Dave or Spidroth are, but Alex has probably been captured. She may have a brain like a moldy potato, but she's one of the best fighters around. She probably kept Marie and her forces back for a while, but even Alex wouldn't be able to fight on forever. Once Marie realized that Alex couldn't be killed, she probably ordered her soldiers to capture her instead."

"Well, if they captured her, they'll probably bring her to the same place they brought me," said Liza. "Mad Mulligan's hideout."

"I guess that's where I'll have to go then," said Carl. "Maybe Mad Mulligan brought Dave there as well, so I can save both of those idiots at the same time."

"Either way, I'm coming with you," said Liza. "Alex came to save me when I was captured, so it's the least I can do."

"Suit yourself," shrugged Carl. "But if you get killed, don't blame me."

Liza raised an eyebrow.

"Do you always act like this?" she asked.

"Like what?" asked Carl.

"Like you don't care about anyone," said Liza, "when it's clear that you actually do."

"The only thing I care about is baked potatoes," said Carl. "Speaking of which..."

He reached into the neck hole of his suit and pulled out a potato.

"I might as well have some lunch," said Carl.

"What is that strange thing?" said Liza, looking at the potato.

"A potato," said Carl. "Unfortunately, they're poisonous to illagers, so I can't let you have any. Sorry."

After they'd had some lunch – Liza ate some porkchops she had in her backpack – Carl and Liza began digging diagonally upwards, heading towards the surface. Carl had a couple of iron pickaxes in his suit, which he and Liza used to dig up through the stone. Finally, they reached the surface and found themselves in a wooded badlands plateau – a biome full of red sand, flat-topped hills made from layers of different color terracotta, and the occasional patch of dry, yellowy-green grass with clusters of small oak trees.

"Okay, which way do we go?" asked Carl.

"Mad Mulligan's base was north of Dead Bush," said Liza, "so I guess let's head north."

Both Carl and Liza knew that the sun rose in the east and set in the west, and the blazing hot sun above them had just started to set. They began walking north, walking across the dry grass and using the oak trees for cover when they could. Before long, they came to the end of the grass and the trees, and all they could see in front of them was a badlands plateau – an endless flat desert of red sand and the occasional bush or cactus.

Carl and Liza walked for as long as they could, but eventually, the sun set completely, and zombies and skeletons began to attack them. With his netherite golem suit, Carl could easily fight them off, but he knew it would be safer if they stopped for the night. Carl just about had enough blocks in his bag to build them a small house, but he didn't have any beds, so they both had to sleep on the floor. Unlike the nice wooden houses that Dave normally built, the makeshift house that Carl had created was made from a patchwork of different types of block – cobblestone, netherrack, pumpkins and other random materials. He also didn't have any glass, so the house had no windows. It was no palace, but at least it would shelter them for the night.

Carl crawled out of his netherite golem suit, leaving it sitting in the corner of the room, then he and Liza laid down on the hard floor.

"So," said Liza, "you're a creeper."

"Well spotted," said Carl. "I can see you've got a keen eye."

Liza laughed.

"I only meant that it's not often that you see a talking creeper," said Liza. "All the creepers I met before you were mindless beasts who tried to blow me up."

"Well, all the illagers I met before you were bad guys who tried to kill me," said Carl. "Although that's not strictly true — there was Chonky and Ivy. They didn't try to kill me; they were just really, really annoying."

"Father tells me that back on your continent, illagers are treated like criminals," said Liza.

"I think illagers and villagers just don't like each other very much for some reason," said Carl. "But if it makes you feel any better, everyone hates creepers."

"Yes, but that's because you're always trying to blow everyone up," said Liza, with a giggle.

"I guess that's a fair point," said Carl. "In fact, that's how Dave and I met. I tried to blow him up and couldn't, and somehow that led to us becoming friends. Don't get me wrong, I still think he's an idiot, but he's a lot less of an idiot than most of the idiots I know."

"Are there many creepers like you?" Liza asked. "Ones who can talk, I mean."

"Yeah, there're quite a few of us," said Carl. "Most of my family could talk — although I would have preferred it sometimes if they couldn't. A lot of creepers are born as mindless, feral monsters, though, and all they can do is hiss. One of my uncles was a feral creeper, but he was still pretty friendly. Well, until he ate too much mushroom stew and exploded. We were cleaning mushroom gunk off the walls for weeks."

Liza laughed.

"You're funny, Carl," she said.

"That wasn't a joke," said Carl. "These are the kind of awful things that happen in my life all the time. And then I met Dave, and every five minutes we ended up getting captured or running away from monsters. And then he ended up forcing me to go to a continent without any potatoes. Will my suffering never end?"

"Goodnight, Carl," said Liza, laughing.

“Goodnight,” said Carl.

The next day, Liza and Carl continued their journey across the badlands. The sun was beating down on them, and it was becoming hard to go on, but thankfully around lunchtime they found a small pool of water. They drank as much as they could, then put some of the water in a bucket, which they stored in Carl’s golem suit.

Finally, just as the sun was beginning to set, they could see the tall, striped terracotta spires of an eroded Badlands biome in the distance and a cluster of buildings nestled around the foot of a small mountain. Between the terracotta spires were wooden watchtowers and white tents.

“That’s Mad Mulligan’s base,” said Liza.

“It looks well guarded,” said Carl.

“Maybe we should build a house and wait until morning?,” suggested Liza.

“No,” said Carl. “In the daylight we’ll be too easy to spot. We need to sneak into the base at night. That’s our only chance. We’ll almost certainly get killed or captured, but I guess it’s worth a try.”

Carl didn’t like the idea of sneaking into a heavily-guarded criminal base, but he knew that Alex and Dave would do the same for him. If there was any chance that he could save his friends, he had to take it.

“Come on,” said Carl. “Let’s go a little closer. And when the sun goes down, we’ll sneak into the base. What could possibly go wrong?”

CHAPTER SIX
The Villager and the Illager

"Are you all right back there, Dave? Mad Mulligan asked. Dave couldn't see the illager's face, but his voice was full of mocking laughter.

Dave didn't respond. He couldn't have responded even if he had wanted to, as he had a piece of cloth tied around his mouth. It felt like he had been tied to the back of the ravager for days, but he knew that it could only have been a few hours, as the sun was only now starting to set. Dave was dusty, thirsty and felt ill from the movement of the ravager. He was also worried about Spidroth and the rest of his friends.

Dave had been in bad situations before, but he'd never felt as helpless as he felt now: tied to the back of a ravager with no idea what was happening to his friends.

They rode for a few more hours until finally the sun began to set over the badlands. Mad Mulligan brought the ravager to a stop, jumped off the saddle, then went around to see Dave. Dave was tied to the back of the saddle with ropes. He'd been trying for hours to break free from them, but they were just too tight.

"Hey Dave," said Mad Mulligan, grinning down at him. "I'm going to untie you now, but you have to promise not to attack me. Okay?"

"Mmmh, mmmh!" said Dave angrily.

"Remember," said Mad Mulligan, "if you kill me or escape from me, your girlfriend is going to be trapped in that ender chest forever. Or at least until she starves. So, are you gonna behave?"

Dave said nothing.

"Are you going to behave, Dave?" Mad Mulligan asked again.

Reluctantly, Dave nodded his head.

"Great," grinned Mad Mulligan. He reached up and untied the ropes holding Dave to the ravager. They unraveled, and Dave fell onto the hard red sand. Now his arms were free, Dave immediately reached up and pulled the piece of cloth from his mouth.

"You want some of this?" Mad Mulligan asked, offering Dave a bucket of water. Dave grabbed the bucket and greedily poured it into his mouth, gulping it down as quickly as he could. His throat felt as dry as the sand they were standing on.

"I'll build us a fire," said Mad Mulligan. He reached into one of the pouches hanging from the ravager's saddle and pulled out a tiny campfire block, placing it down on the ground where it grew to full-size.

With Mulligan's back turned, Dave realized this was his big chance. He charged at the illager, hoping to grab the red sword from Mad Mulligan's belt. But before Dave could grab the blade, Mad Mulligan turned around and whacked Dave with the flat end of his sword. Dave's head exploded in pain, and he fell backward, landing with a thump on the hard sand.

"Come on, Dave," grinned Mad Mulligan, "you did promise to behave."

"Rrrragh!" Dave yelled, and he jumped up and charged at Mad Mulligan once more. The illager lazily stepped to the side, and Dave ended up charging into thin air instead, and he tripped and fell back onto the ground.

"Dave, this is going to be a long night if you keep trying to kill me," said Mad Mulligan with a shrug. "I don't want to bruise your ego, but I'm just a better fighter than you. I've been using the Sight for years, and you've been using it for what, a few days? A few weeks? There's no way you can beat me. It's impossible."

"We'll see about that," Dave snarled, although he didn't try to attack Mad Mulligan again. He was going to have to bide his time and attack at the right moment.

"You and I want the same thing," said Mad Mulligan. "To go to the End and see all the cool stuff there. Think about it — there are treasures there that haven't been seen for thousands of years. Doesn't that fill you with excitement?"

Dave said nothing.

Mad Mulligan leaned down and lit the campfire. He pulled a couple of raw chickens out of one of the pouches on the side of the ravager's saddle and then placed them next to the fire. The ravager was lying down now, and it looked like it was starting to fall asleep.

Mad Mulligan sat next to the campfire.

"Isn't she a magnificent beast?" he asked Dave, nodding towards the ravager. "Big Bessie, I call her. It's not the most fearsome name, but I think she likes it."

"What do you want from me?" Dave asked, giving Mad Mulligan a look of pure hatred.

"I've told you before," said Mad Mulligan. "I've got an end portal, and I want you to help me open it. If you do that, I'll let your girlfriend out of the ender chest, and you and she can go on your way. I'm a man of my word."

"No, you're not," said Dave, "you ordered your soldiers to destroy Dead Bush after you promised you wouldn't."

"I guess you're right," shrugged Mad Mulligan, a faint grin on his lips. "Okay, so I'm not always a man of my word. But I gave the people of Dead Bush plenty of chances. They knew what would happen if they rebelled against me, and now they're paying the price."

Dave said nothing. He'd faced plenty of horrible bad guys in his time, but none of them made him as angry as Mad Mulligan did. Not even Herobrine. It was probably the smug smile Mad Mulligan constantly had on his face – the smile of someone who thinks they're better than everyone else.

"Come on, sit down and have some chicken," said Mad Mulligan. "This is no ordinary chicken; it's cluckshroom. It's good stuff."

"I don't want anything from you," said Dave.

"Suit yourself," said Mad Mulligan, taking a bite out of one of the chickens. "Your rucksack is in that middle pouch."

Dave looked at where Mad Mulligan was pointing: at the pouches hanging off the saddle of the sleeping ravager.

Being careful in case it was a trap, Dave went over to the pouch and opened it. Sure enough, his backpack was inside.

Is Mad Mulligan really going to let me keep all my belongings and my weapons? thought Dave, feeling confused. *Isn't he worried I'll attack him?*

"Take your sword out if you think it will make you feel safer," said Mad Mulligan. "As I said before, you couldn't land a blow on me even if you tried. That's not me being arrogant — that's the truth."

Dave took his rucksack out of the pouch and placed it down on the ground. He opened it and immediately saw what he was looking for.

I'm only going to get one chance at this, Dave thought. He reached into his bag, grabbed his crossbow, then pulled it out and fired an arrow at Mad Mulligan. But Mad Mulligan wasn't there — he'd moved out of the way while Dave's back was turned and was now standing again. The arrow struck the red sand instead.

"Come on, Dave," said Mad Mulligan. "Am I really going to have to tie you up again? It's going to be a boring journey for both of us if you're tied up the whole time. And remember, if you do slay me, Spidroth will be trapped in my ender chest. So why don't you calm down and join me for some chicken?"

Mad Mulligan was right, Dave knew. As long as Spidroth was trapped in the ender chest, there was nothing he could do. Dave was going to have to go along with the smug illager for now until he could come up with a plan. Reluctantly, Dave sat down by the campfire and began to eat his chicken.

Mad Mulligan grinned and sat down on the other side of the campfire.

"Great," he said. "Now, I'm sure you must have plenty of questions for me?"

"What questions could I possibly have for you?" said Dave sourly.

"Well, maybe you're wondering how I got the Sight? Or where I got this awesome red sword from? Or how I visited you inside your dream?"

Dave said nothing. He did want to know the answer to all those questions, but he wasn't going to give Mad Mulligan the satisfaction of asking.

"I get it; you don't like me very much," Mad Mulligan grinned, "so you just keep on eating your chicken, and I'll do the talking. I don't know if you've noticed, but I do love to talk. Anyway, I'll start at the beginning. I came to this continent when I was a teenager. Villagers don't know this continent exists, but we illagers have been coming here for generations. Anyway, some friends and I decided to travel over here to see if we could make our fortune. Instead, we all ended up as footsoldiers for an illager gangster named Big Nose. I've no idea why he was called Big Nose, because his nose was pretty normal-sized. I guess criminals just like to have interesting nicknames. I mean, I'm guilty of that myself, so I can't criticize. I call myself Mad Mulligan, but I'm actually pretty sane. To be honest, I just think it sounds scary. When you're a criminal, it's important to make sure people are scared of you."

"I'll bear that in mind if I ever decide to embark on a life of crime," said Dave sarcastically.

Mad Mulligan grinned.

"See, Dave?" he said. "You can be funny when you want to be – you don't have to rely on Carl to make the jokes all the time. Anyway, I was one of the lowest members of the organization. Most of the time, I was just carrying stuff for people more important than me or cooking them food. I was half tempted to return to my own continent, but then my life changed. Some of Big Nose's soldiers discovered something strange out in the far west: an entire city made from bedrock. The city was huge, with so many colossal buildings that it would take several lifetimes to search them all. Big Nose knew that the city would be full of treasure, and he didn't want anyone else to get it. So he sent a platoon of his soldiers to the city to guard it – and I was one of those soldiers. Anyway, we were stationed at Bedrock City and told to guard it, although the city was completely abandoned and there weren't any settlements for miles around. Bedrock City was the name we gave it, I should point out – I've no idea what the original inhabitants called it."

"How could there be a city made from bedrock?" asked Dave. "It's impossible to mine."

"It's impossible for *us* to mine," said Mad Mulligan, "but I suppose the people who built it didn't have that problem."

Dave thought back to the bedrock fortress where Herobrine had imprisoned him and his friends near the start of their journey. At the time, he'd assumed that Herobrine must have used his magic to create the fortress, but maybe it had been built by the same people who'd built this bedrock city.

It must have been the Old People, Dave thought. Whenever there was some ancient and mysterious structure, it always seemed to be the Old People who'd built it.

"As Big Nose had suspected, the city was full of treasure," said Mad Mulligan. "The other soldiers and I went from building to building, collecting all the treasure we could and putting it in chests. Every so often, some of Big Nose's soldiers would come and collect the chests. The city was so vast that there was no end of treasure for us to find. Most of it was gold, diamonds, emeralds and other normal stuff like that, but there were a few unique items as well. We weren't meant to keep any of it ourselves, but when I found this, I hid it away so that I could collect it later."

Mad Mulligan held up the red sword.

"From the texts I've read, this beautiful sword is made from things called rubies," said Mad Mulligan. "As far as my researchers can tell, the Old People used to mine rubies so much that they ran out. That's why we don't have them anymore. Or at least that's what they suspect anyway. This sword is about as powerful as a diamond blade, but the great thing is that it doesn't break. I've been using it for years, and I've yet to see a crack on it. Anyway, one day, when we were searching the city for treasure, we came across a strange stone room underground. In the middle of the room, a stone-brick staircase led up to a square frame made from bizarre blocks, which rested above a small pool of lava. As you've probably guessed, it was an end portal. We only found that out later, after looking through some old scrolls in a nearby library. We tried and tried, but nothing we did got the portal to activate. I guessed that the portal wasn't working because some of the blocks were missing their strange eye things, but we had no idea what the eye things were or how to make more of them."

Dave said nothing.

Mad Mulligan grinned. "I'm sure you know the answer, Dave," he said, "but we'll come onto that later. I don't want to interrupt my fascinating life story — I know how interested you are. So, we'd found this portal that we knew was probably valuable, but we had no idea how to turn it on. So my commander ordered me to guard it. Every night, I had to sleep next to the portal in the dark underground room. At first, I didn't like it, because I wished I was sleeping with the others outside where I could see the stars. But then, after a few days, the strange dreams began. I had visions that I eventually realized were premonitions about my future. I saw other things too, such as images of a vast desert made from yellow rock with a black sky above it and a terrifying black dragon. It took me a while, but I eventually realized what was happening — the portal was giving me visions. Over time, I became better at reading the visions, and I realized that even when I wasn't near the portal, I was still getting glimpses of my future. When I was finally posted to a new location, I use my new powers to become a spectacular warrior and quickly moved up the ranks in Big Nose's gang.

Eventually, Big Nose made me his second-in-command, and finally, I defeated him and took control of his gang. Using my abilities, I was able to take over this entire region, and the gang became far more powerful than Big Nose had ever dreamed."

"And that makes you happy, does it?" said Dave bitterly. "Ruling over people and threatening them?"

"Yes, it does," Mad Mulligan grinned. The sun had almost set now, and Mulligan's white teeth shone in the moonlight. "Let me tell you something, Dave. There are two types of people in this world – sheep and wolves. The wolves rule over the sheep, and the sheep do what they're told. I know you probably don't agree, but that's the way life is. It's not about being a hero or doing the right thing or fighting for some stupid cause; it's about power. That's why I had to destroy Dead Bush — because my power comes from fear. The settlements under my control do what I tell them because they fear me. If I were to show weakness, they would seize upon that weakness and rebel against me. That's the way the world works."

"You have a pretty miserable way of looking at the world," said Dave.

"You're only young," grinned Mad Mulligan. "One day, you'll realize that I was right. If you live that long, of course. Anyway, it's getting late. I'll build us a shelter."

Mad Mulligan took some wood blocks out of one of the ravager's pouches and built them a quick house, with torches around the outside.

"Come on, Dave, you must be tired," said Mad Mulligan, opening the door for him. "You've had a long day."

Dave wanted to pull out his sword and fight the grinning illager, but he knew it was no use. Also, he had to think about Spidroth. For now, she was Mad Mulligan's prisoner, trapped in the ender chest, and the only person who could open that chest was Mad Mulligan himself. No, for now, Dave was going to have to do whatever Mad Mulligan told him. He didn't see what other choice he had.

Dave walked into the shack and saw two beds on either side of the room.

Mad Mulligan doesn't fear me at all, Dave thought to himself. The illager had given Dave his weapons back and was letting him sleep in a bed in the same room. It was clear that Mad Mulligan thought that Dave didn't stand a chance against him.

"You're not afraid that I'll attack you in the night?" Dave asked.

"You can try if you like," Mad Mulligan grinned. "But I'll save you some time – it won't work."

Dave crawled into one of the beds and pulled the blankets over him. Mad Mulligan climbed into the other bed.

"Sweet dreams Dave," said Mad Mulligan.

Dave wanted to close his eyes and go to sleep, but there was a question that he just couldn't get out of his head.

"So, how did you get into my dream the other night?" Dave asked. "And how do you know so much about my friends and me?"

In the darkness, Dave could see Mad Mulligan grinning. He wished more than anything that he could wipe that stupid grin off the illager's face.

"Those are two questions, Davey boy," said Mad Mulligan. "Let's start with the easy one. Using the Sight, you can broadcast yourself into other people's dreams. I can't read your mind or go snooping through your thoughts or anything like that, but I can send visions of myself. It's a technique I use to keep in touch with my commanders, no matter how far away they are. If you're good, perhaps I'll teach it to you."

"No thanks," Dave scowled.

"Fair enough," said Mad Mulligan. "The answer to the other question is a bit more complicated. As I said, the Sight doesn't allow you to read minds, so I had to be a bit cleverer to find out who you and your friends were. I'd had reports of a group of strange heroes defeating my men at the pyramid. I wanted to find out who you were, so I reached out with the Sight. As you know, the Sight allows you to see visions of the future, but you can also see visions of the present. I reached out with the Sight until I found you and your friends, and then I just watched you guys for a while. That's how I learned your names and about your different personalities and your quest."

"So, the Sight allows you to spy on anyone you want?" asked Dave.

"Within reason," said Mad Mulligan. "You have to be near the person, or at least know where they are. I sent my men to look for you and your friends, and when they found you, they reported back to me. That's all I needed, and then I used the Sight to watch you."

"So, can you see what's going on in Dead Bush right now?" Dave asked. "Do you know what's going on with my friends?"

For the first time, Mad Mulligan's grin vanished. Now it was Dave's turn to smile.

"The attack's not going as easily as you planned, is it?" asked Dave. "My friends are putting up a fight."

"It does seem that Marie and her forces are having a few problems," said Mad Mulligan, "but I'm sure that it's nothing that they can't handle. Before long, your friends will be dead, don't you worry about that."

Dave turned to face the wall, a big smile on his face.

I knew they wouldn't go down without a fight, Dave thought to himself. He tried to use the Sight in the same way that Mad Mulligan had described — to reach out to his friends and see what was happening with them, but he couldn't. Eventually, he gave up, then drifted off into deep and dreamless sleep.

CHAPTER SEVEN
Spidroth Alone

Come on, Spidroth told herself, *you've gotten out of worse situations than this before. You can do this.*

Spidroth was lying on the ground with her arms and legs bound by rope and a piece of cloth tied around her mouth. All around her was nothing but a vast, black, empty space, but she didn't have time to worry about where she was at the moment – her immediate concern was to break free of her bonds.

The ropes around her arms and legs had been tied well, and as much as she tried, she couldn't wriggle free or break them.

Is this how the great Lady Spidroth meets her doom? she thought bitterly. She thought about how her father would have laughed if he could see her now, which made her all the angrier.

Finally, Spidroth realized that there was no way she could break these bonds on her own, so she decided to have a closer look at her surroundings. At first, it looked like she was alone inside the black void, just as she had been in the void underneath the bedrock for all those years, but then she noticed some shapes in the distance. They seemed to be some sort of buildings, but the lighting was so bad that she couldn't make out what they were. Also, the place she was in wasn't completely dark, even though there was no visible light source. It reminded her of the Nether, which was always evenly lit, no matter where you were.

Spidroth decided to make her way over towards the buildings, or whatever they were. Of course, this wasn't easy because her arms and legs were tied up, but she managed to roll across the ground slowly. It was a long and uncomfortable process, and each roll took all her strength, using her leg muscles to flip herself over. Before long, she was covered in sweat and her limbs ached.

Push past the pain, she heard her father's voice say in her head, an echo of a memory from long ago. *True warriors don't complain. True warriors do what needs to be done.*

As much as she hated Herobrine, those words were what Spidroth needed to hear. She kept going, using all her strength to roll herself over, again and again, heading slowly towards the buildings in the distance. She had no idea how long she kept going, but it seemed like forever. Finally, she was so tired that she was tempted to give up when she saw something glittering a short way away from her.

Is that... A sword? she wondered. She squinted and saw that yes, it was — there was an iron sword lying on the black ground short way away from her.

Spidroth used all her strength to roll over to the sword. When she finally reached it, she shuffled around so that her tied-up hands were next to the blade, then carefully rubbed her bonds against it.

It took a while, especially as she had to be careful not to cut herself, but finally, Spidroth cut through most of the ropes holding her arms together. Then she used her strength to break the rest of them, and her arms were finally free. She reached up and yanked the piece of cloth away from her mouth.

"That's better," she muttered, finally able to breathe properly again. She picked the iron sword up and used it to cut the ropes around her legs, then gingerly got to her feet. Her legs felt like jelly, but at least she was free.

So, this is what the inside of an ender chest looks like, Spidroth thought, taking in her surroundings. But no, that didn't make sense. Spidroth had used plenty of ender chests in her time, and they could only hold a limited number of items, so, she assumed, they must have a limited amount of space. This black void seemed to be endless. You could hold millions of items inside here.

The wood of the ender chest had a slightly different tint to that of a normal ender chest, Spidroth thought to herself. The wood of Mad Mulligan's chest had been black with a tint of red, rather than black with a tint of green, as ender chests normally were. This was obviously some unique type of ender chest. Judging from the red sword that Mad Mulligan had, Spidroth guessed that he must be a collector of rare items, and she supposed that this chest must be another one of them.

Thinking of Mad Mulligan filled Spidroth with anger. He'd made complete fools of her and Alex when the three of them had fought. It had been a long, long time since Spidroth had been bested in a sword fight, but Mad Mulligan had made her look like a noob. It had been as if he knew exactly where every sword blow from Spidroth and Alex would come from, and he blocked them with ease. As far as Spidroth could see, the only explanation was that Mad Mulligan, like Dave, had the Sight. But unlike Dave, he'd trained himself to use it properly. Thinking of Dave made Spidroth feel upset, so she pushed those thoughts to the side. Feeling upset or angry wouldn't help her now; she had to use all her mental strength to think of a way out of this place.

Taking the sword with her, Spidroth made her way towards the dark buildings in the distance. As she got closer, she realized that she couldn't see the buildings very clearly because there was some kind of smoky black fog in the air. She hadn't noticed it before because everything in this place was black, but the fog seemed to be everywhere.

Finally, she got near enough to the buildings to see them clearly. There were several short, squat rectangular buildings made from a myriad of different blocks. They looked like they'd just been built with whatever blocks the builders had to hand at that moment. As she approached the buildings, an elderly cowman leaned out of a window and waved at her.

"Looks like we've got another newbie," the cowman shouted. In a couple more seconds, the other buildings' doors began opening, and other cowmen and illagers came out, all of them giving Spidroth curious looks.

An elderly illager with a thick white beard and an eye patch walked up to Spidroth and nodded his head.

"Greetings, stranger," he said, his voice gruff. "I'm Big Nose, and this here is Mulligan Town."

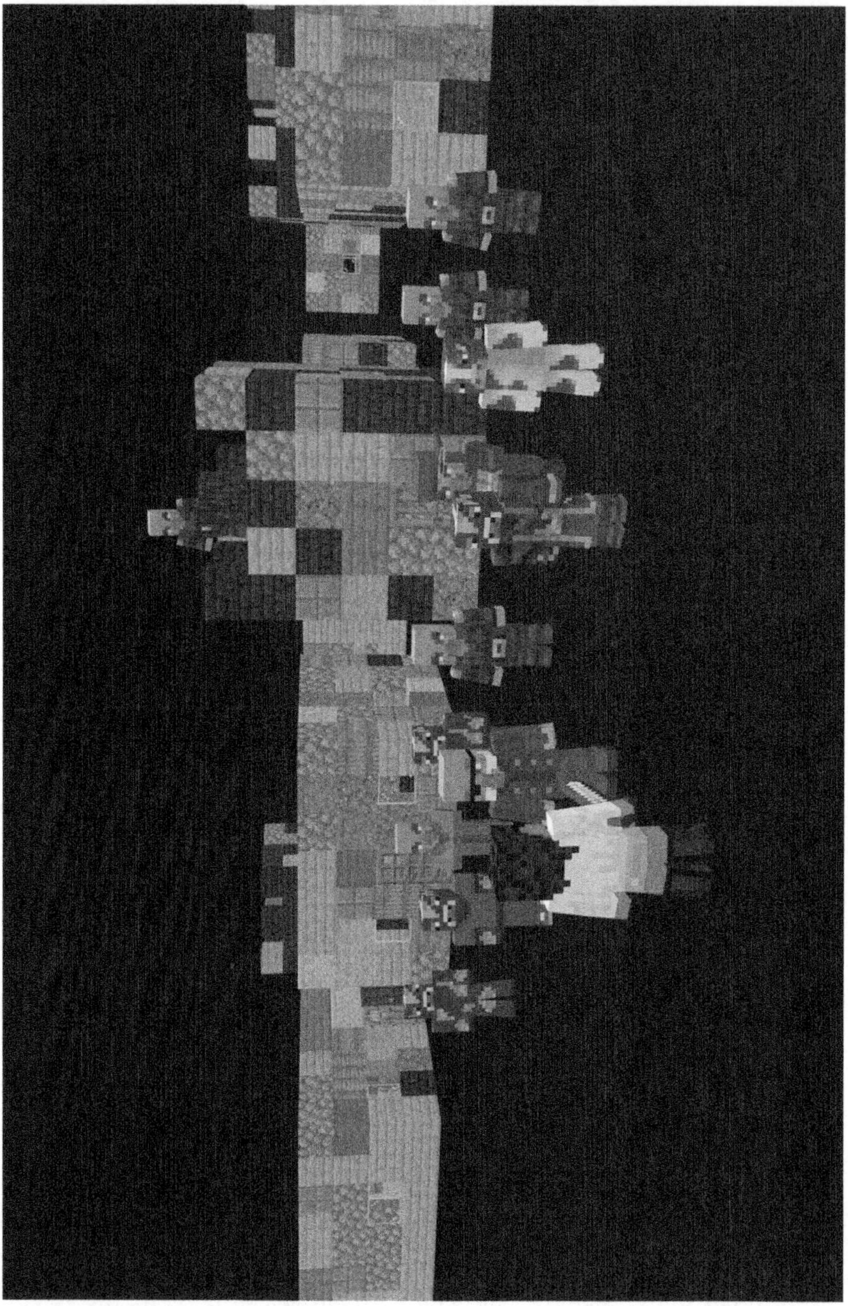

CHAPTER EIGHT
Soul Sand

No matter how long he spent in it, Porkins just couldn't get used to the new Nether. He, Mayor Grady and the rest of the townsfolk of Dead Bush had made their way through the cyan biome with the big mushrooms and were now walking across a great empty desert of brown soul sand. There weren't many plants in this biome, but there were the occasional bones from some huge extinct creature. Porkins had never seen creatures that big in the Nether, so he assumed they must have evolved and then gone extinct during the period when the Nether was fast-forwarding for over a million years. He still found it difficult to get his head around the fact that the Nether he was in now was a million years in the future from the Nether he had grown up in. Thinking about it too much made his brain hurt.

Because of the soul sand, they were only able to walk very slowly through this biome. The sand stuck to their feet, and each step took much longer than it normally would have. There was also a heavy blue mist in this biome, which made it hard to see too far. Porkins had had glimpses of a few ghasts in the distance, but thankfully none of them had tried to attack him and the townsfolk yet. Porkins had made sure that there were archers all around the edges of their group, but he knew from experience how dangerous ghasts could be. Continuous ghast attacks had been part of the reason why his people, the pigmen, had trusted Herobrine. Herobrine had promised that he would give the pigmen the power to fight back against the ghasts but instead, he had turned them all into zombies. Porkins had barely escaped with his life and had had to watch all his tribe, including his father, transform into hideous monsters.

"Do you think we've gone far enough yet?" Mayor Grady asked Porkins.

"Probably," said Porkins, "but it won't hurt to go a little farther, just in case. The last thing we want is to end up back in the caves and get caught by Mad Mulligan's gang or those yellow creeper chaps."

"Agreed," said Mayor Grady. "Let's keep going a bit longer."

So, they kept walking, trudging across the endless soul sand, past patches of blue fire, which burned on the ground in random places, giving the entire biome an eerie feel. With the ghasts floating like huge ghosts in the distance and the thick blue mist, this biome felt to Porkins like it was haunted.

This isn't my Nether anymore, he thought sadly. The Nether he knew was gone, just like his people.

"Are you doing okay, Porkins?" Mayor Grady asked. "It must be tough for you, being back here. I don't know what happened, but I know that a few years ago, all the pigmen in the Nether turned into zombies, and now they've been replaced by some strange pig creatures with tusks."

"Piglins," said Porkins. "I haven't met many of the chaps, but the ones I've met have been jolly nice. A little rough around the edges, but jolly good eggs. But yes, it is a bit tough. Even though the Nether has changed, being here just brings back so many memories."

"There's nothing worse than losing your home," said Mayor Grady. "I don't know what it's like to lose your people, but I have had to leave my home before. I just hope that we can find somewhere safe to build a new town. Dead Bush may be gone, but we can build it again, somewhere new."

Suddenly, their conversation was interrupted by screeching from overhead. Porkins looked up, and to his horror, he saw three ghasts floating above them. The ghasts' eyes, which were normally closed when they were calm, were wide open, and they began firing fireballs down at the townsfolk.

"Watch out, chaps!" Porkins shouted.

DATHOOOM!!!! The fireballs exploded on the ground in the middle of the procession of illagers and cowmen, but, by some miracle, no one was badly hurt.

The townsfolk all began to panic, trying to push and shove out of the way, but they couldn't move very fast because of the soul sand.

"Archers, fire!" Mayor Grady shouted. "We need to take those things down!"

Porkins pulled out his bow and strung an arrow, then he and the other archers in the group began firing at the ghasts. In a matter of seconds, one of the ghasts exploded with a *POOF,* but the other two ghasts weren't dead yet, and they flung more fireballs down at the terrified townsfolk. This time, the illagers and cowmen weren't so lucky, and many were hit by the explosion. As far as Porkins could see, no one had been slain, but it looked like many of them had been badly injured.

"Keep firing, chaps!" Porkins yelled. "Give them what for! Tally-ho, tally-ho!"

Another volley of arrows flew upwards into the air, peppering the ghasts. One of the ghasts was slain, exploding with a *POOF,* but the other ghast survived. It screeched and flung another fireball down. This one hit its target as well, the explosion sending illagers and cowmen flying. Porkins didn't have time to check if the townsfolk were all right, as he was too busy notching his bow and aiming at the ghast.

"Fire!" Porkins shouted.

Once more, Porkins and the other archers fired a volley of arrows at the ghast. This time it was enough, and the third and final ghast exploded with a *POOF.*

"Is everyone okay?" Mayor Grady asked, running towards where the fireballs had exploded against the ground. Porkins ran after him, going as fast as he could on the stodgy soul sand.

Several cowmen and illagers had been injured, but their fellow townsfolk were helping them to drink healing potion. A group of illagers and cowmen were gathered around something on the ground that Porkins couldn't see. He could hear some of them sobbing.

"Mayor Grady," an illager woman sobbed, "come quick!"

Mayor Grady pushed through the crowd of townsfolk, Porkins following behind him. In the middle of the crowd was a badly injured cowman.

"Tom!" Mayor Grady gasped.

"We've tried giving him some healing potion, but his injuries are too severe," said an illager man, with tears in his eyes.

Mayor Grady knelt next to Tom.

"Mayor Grady..." Tom gasped, his voice croaky. "Make sure... you get everyone to safety..."

"I will, Tom," said Mayor Grady, taking Tom's hoof in his hand. Porkins saw that the mayor was crying.

"And tell Liza... tell her that..."

But whatever Tom had wanted to tell Liza, they never found

out. With a faint *poof,* he was gone.

“I’m so sorry,” said Porkins, putting a trotter on Mayor Grady’s shoulder.

Mayor Grady stood to his feet, using his sleeve to wipe away the last of his tears.

“We will honor Tom’s wishes,” said the mayor, addressing his people. “We will find a safe place and we’ll found a new town.”

“Forget founding a new town,” said the illager man who’d been crying before, “we need to get vengeance! Vengeance on Mad Mulligan!”

Some of the townsfolk muttered in agreement.

“Chaps, trust me,” said Porkins, “I know all about the desire for revenge, but the important thing is that you all find a new place to live. The best way you can honor your friend is to go on. That’s what he would have wanted.”

"Don't try and tell us what Tom would have wanted," said a cow woman, looking at Porkins angrily. "We were all fine before you and your friends came to our town. This is your fault!"

There were more mutters of agreement. Some of the illagers and cowmen were looking at Porkins with fury in their eyes.

"Everyone, calm down," said Mayor Grady, stepping in front of Porkins. "We need to stand together."

"Why are we listening to Grady?" snapped the illager man who'd spoken before. "Under his leadership, our town has been destroyed, and too many of us have been killed. I say we need new leadership. Who's with me?"

Many of the other illagers and cowmen cheered.

"We know how to use weapons now," said the illager man, "so we shouldn't be running. We need to regroup and go back and slay Marie and Mad Mulligan and all their forces. We need to have our revenge!"

"Dear boy, Mad Mulligan's forces vastly outnumber your own," said Porkins. "That would be foolhardy."

"You're not one of us!" shouted a cowman. "You don't get to order us about!"

"This is ridiculous," said an illager woman, "we need to listen to Mayor Grady. He knows what to do!"

"Mayor Grady is the one who's led us to our doom!" a cowman shouted back at her.

A scuffle broke out, with illagers and cowmen shouting at each other and fighting.

"Stop it, chaps!" Porkins shouted. "This isn't the time or the place!"

"Everyone, calm down!" Mayor Grady roared.

But things had gone too far. All the townsfolk were fighting now, even the children and the elderly. Thankfully, no one was using their swords or their bows, but they were all throwing punches and wrestling each other. It was complete chaos.

Porkins looked anxiously at the ghasts floating in the distance. Thankfully none of the flying monsters were approaching them yet, but it would only be a matter of time. They needed to get out of this biome, but the townsfolk were so enraged that they wouldn't listen to reason.

"What are we going to do?" Porkins asked Mayor Grady.

"I... I'm not sure," said Mayor Grady. The mayor looked completely lost, a far cry from the confident figure he normally was.

Then Porkins heard a strange sound. It wasn't a sound he normally associated with the Nether – it was barking.

"Are those wolves?" Porkins muttered to himself. He'd never heard of wolves being in the Nether before, but maybe these were some new type of Nether wolves that he hadn't seen before. There were so many new weird and wonderful creatures in the Nether now that he wouldn't have been surprised.

Suddenly a pack of wolves ran around the outside of the townsfolk, barking and snapping their jaws. They were ordinary gray wolves, and they were wearing black collars. The townsfolk immediately stopped their squabbling and looked in terror at the wolves surrounding them and penning them in.

"Good boys," shouted a female voice. Porkins looked over and saw a big army of illager soldiers walking towards them across the soul sand. At the front of the illagers, smiling a smug smile, was Marie. Her army vastly outnumbered the Dead Bush townsfolk, and her archers were aiming their crossbows directly at them.

"Oh no," gasped Mayor Grady.

"Well, you really gave us the runaround," grinned Marie. "But now your little escape plan is over, and you're all going to die."

Marie turned to face her archers.

"Kill them," she said softly, "kill them all."

Marie's soldiers all pointed their crossbows towards the townsfolk, but before they could fire, there was an ear-piercing shriek from above:

SKRIIIIII!!!!!!

Porkins looked up to see a group of at least five ghasts floating above them. The ghasts screeched and began firing fireballs down at Marie's forces and the Dead Bush townsfolk.

"Kill those things!" Marie shrieked, looking up in terror at the ghasts.

Marie's illagers began firing their crossbows at the ghasts instead. The sudden appearance of the ghasts was all the distraction that Porkins needed, and he quickly pulled some obsidian blocks out of his rucksack and built a portal, lighting it up with some flint and steel.

"Into the portal, chaps!" Porkins shouted. "Go, go, go!"

The illagers and cowmen of Dead Bush didn't need telling twice and quickly rushed towards the portal, moving as fast as they could on the soul sand. The ones who could walk helped the ones who'd been injured.

It was taking far too long for the townsfolk to escape into the portal, so Porkins quickly built another portal and lit it so that some of the townsfolk could escape through that one. It was clear that Marie's forces had never seen ghasts before, and they were too busy firing up at the huge mobs to notice what was going on before it was too late. Finally, Marie noticed the townsfolk escaping into the portals.

"Idiots, don't let them get away!" she shrieked, then *DATHOOOM,* a fireball exploded into the ground next to her, sending her flying.

Good riddance, thought Porkins, and he jumped into one of the portals after the last of the townsfolk had escaped.

To Porkins's relief, when he went through the portal, he found himself back in the open air, rather than in a cave. They were all in the middle of a large open badlands plain, and it was the middle of the day: the bright sun shining down on the red sand. Porkins quickly pulled out his pickaxe and broke a block from the portal frame, deactivating the purple liquid.

"Get ready, chaps," said Porkins. "Once Marie and her scoundrels deal with the ghasts, no doubt they'll be building portals of their own to come and get us. As my chum Dave would say – battle stations!"

The illagers and cowmen all got into formation, following the training that Porkins and his friends had given them over the past week.

"I... I'm sorry about before," said the illager man who'd tried to overthrow Mayor Grady. "I got carried away."

"It's okay," said Mayor Grady. "We've all had a tough time, but we need to stick together."

They all stood in formation, watching the broken portal. Even though Porkins had built two portals on the other side, only one portal had appeared in the Overworld. Porkins had never quite got his head around how portals between the Overworld and the Nether worked, but if you didn't put enough distance between your portals, they would bring you to the same place. That was how he knew that Marie's forces would be coming through the broken portal, so they would have to be ready.

"Aim your bows at the portal," Porkins shouted to his troops.

They all stood there, anxiously waiting. Once Marie fixed one of the other portals on the other side and lit it, this portal in the Overworld would fix itself and reactivate, Porkins knew. Even though the enemy vastly outnumbered them, at least they would all be coming through the same entrance, so Porkins and his archers would be able to attack them with arrows as they came through.

So, they waited, and waited... but no one came through.

Is this some kind of trap? Porkins wondered. *Are they trying to bait us, to make us go back in?*

Then, suddenly, the missing obsidian block in the portal reappeared back in place, and the purple forcefield sprung into life. An illager emerged from the portal — or rather, half emerged. It was a male illager, and he was crawling along on his stomach, and his legs were still on the other side of the portal, back in the Nether.

"Help me..." he said, his eyes full of terror. Then *woosh*, something yanked him backward, and with a scream, he disappeared back into the portal.

"What's going on?" said Mayor Grady. He sounded scared.

Porkins was scared too, but he slowly, carefully approached the lit portal. Then he stood on the frame and poked his head through. On the other side of the portal, back in the soul sand biome, all the illagers in Marie's army had disappeared, although their armor, weapons and belongings were scattered across the ground. In their place stood hundreds of hideous pig creatures. It took Porkins a moment to realize what they were — they were piglins, but parts of their flesh had rotted away, exposing the bone underneath.

Zombified piglins, thought Porkins. He and the Dead Bush townsfolk had escaped just in time, it seemed — these hundreds of zombified creatures had slaughtered Marie's forces.

"Get back, you ugly fiends!" Porkins heard a female voice shout. In the distance, he saw a lone illager fighting off hordes and hordes of zombified piglins. To his surprise, it was Marie. The rest of her forces had been destroyed, but she was still fighting on to the end.

"You'll never defeat me!" Marie screeched as she cut down piglin after piglin. "I'll kill you all!"

But as good as a fighter as Marie was, she was overwhelmed. Finally, the zombified piglins managed to grab her from behind, and then it was all over. The rest of them piled onto her, and Porkins couldn't see her anymore. All he could hear was her terrified screams.

"How awful," Porkins gasped. For the first time, some of the zombified piglins noticed he was there. They all began to turn towards him, staring at him with their blank eyes and snorting and grunting in anger.

All at once, the zombified piglins charged towards him.

"Oh my," said Porkins. He quickly pulled his head out of the portal, re-emerging back in the Overworld. Then he took out his pickaxe and hacked away at one of the obsidian blocks in the portal frame. As soon as the block broke, the purple forcefield disappeared, and the portal was no more.

"What happened to them?" Mayor Grady asked.

"Let's just say we won't have to deal with Marie's forces anymore," said Porkins. "They were all destroyed by zombified piglins. A pretty awful way to go, but no more than those blaggards deserved."

"Well, at least that's over," sighed Mayor Grady. He took a look at the vast desert of red sand around them. "I guess here is as good as anywhere to build a new town. What does everyone think?"

All the illagers and cowmen nodded. They were tired and exhausted and eager to stop fleeing.

"There's just one thing," Mayor Grady said to Porkins. "I don't know if my daughter is still alive, but if she is, I need to rescue her. Will you go with me, Porkins?"

"Of course, dear chap," said Porkins. "Do you have any idea where she'll be?"

"No," sighed Mayor Grady, "but I would guess that Mad Mulligan's soldiers would take her back to his base as a prisoner. We can head there."

"That sounds like a good plan," said Porkins. "If they're keeping prisoners there, my friends might be there as well. We can rescue them and teach Mad Mulligan a lesson while we're at it."

"That would be good," smiled Mayor Grady. "But we'll have to be careful. With Marie's forces gone, there will be a significant dent in Mad Mulligan's army, but I'm sure he'll still have plenty more soldiers back at his base. This won't be easy."

"In my experience, not many things are," said Porkins. "But we will do the best we can."

Mayor Grady made sure that his people were okay and safe, and then he and Porkins headed off across the badlands, heading north, as that was where Mayor Grady said that Mad Mulligan's base was.

Don't worry, chaps, I'm coming for you, Porkins thought, thinking of his captured friends. He didn't know what trials lay ahead, but if anyone could defeat Mad Mulligan and his forces, it was him and his friends.

CHAPTER NINE
Breakout

Alex tried to move, but her hands and legs had been bound together tightly by rope. She was lying down in the same cell that she and Spidroth had rescued Liza from earlier.

"Help!" she shouted. "Somebody help me!"

An illager's face appeared at the bars of one of the windows.

"Can you let me out?" Alex asked the illager.

"Er, no," said the illager. "I've been told to guard you."

"Oh," said Alex. "I don't suppose you've got any comic books, do you? It's a bit boring in here."

"No," said the illager.

"Okay," said Alex, "but do you have any cake? I'm a bit hungry."

"No," snapped the illager. "Now, can you please shut up?"

The illager's face disappeared from the bars, and Alex was alone once more.

How am I going to get out of this one? she wondered. She thought back to all the comic books that she'd read: to all the fantastic and unlikely ways that heroes like Seth the Elf and Captain Cowman had escaped. In one issue, Seth the Elf had escaped by sending a message to his friends via a talking bat, but, as far as Alex knew, bats didn't talk in real life. In one issue of *Captain Cowman,* Captain Cowman had escaped a prison cell by pretending he was sick and then overpowering the guards when they came to check on him. Maybe she could try that?

"Help!" Alex shouted. "I feel sick! I think, um, my head is going to explode or something!"

Once more, the illager's face appeared at the bars.

"What is it now?" he demanded.

"I think I'm sick," said Alex. "You'd better untie me and check that I'm okay."

"No," said the illager, and then he disappeared once more.

So much for that idea, thought Alex.

Then she heard some sort of commotion outside. Some illagers were talking to each other, but she couldn't hear what they were saying. Then, the next thing she knew, the iron door to her cell swung open, and another prisoner was thrown inside. It was a small yellow creeper. At first, Alex tried to roll out of the way of the creeper, worried that it would electrocute her, but then she realized that she recognized it.

"Creepo Jones?" said Alex in disbelief. "Is that you?"

"It is," said the little yellow creeper. "Those swine may have captured me, but no cell can hold the great Creepo Jones!"

Suddenly, something else was thrown through the door, and it landed on Creepo Jones.

"Oof!" the little creeper grunted.

"I'm sorry, Master," said the person who had landed on Creepo Jones, quickly rolling to the side. Alex realized that she knew this person as well: it was the cowman named Milo – Creepo Jones's loyal assistant.

The iron door swung shut, and the three of them were alone.

"You won't get away with this!" Creepo Jones shouted. "You haven't heard the last of Creepo Jones!"

"Oh, hello Alex," said Milo, noticing her for the first time. "Did those horrible illagers capture you too? Are Dave and the others here as well?"

"Just me, I'm afraid," said Alex.

"Mad Mulligan's soldiers captured Master Creepo and me while we were on our way back to Spectrite City," said Milo. "They seemed to know exactly where we were. I've no idea how."

"And they stole the Trident of Emeros," said Creepo Jones angrily. "That is a priceless artifact, and those criminals stole it!"

"So, what's the escape plan?" Alex asked.

Creepo Jones gave her a curious look.

"What escape plan?" he asked.

"You said that no cell can hold you," said Alex, "so I assume you have a plan to escape?"

Creepo Jones's cheeks glowed red.

"Well, I don't have a plan yet," said the little yellow creeper, "but I'm sure I'll think of something. It's a bit difficult to do anything without my trusty suit, but for an explorer as great as me, I'm sure it won't stop me for long."

The last time Alex had seen Creepo Jones, he'd been wearing a suit which gave him villager-sized arms and legs. Now he was just in his normal creeper form.

"So what happened to you, Alex?" Milo asked.

Alex explained all about Dead Bush and how she and her friends had tried to organize a rebellion before Mad Mulligan and his forces had defeated them all.

"So, you've no idea where your friends are?" Milo asked her.

Alex shook her head.

Through the bars of the cell, Alex saw that the sun was beginning to set. At first, she, Milo and Creepo Jones discussed possible escape plans, but they couldn't come up with anything. For all Creepo Jones's big talk, it seemed that he didn't really have any plans at all.

Finally, it was night time. Alex felt her eyelids begin to droop. It had been a long day, and there wasn't much more she could do until she could think of an escape plan, so she allowed herself to drift off to sleep.

DAKOOM!!!!

Suddenly, one of the walls of their cell blasted open. Alex jolted awake and sat up.

"Carl?" she said in disbelief.

Standing in the middle of the broken wall was Carl the creeper in his netherite golem suit. Liza the illager was standing behind him.

"Carl, we were supposed to break them out quietly," Liza hissed angrily.

"I was trying to be quiet," said Carl, shrugging. "It's a bit hard when you're wearing a golem suit. Golems aren't designed for stealth. Anyway, I'm sure no one heard us."

Suddenly a bell began ringing somewhere in the camp. Then another bell joined it, then another.

"Alarm bells," said Creepo Jones. "We need to get out of here!"

"Oh no, not you," said Carl, noticing Creepo Jones.

Liza ran over and cut Alex, Creepo Jones and Milo's ropes, and they were all able to stand up.

"I don't suppose Dave or Spidroth are around here as well?" Carl asked Alex.

Alex shook her head sadly.

"Some illagers are coming this way!" Milo whimpered, looking through one of the barred windows.

"What happened to the guards, anyway?" Alex asked.

"I biffed them," said Carl. "That's definitely going in the comic book. We can call the issue *Carl saves the day*."

"Can you save the day first, and think about your stupid comic book later?" said Liza. "We need to get moving!"

They all left the prison cell through the hole that Carl had made. Two illagers holding torches in one hand and diamond swords in the other, charged towards them.

"Stop right there!" one of the illagers shouted. Carl stepped forward, and *POW, POW,* biffed both of the illagers, sending them flying.

"Good job, Carl," said Liza, "but there are a lot more of them on the way."

Liza was right, Alex saw. More illagers with torches were rushing up the hill towards the prison cell.

"We passed some stables on our way here," said Liza. "Come on!"

Liza and Carl led them around a small terracotta hill. When they got to the far side, they saw a wooden stable in the distance, with some horses in pens and illagers standing guard.

"We can easily take those guys on," said Creepo Jones. "I could probably take them all single-handedly."

"Um, Master," said Milo, "remember, you don't have your suit."

"I don't need it," said Creepo Jones.

"Well, we can't waste any more time," said Carl. "Let's give those idiots a beating and then get out of here. Attack!"

Carl, Alex, Liza, Milo and Creepo Jones all ran down towards the stables. Liza was the only one with a weapon, but Carl had his golem suit, and Creepo Jones was riding on Milo's shoulders. The illagers guarding the stables looked around at them in shock.

"Throw me, Milo!" Creepo Jones demanded.

Milo tossed Creepo Jones towards one of the illagers. The illager automatically caught the little creeper in his hands. Then *ZZZAAAP,* Creepo Jones shocked the illager with a blast of blue electricity. The illager let go of Creepo Jones and went flying backward, banging his head on one of the wooden poles holding up the stable roof, and falling to the ground unconscious. Carl used his huge netherite fists to bash the other illagers who came running towards them, sending them flying, and Alex used her ninja skills to take out the remaining illagers, sending them flying with her kicks. In a few seconds, all the illagers were dazed or unconscious on the ground.

"You can ride behind me, Master," Milo said to Creepo Jones, placing the little yellow creeper on the saddle of one of the horses.

"Of course I'm going to ride behind you," said Creepo Jones, sounding annoyed, "I can't ride a horse without my suit. Come on, Milo, use your brain!"

"Yes, Master Creepo," said Milo, climbing onto the horse.

Alex thought that Creepo Jones was being very mean to Milo, but there was no time for arguments at the moment. She jumped onto another horse, and Liza jumped onto another. Carl's golem suit was far too big for him to ride a horse, but his golem legs could run as fast as a horse anyway.

"This way," said Liza, tugging at the reins of her horse. The horse went galloping forward, down the dirt track that led along the outside of the base. Alex and Milo pulled at the reins of their horses and rode along behind her, with Carl running beside them in his golem suit. For a moment, it looked like they were going to escape the base safely, but then they heard galloping behind them. Alex looked around and saw a huge group of illagers on horseback chasing them.

"We've got company!" Milo whimpered.

They rode through the main road that led to the base, passing the watchtowers and the illagers stationed in their white tents. The illagers in watchtowers began firing arrows at them, and the illagers by the tents tried to grab them or attack them with swords as they rode past, so they had to keep dodging out of the way. Alex looked behind her again and saw that more illagers on horseback had joined the others, and as they made their way past the watchtowers and the tents, more and more illagers on horseback joined the big group, until there were hundreds of them.

Finally, they left the outskirts of the base and were riding their horses across the vast open badlands plains. The illagers on horseback were still pursuing them and seemed to be getting nearer every second. There was nothing ahead of them but endless badlands, and Alex had no idea how they were going to lose their pursuers.

"What now?" Liza shouted. "We can't just keep riding forever!"

"Maybe they'll get tired before we do?" suggested Milo.

"I doubt it," said Carl miserably, "we never get that lucky."

"They won't capture the great Creepo Jones," said Creepo Jones. "Nobody captures the great Creepo Jones!"

"I don't want to burst your bubble, but they've already captured you once already," said Carl.

"Well, nobody catches the great Creepo Jones twice," said Creepo Jones.

"Um, Master," said Milo, "what about that time you got captured twice by the Zombie Prince?"

"Shut up, Milo!" snapped Creepo Jones. "That was just very bad luck!"

As it was dark, and they only had the light from the moon to guide them, they weren't sure which direction they were going, and soon ended up in a place that none of them had passed through before — a vast swamp biome with a shallow layer of water on the ground and trees with vines hanging down. Their horses splashed across the ground, their hooves sending up great sprays of water.

"I didn't know you had swamps around here," said Alex. "I thought this was all badlands."

"This must be Lily Pad Swamp," said Liza, "it's one of the only non-badlands biomes around here. During the dry seasons, people often go here to collect water."

Alex looked behind her again and saw that the illagers on horseback were still pursuing them through the swamp, the hundreds of horses sending up such a big cloud of water that it looked like they were surrounded by a living fog that followed them as they went. Alex's horse was starting to make whimpering noises now — it was clear that it was getting very tired. They couldn't continue this chase much longer.

"Maybe we can lose them in the trees," Alex suggested.

"I doubt it," said Liza. "This biome isn't very big. "Before long, we'll be back in the badlands, on the open plains again."

"Then perhaps it is time for the great Creepo Jones to step up and save the day," said Creepo Jones.

Carl scoffed.

"And what are you going to do?"

"Watch and learn," said Creepo Jones. "I'm going to stay behind, but the rest of you have to keep going."

"Master, no," said Milo. "I'm not going to leave you behind."

"That's an order, Milo," said Creepo Jones. "You have served me well, but you need to live on and make sure the Trident of Emeros gets back where it belongs. Do you promise you will?"

"I promise, Master," said Milo. It sounded like he was crying.

"What are you two idiots blabbing about?" said Carl. "I don't think one little yellow creeper is going to be able to stop all those illagers. But if you want to sacrifice your life in vain, I'm not going to stop you."

"It won't be in vain," said Creepo Jones. "Make sure you tell everyone how spectacular I was!"

Then, without a word of warning, the little yellow creeper jumped off of the back of Milo's horse and landed in the swamp water.

"What's he doing?!" Liza asked Milo. "We need to go back for him!"

"No!" Milo shouted. "We must keep riding, or Master Creepo's sacrifice will be for nothing!"

Alex turned to look behind her. Creepo Jones was walking through the swamp water, towards the hundreds of illagers on horseback.

He's going to get trampled to death, she thought. *What is he doing?*

Then Creepo Jones began to glow blue, and Alex understood. He crackled with electricity, then the electricity spread across the water of the swamp, moving so fast that the illagers didn't have time to react. The illagers and their horses were electrocuted. The horses reared up, and their riders went flying, landing in the water where they were electrocuted some more.

"He stopped them all!" said Alex happily. "Let's go back to get him!"

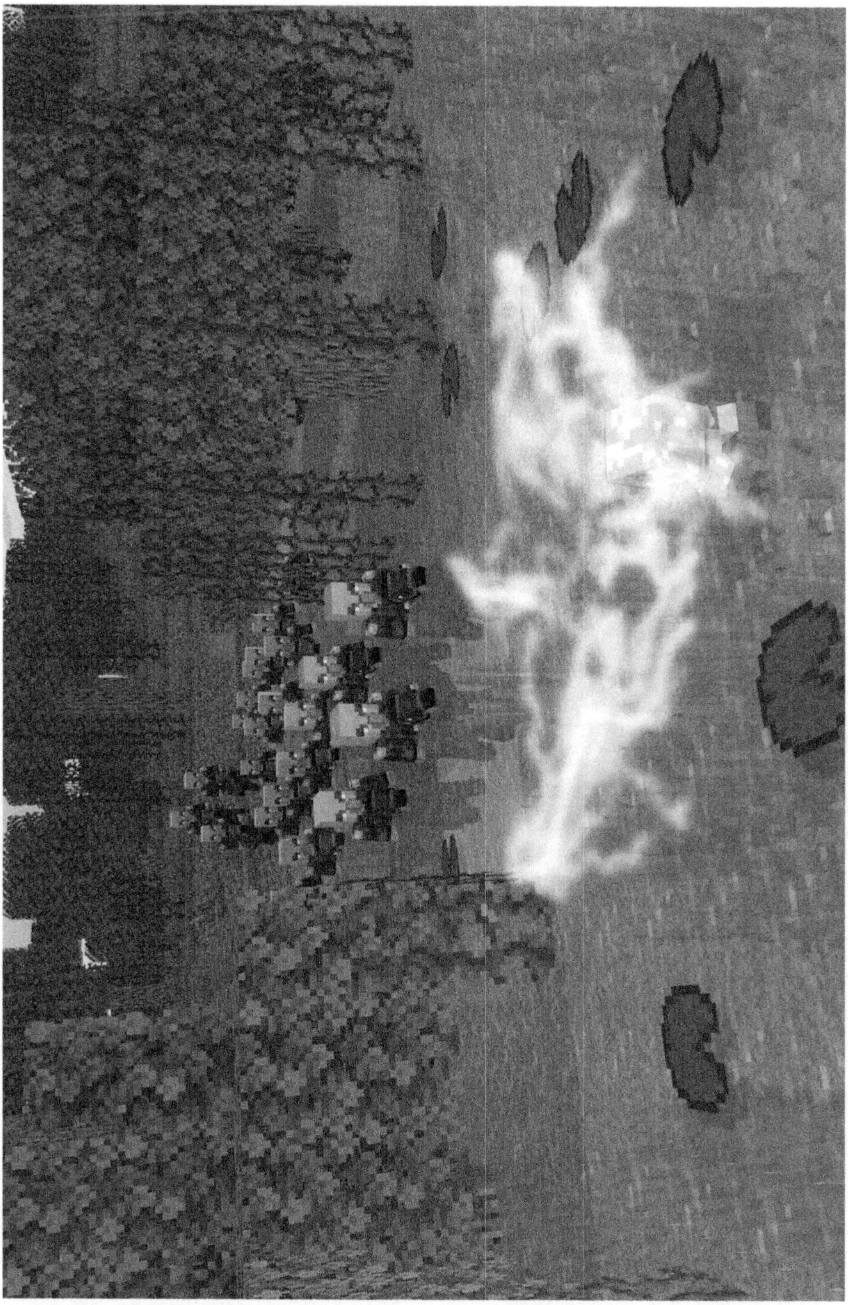

"I wish we could," said Milo, "but the illagers will be back on their feet and their horses soon. Master Creepo has bought us enough time to escape, so escape we must. I can only hope that they capture Master Creepo rather than kill him, but they may be so angry that they take it out on him."

The cowman sounded so sad that Alex wanted to go over and hug him, but they were riding on separate horses.

"I said a lot of bad things about that little guy, but he was a real hero in the end," said Carl.

"He was," Liza agreed. "Let's just hope that one day we're in a position to avenge him and teach Mad Mulligan's forces a lesson once and for all."

CHAPTER TEN
Mulligan Town

"Mulligan Town?" said Spidroth. "What kind of stupid name is that?"

The old illager with the white beard and the eyepatch laughed.

"To be honest, we first gave it that name for a joke, but the name just stuck," he said, shrugging. "All of us have been imprisoned here by Mad Mulligan over the years. I was the first, and when I came here, there was nothing but empty black space. Eventually, Mulligan began storing all sorts of bits and bobs in this chest, and he began imprisoning more people down here as well, so we all worked together to build this town. If we're going to be stuck here until the end of our days, we might as well have somewhere nice to live."

"Well, I'm not going to be stuck here for the rest of my days like you fools," said Spidroth. "I'm going to find a way out."

The old illager laughed again.

"That's what everyone says when they first get here," he said, "but there is no way out unless Mulligan lets you out – and he's never let anyone out. One of his favorite blackmail techniques is to put a loved one of someone he wants to manipulate in this chest, with the promise that he'll free the prisoner once that person cooperates. But he never does. Mulligan is a liar. He used to work for me once, and, being the fool I am, I kept on promoting him. Finally, he defeated me in combat and imprisoned me in here, taking control of my gang."

"Mulligan imprisoned me here when I refused to burn a village to the ground for him," said a blonde-haired illager with a long scar across her face.

"And he imprisoned me when my town refused to pay him protection money," said a cowman with black fur with white spots.

"I'm sure you've got a story to tell too," Big Nose, the old illager, said to Spidroth. "Why don't you come to the inn for a glass of milk, and you can tell us all about it?"

Spidroth was anxious to find a way out of the ender chest, but she knew that she should probably get the lay of the land first and find out what these exiles knew.

Big Nose and the others led Spidroth to a one-story building made from an assortment of blocks. A sign above the door said *The Mad Dog Inn.*

Inside the inn, there were lots of tables, with illagers and cowmen sitting around them. At the far end of the room, a cowman stood behind the bar, polishing glasses. As Spidroth entered, everyone turned to look at her.

"A mug of warm pumpkin milk for our new citizen," Big Nose said to the cowman behind the bar.

The cowman nodded and began pouring frothy orange liquid from a tap into a mug.

Big Nose sat down at a table, and Spidroth sat down opposite him. All the other illagers and cowmen bustled forward, trying to get as close to the table as they could, surrounding them. The cowman behind the bar came over with a mug and placed it in front of Spidroth.

It could be poisoned, she thought, looking down at the frothy orange liquid.

"Don't worry," grinned Big Nose, "there's no poison in there. If we wanted to hurt you, we do vastly outnumber you, so it wouldn't be too hard."

I could take all of you fools on, Spidroth thought to herself. But she picked up the mug and sipped the frothy orange liquid. It tasted surprisingly sweet and delicious.

"That's Paul's own recipe," said Big Nose, nodding to the barman. "Being stuck in here, we all have to find ways to kill time. Paul's hobby is coming up with recipes for delicious drinks. You'll have to try his beetroot cocktails — they're delicious."

"I'm sure they are," said Spidroth. Although in reality, she couldn't imagine anything worse. She'd never been a fan of beetroot.

"So, what's your name, stranger?" Big Nosed asked Spidroth. "And what did you do to tick Mad Mulligan off?"

"My name is Spidroth," said Spidroth. She almost introduced herself as Lady Spidrothbrine, daughter of Herobrine, but she stopped herself just in time. There was no need to overcomplicate matters. "My friends and I tried to free a town called Dead Bush from Mad Mulligan, but he ended up besting my companion Alex and me in combat."

"Yeah, Mulligan can best pretty much anyone in combat," said the blonde-haired illager. "I was foolish enough to get into a battle with him, and that's how I got this scar on my face."

"How is Mulligan so good at fighting?" Spidroth asked. "Is it the Sight?"

"You know about the Sight?" Big Nose said, raising an eyebrow. "It's not a very well-known phenomenon these days."

"Let's just say I'm older than I look," said Spidroth.

"Fair enough," said Big Nose. "Yep, Mulligan does have the Sight. He practiced with it for years, turning himself into the ultimate fighting machine. You can't outsmart him or surprise him because he'll see you coming. When I ran his gang, we were a small operation, mostly concerned with robberies and stealing treasures from ancient ruins. But, from what I hear, Mulligan has turned it into his own empire."

"Well, all empires fall one day," said Spidroth. "It's only a matter of time."

"I hope you're right," grinned Big Nose. "It would be brilliant if someone could wipe that smug smile off Mulligan's face one of these days. Even though I probably won't be around to see it."

"Now," said Spidroth, "how do I get out of this place? There must be a way."

"I'm afraid there isn't," said Big Nose. "Trust us, if there was, we would have all escaped by now."

Spidroth had feared as much. But she was sure there had to be a way out. There was no way that she was going to spend the rest of her days here, in this town inside a treasure chest.

Spidroth pushed her chair back and stood to her feet.

"Does no one know of a possible way out?" she demanded. "Does no one have any theories or any ideas about how to escape? Don't tell me you've all been down here for years, and you haven't come up with any ideas on how to get out of here?"

There was a long silence, all the illagers and cowmen looking at her blankly.

"Well, there is the crack," one cow woman said.

"We've been over this a million times," replied a female illager. "Even if the crack was a route to a way out, there's no way of getting up there. It's just too high and too dangerous."

"Tell me everything about this crack," Spidroth said, turning towards the cow woman.

"It's impossible to get up there," the female illager repeated. "Many have tried, and they've all failed."

"Yes," said Spidroth, "but none of those people were the Lady Spidrothbrine. And the Lady Spidrothbrine does not fail."

CHAPTER ELEVEN
Written by the Victors

Dave had never ridden on a ravager before, and he wasn't enjoying the experience. He was sitting behind Mad Mulligan on the ravager's saddle as the huge beast made its way along a narrow ledge. On one side of them was a huge drop, down to the badlands valley below, and on the other side was a sheer rock face. They were traveling through a mountainous region of the badlands now, with cliffs and drops everywhere. If it had been up to Dave, he would have got off of the ravager and walked along on foot, but Mad Mulligan insisted that they ride on the huge beast to conserve their strength.

"We've got a long way to go to get to Bedrock City," Mad Mulligan had said. "We need to rest our legs whenever we can."

Sitting behind Mad Mulligan on the saddle, Dave could easily have just reached out and grabbed the illager's red sword. But every time he was tempted to do so, he remembered that Mad Mulligan would probably see the attack coming, and even if he did defeat him, Mad Mulligan was the only one who could free Spidroth from the ender chest. For now, Dave had to do what he was told and behave himself.

Ever since Mad Mulligan had told him that the Sight could be used to speak to people across vast distances, Dave had been trying to reach out to Carl, Spidroth, Porkins and Alex, but so far, he'd had no success. It seemed that this was a skill he was going to have to practice over time. He desperately wanted to know what was going on with his friends, but if Mad Mulligan knew, he wasn't telling him.

Dave had noticed a slight change in Mad Mulligan's mood. The illager seemed to be less smug than before, and he often seemed distracted, as if the things he saw with the Sight were making him unhappy.

Maybe my friends are fighting back, Dave thought hopefully. *Maybe Mad Mulligan is starting to realize that his empire isn't quite so invincible after all.*

One thing about Mad Mulligan was that he loved to talk, and Dave was trying to use this to his advantage. Dave knew little about the Sight, and Mad Mulligan had been using it for years, so Dave thought he might as well use this opportunity to learn more about how he could use his abilities.

"Tell me," Dave said, as the ravager walked slowly around a particularly tight ledge, "when we fought outside of Dead Bush, how did you trick me into thinking you were going to attack from a different direction? I was using the Sight and thought you were going to attack from my left, but instead, you attacked from my right. Did you use the Sight to send me the wrong vision?"

Mad Mulligan chuckled.

"I was pretty pleased with that," the illager said. "I've never fought anyone else with the Sight before, so I had to think up new tactics. The Sight lets you see the future, but, as you know, the future is hard to predict. People are always changing their minds and doing unexpected things, so predicting the future can be a dangerous game. Some actions are more set in stone than others. For example, a few years ago, a group of cowmen decided that they would sneak into my base and assassinate me. They'd been making their plans for months and had everything organized down to the smallest detail. Unfortunately for them, it meant that it was very easy for me to know when and how they were going to attempt the assassination. I had my men waiting for them, and that was the end of that. The events that are harder to predict are the unexpected ones. If one of my soldiers suddenly decided, at that very moment, that he wanted to attack me with his sword, I'd have trouble predicting that.

"So, to answer your question, I knew that I'd have to be unpredictable to beat you. I fully committed myself to attack you from the left, but then, at the last minute, I randomly decided to switch to the right-hand side instead. I didn't plan it ahead of time, or you'd have been able to predict what I was doing. I had to act in the moment. When people act in the moment, it's hard for the Sight to anticipate that."

Dave couldn't help but smile. Whether knowingly or not, Mad Mulligan had just given him the advice he needed to beat someone with the Sight.

"I know what you're thinking," chuckled Mad Mulligan, "you're thinking that you should unexpectedly grab my sword and attack me before I can see it coming. That would be a good idea, but you've got to remember about poor Spidroth. If you don't behave yourself, she's trapped forever."

That's true, Dave thought to himself, *but you've given me the information I need to defeat you when the time comes, Mad Mulligan. And you're going to regret that.*

Dave looked off to the side and immediately regretted it. The ledge they were riding along overlooked a vast valley, which was a long, long way down. If the ravager took one wrong step, they would plummet to their doom. Mad Mulligan didn't seem to be worried, though — Dave supposed that the Sight would allow him to see a fall coming before it happened.

Then Dave asked Mad Mulligan something that had been on his mind for a while.

"If all you want from me is the knowledge of how to open end portals, then why go to all this trouble?" Dave asked. "Couldn't you just have threatened me or my friends and forced me to tell you?"

"Oh, I could have," said Mad Mulligan. "But using the Sight, I saw that threatening your friends, even Spidroth, wouldn't work. You're so terrified of what someone like me could do if they reached the End that you would have refused to tell me the secret."

Dave had never really thought about it before, but Mad Mulligan was right. There was something in the End that Herobrine had thought could help him destroy the entire universe, so Dave would have done whatever it took to make sure a bad guy like Mad Mulligan couldn't get there.

"So, if you know that I'm never going to tell you the secret to getting the end portal to work, then why are you bringing me along?" asked Dave.

"Because I had another vision," said Mad Mulligan. "I saw a vision of you activating the end portal and going through it. Unfortunately, the vision wasn't clear enough for me to see how you activated it, but you did. So somehow, I don't know how or why yet, you are going to activate the end portal, and you are going to go through it – and I'm going to be there when you do."

Dave found it interesting that Mad Mulligan still couldn't see the future perfectly even with all his practice with the Sight. Just like Dave and the vague visions he'd had of the End and the Ender Dragon, the visions Mad Mulligan had had were equally unclear. It seemed that even an expert with the Sight was unable to predict everything perfectly.

"And why do you want to get to the End so badly anyway?" Dave asked.

"Well, one of the main reasons is that I want a dragon," Mad Mulligan shrugged. "I mean, I'm pretty powerful now, but if I had a dragon, there would be nothing that could stop me. I could take over Spectrite City and the rest of this continent as well... But, to be honest, I'm more excited about all the ancient stuff there will be there. No one's been to the End for thousands and thousands of years, so think of all the amazing Old People technology that's probably been left behind there. I find history and historical artifacts endlessly fascinating."

"I don't believe you," Dave scoffed. "You're just a thug and a killer."

"Can't a thug and a killer be interested in history?" Mad Mulligan shrugged. "History is *full* of thugs and killers. They say that history is written by the victors — the strongest warriors and the strongest leaders defeat their enemies, and they're the ones who get to write the history books. One of the things I find fascinating about history is that there is still so much we don't know. Who built this red sword that I have? Was it used in any important battles or wars? I have no idea — that knowledge has been lost to history. Historical stories change over time, as well. Just look at Herobrine and Steve. In many cultures, they are both thought to be mythological figures who never existed. Some societies believe that they are one being, who is good on one day and evil on the next. Others believe that the two of them are brothers, whereas some say they were one single person who was split in two. Will we ever know which stories are true? Even Herobrine and Steve themselves don't remember their origins, from what I hear, so perhaps we'll never know.

"Let me give you another example of how legends can change over time," Mad Mulligan continued. "Imagine, if you will, a little village in the middle of nowhere. They haven't even invented swords yet, and they fight each other with sticks. Then, one day, a stranger comes to the village. He's from a more advanced village, and he has a fishing rod. The villagers are amazed at this fantastic invention and marvel at how many fish he can catch. When the stranger leaves, they continue to tell stories about him. But the stories grow in the telling, and now, instead of being a simple man with a fishing rod, he's a mighty wizard who can control the waves and speak to sea creatures. History gets molded and exaggerated over time until it becomes impossible to tell what is fact and fiction.

Who knows — one day, people might tell tales of your deeds, Dave. In the stories, you'll be a mighty warrior as tall as a tree who was unbeatable in combat. Or perhaps you'll be a cowardly villain who let the evil Mad Mulligan into the End to steal a dragon."

Mad Mulligan chuckled.

"Fascinating, isn't it?"

Dave didn't think it was very fascinating at all. While Mad Mulligan had been talking, he'd been more concerned with trying to come up with a plan to rescue Spidroth. But he still had nothing. Dave wasn't worried about how history would see him or anything like that; he just wanted to make sure his friends were safe.

Suddenly, Mad Mulligan pulled at the reins, and the ravager came to a stop.

"Did you see that?" Mad Mulligan whispered. There was a note of fear in his voice.

"See what?" asked Dave.

"I just had a vision," said Mad Mulligan, taking out his red sword. "Grey zombies. Hundreds of them, climbing towards us."

"Zombies can't climb," said Dave.

"Bouldering zombies can," said Mad Mulligan. "Even so, they can't come out in the daytime, so we're safe for now. But when the sun sets, we will need to defend ourselves."

Dave had never heard of bouldering zombies before, but perhaps an attack like this might be just what he needed. If Mad Mulligan was too busy fighting off zombies, perhaps he would be distracted, and Dave could finally take advantage of him. If he could get Mad Mulligan at sword point, he could force the illager to open the ender chest and free Spidroth. It wasn't much of a plan, Dave had to admit, but it was the first solid plan he'd had since Mad Mulligan had captured him outside of Dead Bush, and Dave wasn't going to let this opportunity go to waste.

I'll get you out of there, Spidroth, Dave thought to himself. *I promise.*

CHAPTER TWELVE
The Crack

"That's the crack up there," said the cow woman, who Spidroth had found out was called Noer.

Spidroth looked up towards where Noer was pointing. Above them, the sky was an endless void of black, apart from a small scar-shaped hole that glowed with white light.

Spidroth and the exiles were gathered outside the inn, all of them looking up at the sky.

"About five years ago, Mulligan accidentally hit the ender chest with that red sword of his and created the crack," said an illager with a red bandanna. "On the outside, it's only a small crack, but in here, it's a lot bigger. I was a member of his crew at the time and saw it happen. That was before I tried to cheat him out of some emeralds, and he imprisoned me down here."

"A while back, we had a theory that if we could shove enough TNT into that crack, we could blow it up and destroy the entire chest, setting us all free," said Big Nose.

"Then why didn't you do it?" Spidroth asked.

"Many of us tried," said Big Nose, "but most of those who tried have ended up dead. You can't see it from down here, but the area around the crack is a cluster of vicious storms and constant bolts of lightning. It's far too high to build a tower up there, even if we took the town apart and used all the blocks we have, so the only way to get up there is to fly. But once you fly up there, you have to swerve around the lightning. And even if you manage that, you have to get to the crack, place the TNT and light it, all while avoiding being hit. It's just not possible."

"Not possible for you, maybe," said Spidroth, "but Lady Spidrothbrine isn't so easily defeated. You said that people flew up there – how?"

"Mad Mulligan keeps a lot of his treasures in here," said Big Nose, and one of those treasures is a pair of elytra."

"I thought elytra were only useful for gliding," said Spidroth. She'd never used elytra before, but she'd read plenty about them in books and heard stories from her father. "How do you get enough height to get up there?"

Big Nose grinned.

"It turns out that elytra work quite well with firework rockets," he said. "We attached a firework to the wings, and then the wearer could boost up into the sky."

Flying up into a lightning storm wearing a pair of firework-powered wings didn't sound like a very clever idea to Spidroth, but she wasn't sure what other options she had. Blowing open the crack in the sky might be her only chance to escape from this cursed chest.

And my only chance to see Dave again, thought Spidroth sadly. She had to try.

"Get me the elytra and a rocket," Spidroth demanded. "You fools are about to witness true greatness in action – the greatness of Lady Spidrothbrine, Spider Queen and daughter of Herobrine."

"Er, Spider Queen?" said Noer. "What does that mean?"

"Daughter of Herobrine?" said Big Nose, raising an eyebrow. "Are we talking about Herobrine, the evil guy from all those stories?"

"None of that's important right now," said Spidroth. "Now, get me those elytra, fools, before I lose my patience. It is time for Lady Spidrothbrine to fly."

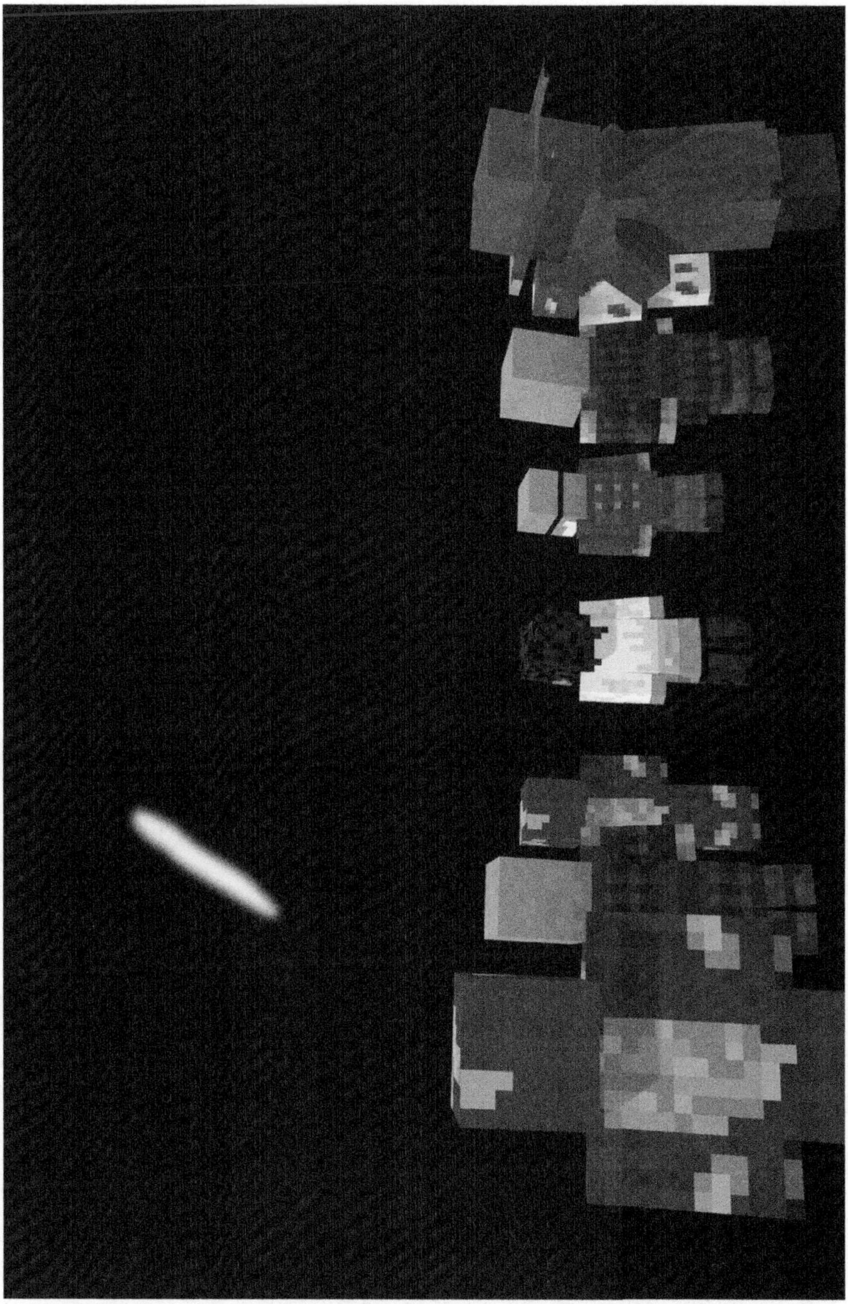

Epilogue

Captain Preston was cursing his bad luck. Two days ago, he'd been promoted and was looking forward to proving himself, and today it had all gone wrong. It had all started when the troops under his command had failed to stop Creepo Jones and the pale girl with the orange hair from escaping, but at least at first, it had looked like they wouldn't be getting very far. Captain Preston and his soldiers had chased the escapees on their horses and had been slowly gaining on them as they crossed the badlands. But then the escapees had fled into a swamp biome, and the next thing Preston knew, his soldiers were being electrocuted and thrown off their horses. They'd managed to recapture Creepo Jones, as it had been the little yellow creeper who'd electrocuted them, but the others had all escaped. Preston thanked his lucky stars that Mad Mulligan was currently off on a mission and probably wouldn't be back for a few weeks. Preston might be able to recapture the girl with the orange hair and her friends in those few weeks. He already had a load of his soldiers out looking for them.

Preston and his fellow horseriders were almost home now. They could see the base in the distance, lit by the glow from the rising sun. It had been a long night, and Preston's clothes were cold and damp. He was looking forward to a long soak in a warm bath.

Then, ahead of them on the red sand of the badlands plains, Preston spotted a single figure walking in the direction of the base. As they rode closer, he saw that it was a female illager. As she heard the hooves approaching, she turned around, and Preston had the shock of his life.

"Marie?" he gasped. The last time he'd seen Marie, she was heading off to attack the town of Dead Bush, but now here she was, all alone without a horse or a ravager. There seem to be something else wrong with her too, but Preston couldn't put his finger on what it was. Then he realized: Marie was missing an arm. She was clutching the space where her left arm had been with her right hand. As he got closer, Preston saw that her clothes were torn in places, and she had a few new scars across her face and remaining arm.

"Boss, what happened to you?" asked Preston, jumping off of his horse and running over to Marie.

"My arm got bitten by a pig zombie," Marie said, matter-of-factly. "I had to chop it off."

"You... you chopped off your own arm?" said Preston in disbelief.

"That's what I said, didn't I?" Marie snapped. She looked angrier than Preston had ever seen her, but he supposed he'd be pretty angry too if he'd been forced to chop his own arm off.

"Give me your horse," Marie demanded.

"Yes, boss, as you say," said Preston. He grabbed the reins of his horse and led it over to Marie. She tried to climb up onto it but was unable to do so with only one arm.

"Help me up, idiot!" she shouted.

Preston quickly helped push Marie up onto the horse. Once she was on, she turned her horse around to face the rest of the illagers on horseback.

"Mad Mulligan has gone and won't be back for some time," she announced. "So I'm in charge now. We are going to go back to the base, gather every single soldier we have, and then we are going to burn every single village, town and settlement in the area down to the ground."

"Um, boss, are you sure that's wise?" Preston asked. "Doesn't Mad Mulligan need all those villages and towns to make regular payments to him? How is he going to run his operations without all that money?"

"Are you questioning my orders?" Marie shouted at him. Her eyes were bulging, and she seemed to be half-crazed. It was clear to Preston that whatever had happened to her had driven her even crazier than she normally was.

"N-no, boss," he stammered.

"We will have revenge on all those who have defied us," she told the troops. "There will be no mercy! There will be no prisoners! We will leave nothing behind but destruction! We will destroy it all!"

She raised her fist in the air, and all the other illagers cheered. Preston was sure that if Mad Mulligan was here, he wouldn't agree with what was happening at all. But Mulligan was gone, and Marie was in charge now.

Marie tugged at Captain Preston's horse's reins and began galloping across the red sand, back towards the base. The other illagers on horseback all follow behind her, kicking up a huge cloud of red dust.

"Wait!" Captain Preston shouted. "I don't have a horse! Can someone give me a ride?"

But no one was listening to him. Before long, all the horses and their riders had ridden off into the distance, leaving Captain Preston alone in the middle of the vast red desert.

"Looks like I'm walking then," he sighed. And he began the long, lonely trek back to the base.

To be continued...

BOOK 34

The Battle for the Badlands

Warning!

In this book, Spidroth does some crazy things with firework rockets. These are video game fireworks, which work in the same way that fireworks do in the Minecraft video game. In real life, you should never play with fireworks. And you especially shouldn't play with fireworks while you have a backpack full of TNT and are flying into a lightning storm using a flimsy pair of wings. That would be very dangerous indeed...

(But seriously, don't mess around with fireworks!)

Prologue

Marie lowered herself into the bath. She could feel the sweat and grime wash away into the soapy water and immediately felt better. Picking up some water with a cupped hand, she rubbed it against the scar where her left arm had been. Marie was still coming to terms with the loss of her arm and wanted to scream and rage. She had been a great warrior, but would she still be able to fight with only one arm? Only time would tell, she supposed.

We should never have followed those scum from Dead Bush into the Nether, she thought bitterly. While searching the caves under Dead Bush for the escaped townsfolk, she and her soldiers had come across an unlit nether portal in a cavern full of yellow creepers. After defeating the yellow creepers, Marie had lit the portal, and then she and her soldiers had gone through. Marie had never been to the Nether before, but she thought with all the soldiers she had, they would be fine.

That had been a huge mistake. Marie and her troops had been ambushed by a group of zombie pig creatures. They hadn't even been able to run away, as the brown sand they'd been walking on stuck to their boots. The pig creatures had massacred them in a matter of seconds, and only Marie had survived. One of the pig creatures had managed to bite her on the arm, though, and she'd had no choice but to cut it off before the infection could spread.

Marie climbed out of the bath and put her clothes and boots back on. Then she opened the wooden door of her tent and walked out into the blazing sunlight. The illager army had started to get in formation, all of them ready to go to war.

"The troops are almost ready, boss," said Zara, one of Marie's captains.

"And is this all of them?" Marie asked. "I want every single soldier we have."

"Nearly all of them, boss," said Zara. "I've left a small group to guard the prison cell."

Marie raised an eyebrow.

"I didn't know we still had any prisoners," she said.

"Just Creepo Jones, the yellow creeper," said Captain Zara. "He was recaptured after the incident at the swamp."

"Bring those soldiers here," Marie commanded. "They're no use to me guarding the prison."

"But what about the creeper?" Zara asked.

"Execute him," said Marie.

"Boss... Mad Mulligan wanted us to keep Creepo Jones alive," said Zara nervously.

"Well, Mad Mulligan isn't here, is he?" said Marie. "I'm in charge now, and I'm commanding you to kill him."

"As you say, boss," said Zara. She bowed her head, then left.

Marie respected Mad Mulligan, but she thought that he had gone soft recently. He should have destroyed Dead Bush as soon as the town defied his orders, rather than waiting. Marie knew from experience that the only way to truly control people was through fear. The only way that Mad Mulligan's gang was going to restore the fearsome reputation that they once had was by finding the escaped Dead Bush townsfolk and destroying them all. There could be no mercy, and no survivors.

The last time Marie had seen the Dead Bush escapees, they'd been in the Nether, but she knew that they'd have to travel back to the Overworld eventually. The Nether was far too dangerous to settle in, especially for young children and old people. No, they had probably returned to the Overworld by now, and they probably thought they were safe. But Marie was going to find them, and she was going to wipe them out.

"Boss," said a male illager with an eye patch, running over to Marie, "we were wondering what to do with the trident. We were going to store it in Mad Mulligan's treasure room back at the base, but with no one to guard it, we should take it with us."

"What trident?" Marie asked.

"The Trident of Emeros," said the illager. He yelled at some of his fellow illager soldiers, and they walked over. One of them was holding a large green trident.

It's beautiful, Marie thought, taking the trident from the soldier holding it. Mad Mulligan had been obsessed with finding this thing, and now she knew why.

"What can it do?" Marie asked. "Does it have any powers?"

"It can shoot blasts of energy," said the illager with the eye patch. "You just have to hold it and point."

"Interesting," said Marie. She pointed the trident at the illager with the eye patch.

"No, wait!" the illager shouted, but before he could say anything more, a blast of green energy shot out of the end of the trident, exploding him to bits. The other soldiers looked on in disbelief, their eyes wide with fear.

Marie grinned. *Fear,* she thought to herself. *That's what's*

going to win us this war. The soldiers were afraid of her now, and that was good. The story of her exploding a random officer would spread, and the other soldiers would fear her too. People who were afraid did as they were told.

"Someone bring me my horse," Marie commanded.

The soldiers nearby ran as quickly as possible, untying Marie's horse from the fence post it had been attached to, then leading it over to her. Marie climbed up onto the horse's back and sat on the saddle. It was difficult with only one arm, but she didn't want to ask anyone to help her. She didn't want to seem weak.

"Spread the word," Marie told the soldiers below her. "We move out at midday. I want everyone ready by then. Lateness will not be tolerated."

"Y-y-yes, boss," one of the illagers stammered, and they all ran off to deliver her message.

Marie smiled to herself. She had suffered a humiliating defeat in the Nether, but now she was going to have her vengeance. The people of Dead Bush and those new friends of theirs would pay. Marie was going to make them suffer for what they'd done, and by the time the battle was over, every last one of them would be dead. She might no longer have a left arm, but she had a magical trident and an enormous army of soldiers willing to do her bidding.

"It's time to get some revenge," Marie grinned to herself. "It's time to put an end to this once and for all."

CHAPTER ONE
Bouldering Zombies

Mad Mulligan had barely said a word for the past hour, which was not like him. Dave and the illager were building a makeshift fortress at the top of the mountain, using terracotta blocks that they'd dug up. According to Mad Mulligan, bouldering zombies could climb up walls as fast as spiders and were far more dangerous. Mulligan had had a vision of bouldering zombies attacking them that night, and he wanted to be ready when the attack came.

Dave looked up at the sky. The sun had almost set now, and soon it would be dark, and darkness meant zombies. Dave had never fought bouldering zombies before, although he'd fought plenty of regular zombies. Zombies weren't that hard to defeat, but there was always the danger that you would get bitten. So, the idea of zombies who could climb like spiders did make Dave feel a bit scared.

Dave was adding some more terracotta blocks to the fortress when he heard a voice nearby. He followed the sound of the voice and found Mad Mulligan standing by himself behind a cactus, speaking in an angry whisper.

"Marie, stop this right now!" Mad Mulligan hissed. "You can't leave the base unguarded! Marie!"

Mulligan's talking to Marie using the Sight, Dave thought to himself. It sounded like Marie was disobeying Mad Mulligan's orders. Dave had no love for Marie, but it did make him happy to see Mad Mulligan so angry.

Mad Mulligan roared in frustration then punched the cactus, breaking it into blocks.

"Something on your mind?" Dave asked, grinning.

Mad Mulligan gave Dave a furious look. He reached down to

the hilt of his sword but then took a deep breath and composed himself.

"Sometimes being the boss is tough, Dave," Mad Mulligan said, forcing himself to smile. "But things always work out for me in the end."

"Things have always worked out for you so far," Dave corrected, "but who knows? Maybe this time they won't. It sounds like even Marie isn't obeying you anymore. What a shame. Maybe this is the end of your criminal empire?"

"Maybe," said Mad Mulligan, "but if it is, I'll just build another one. That's the thing about me, Dave — I never give up. And besides, when I return to the badlands, it'll be on the back of a dragon. No one will dare defy me then."

"Even if you get to the End, how do you know the dragon won't just gobble you up?" Dave asked.

"Because I've seen a vision," Mad Mulligan said, his smug grin returning. "A vision of me riding on the back of the dragon into battle. Now come on, we need to get this fortress built before the zombies arrive."

Dave and Mad Mulligan continued to build their terracotta fortress on the top of the mountain. It wasn't that big but was wide enough so that Big Bessie, Mad Mulligan's ravager, would fit on the top. The fortress itself was ten blocks high, with a spiral staircase in the middle of it. From the top, they could see the entire mountain range and would have an excellent view of the zombies below. Mad Mulligan placed torches all around the bottom of the tower, as well as placing them all around its walls. The top of the tower had one-block-high walls that Dave and Mad Mulligan would be able to lean over to fire arrows down at the zombies.

The sun had almost set now, and there wasn't anything else for them to do but wait on the top of the tower. Mad Mulligan had sealed the entrance at the bottom of the spiral staircase with blocks, so the zombies would be unable to get in. Now the only way up the tower was to climb up the outside.

While he waited, Dave thought again about his plan. It wasn't much of a plan, but he knew that if he plotted out what he was going to do too much, Mad Mulligan would be able to see it coming with the Sight. No, Dave was going to have to be unpredictable. Sometime during the battle with the zombies, he was going to have to overpower Mad Mulligan, take his weapon and force him to free Spidroth from the ender chest. Dave purposefully tried to leave the plan as vague as possible in his mind, so it would be more difficult for Mad Mulligan to predict. He didn't know if it would work, but he had to try. Mad Mulligan had promised to release Spidroth from the ender chest once Dave activated the end portal, but Dave didn't want to let Mulligan into the End and doubted very much that Mad Mulligan would keep his promise anyway. Mad Mulligan had already demonstrated that he was more than willing to lie when it suited him, and Dave didn't trust him at all.

Dave tried to reach out with the Sight to see what was happening with Carl and the others, but he didn't have any luck. From listening to Mad Mulligan earlier, he knew that Marie was leaving Mulligan's base undefended. Dave didn't know if this was useful information, but he thought it might be something that would be useful for Carl and the others to know.

Maybe Carl is dead, and that's why I can't reach him, Dave thought sadly. For all he knew, all his friends were dead. Even Spidroth. He had no way of knowing.

Dave walked over to one of the sides of the tower, looking down at the mountain below. The sun was just a faint orange glow on the horizon now, and in a matter of minutes, it would be dark.

"You should put your armor on," Mad Mulligan said to Dave. "To stop yourself getting bitten."

"What about you?" Dave asked.

"The Sight will protect me," said Mad Mulligan.

Dave took his netherite armor out of his backpack and put it on. It felt strange that he was technically a prisoner but was allowed to wear armor and hold a weapon. That was how confident Mad Mulligan was that Dave wouldn't be able to stop him. Not only would the illager be able to see any attacks coming with the Sight, but he also had Spidroth as a hostage. Dave was hoping that this zombie attack would distract Mad Mulligan so much that it would be easier to surprise him, but he was still not completely sure that it would work.

Finally, the last orange rays of the sun disappeared, and it was night. The only light came from the moon and from the torches that Mad Mulligan had put down. Big Bessie the ravager seemed to know that was something was up and was nervously pacing around the top of the tower.

"She's not going to go crazy and knock us off the tower, is she?" said Dave, looking around at the huge beast.

"Bessie will be fine," said Mad Mulligan. "Just get your bow out."

Dave took out his crossbow and notched an arrow. He walked to the side of the tower and looked down but couldn't see any sign of the zombies. There were torches on the ground all around the bottom of the tower, so as soon as the zombies approached, Dave and Mad Mulligan would be able to see them.

"Are you sure your vision was correct?" Dave asked. "I can't see any zombies."

And then he heard the *BURR*ing.

Suddenly the night air was full of zombie *BURR* noises. It sounded like there were hundreds of them. Dave looked down and saw gray figures slowly lurching across the ground towards the tower, lit by the orange glow of the torches. There were just a couple of them at first, then more and more came walking out of the darkness. The first of them reached the tower and tilted their heads to look upwards.

Maybe they can't really climb, Dave thought to himself. *Maybe Mad Mulligan is mistaken.*

And then one of the zombies began climbing, its arms moving faster than Dave would have thought possible as it scaled the tower, rushing towards him. The other zombies followed suit, all of them rushing up the sides of the tower like spiders. Dave could see what they looked like now: they had black eyes like regular zombies, but their foreheads were bigger, and their skin was gray. They were all wearing tattered brown T-shirts and dark gray trousers.

Mad Mulligan had already started firing down at the bouldering zombies with his crossbow, and Dave started doing the same, firing arrows as quickly as he could. His arrows hit some zombies, making them lose their grip and fall off the side of the tower, but for every zombie he hit, more kept coming.

How are we going to defeat them all? Dave wondered. His plan to use the zombie attack as a distraction for attacking Mad Mulligan seemed ridiculous now. It would be all that Dave could do to stay alive during this attack, let alone take Mad Mulligan out at the same time.

Dave fired a few more arrows at the bouldering zombies, but his efforts weren't doing enough to keep them back, and the horde of zombies got higher and higher every second. Finally, the zombies reached the top of the tower. One of them grabbed the crossbow and nearly pulled Dave off the side of the tower. Thankfully, Dave let go of the crossbow just in time, and the zombie holding the crossbow went hurtling down to the ground. The rest of the zombies climbed over the wall and rushed towards Dave. Dave pulled out his netherite sword and *SWOOSH, SWOOSH, SWOOSH,* began hacking away at the zombies. Behind him, he could hear Big Bessie snorting nervously. To his side, he could see that the zombies on Mad Mulligan's part of the wall had climbed to the top as well, and the illager was fighting them off with his red sword.

Dave and Mad Mulligan fought the zombies as best they could, keeping them back with their swords, but they found themselves being pushed further and further towards the center of the tower. Big Bessie was bashing the gray zombies with her horns and shaking off the ones that tried to climb onto her back.

"We need to get onto Bessie's saddle," Mad Mulligan shouted. "It's the only way."

Mad Mulligan ran over and climbed up onto Big Bessie's back. He reached down a hand for Dave to join him. Dave quickly ran over, and Mad Mulligan helped him up onto the saddle behind him.

"Ya!" Mad Mulligan shouted, tugging at Big Bessie's reins. The ravager began to run around in a circle, charging into the gray zombies with her horns and sending them flying off the tower. At the same time, Mad Mulligan resumed firing his crossbow at the bouldering zombies, and Dave pulled a normal bow from his bag and started doing the same. Between the three of them, they were taking out scores of the bouldering zombies, but more of them kept climbing to the top of the tower. There seemed to be no end of them.

Some of the bouldering zombies tried to clamber up the side of Big Bessie, and Dave and Mad Mulligan had to kick them off.

"Don't let them bite you," Mad Mulligan shouted. "I've got a potion of weakness and a golden apple in my bag, but we don't want to take any chances."

Suddenly, Dave had an idea. It was a spur of the moment idea that had just come to him, and he knew that he had to act now or Mad Mulligan would see it coming.

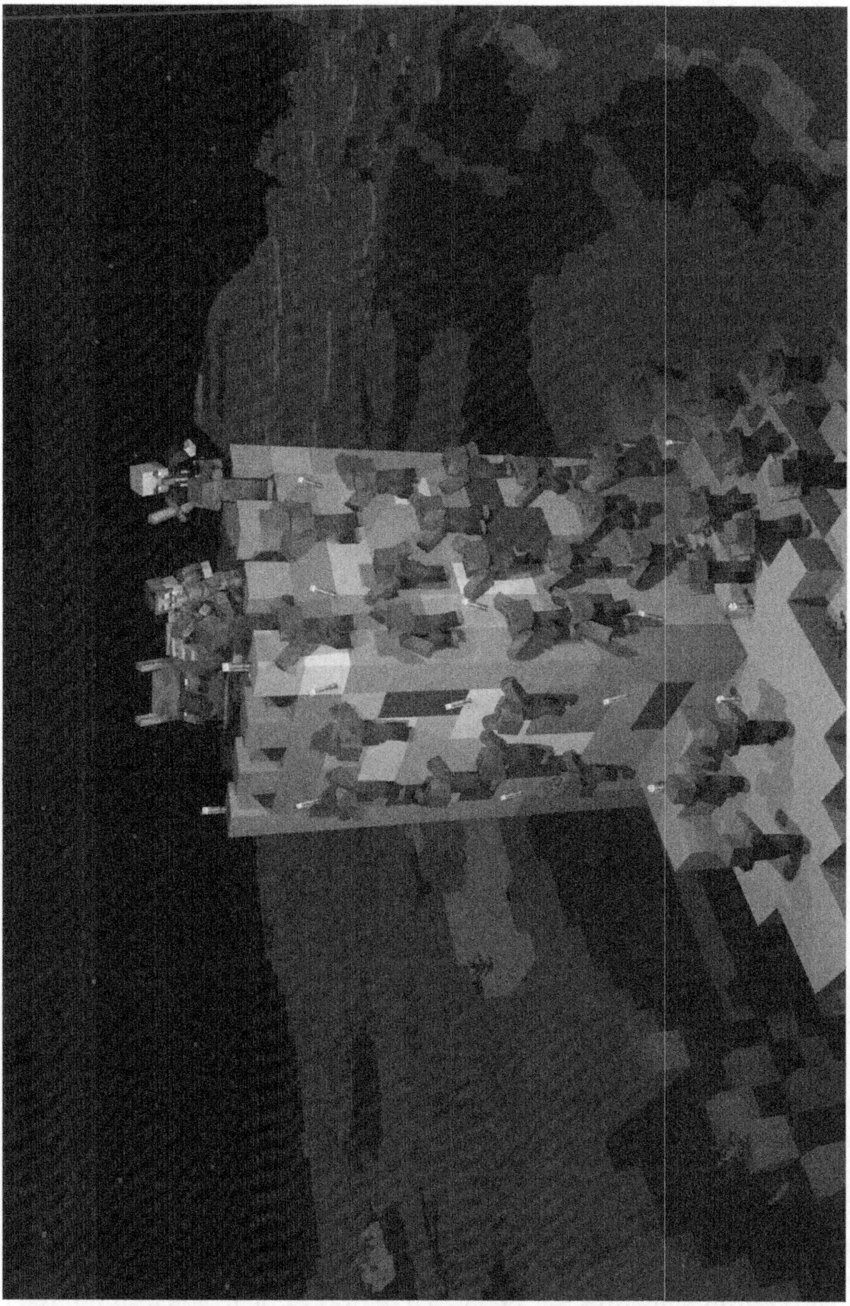

Dave grabbed Mad Mulligan's backpack and yanked it off him, then he shoved the illager off the back of Big Bessie.

"What are you doing?!" Mad Mulligan yelled as he landed on the top of the tower. Immediately the bouldering zombies ran over to him. Mad Mulligan's reactions were quick, but before he could pull out his red sword, one of the zombies chomped down on his shoulder.

"ARRRRGGHH!!!" Mad Mulligan screamed.

I bet you wish you'd worn armor now, Dave thought to himself.

Mad Mulligan pushed the zombie away, then hacked the rest of them down with his red sword, but the damage had been done: he'd been bitten. He looked up at Dave with pure anger in his eyes.

"Did you say you had a potion of weakness and a golden apple in here?" Dave asked, holding Mad Mulligan's bag up. "I bet you'd like them right now, wouldn't you? It wouldn't do much for your plans if you turn into a zombie."

Mad Mulligan charged towards Big Bessie, his red sword drawn.

What now? Dave asked himself. In a couple of seconds, Mad Mulligan would jump back on the ravager's back, grab the backpack off Dave, and he'd be able to cure himself. Bouldering zombies were still rushing at them from every side, and there was nowhere for Dave to go.

Well, there is one place you can go, Dave thought himself. He tugged at Big Bessie's reins, making her charge into another group of bouldering zombies, then he jumped off the back of her saddle, landing on the top of the tower. Mad Mulligan was rushing towards him, but Dave quickly pulled some obsidian blocks from his backpack, built a portal, and then lit it with some flint and steel.

"Come and get me!" Dave shouted, holding up Mad Mulligan's backpack. Then Dave jumped through the portal.

Dave found himself in a biome that looked like the old Nether, with netherrack hills and a big ocean of lava nearby. Dave ran over and stood next to the lava, then turned to watch the portal.

Mad Mulligan ran through the portal. He was clutching his

shoulder, and sweat was dripping down his forehead. He looked furious. Immediately he began hacking away at one of the obsidian blocks that made up the portal frame with his ruby sword. It took quite a few blows since the sword wasn't designed for destroying blocks, but eventually, the block broke, and the purple force field of the portal disappeared.

"Give me that backpack, Dave," Mad Mulligan snarled.

"This backpack?" said Dave, holding the bag over the lava. Immediately Mad Mulligan stopped walking.

Dave reached into Mad Mulligan's backpack and took out the tiny red-tinted ender chest. He threw it to Mad Mulligan, who caught it. Then Dave held the backpack over the lava once more.

"Unless you want to turn into a zombie, you're going to place that ender chest on the ground right now and free Spidroth," said Dave.

"If I turn into a zombie, Spidroth is going to be trapped in that ender chest forever," said Mad Mulligan.

"Well, it looks like we have a stalemate," said Dave. "How does the Sight tell you this is all going to play out?"

Mad Mulligan grinned.

"This was a clever plan, Dave," he said. "You did something completely unpredictable, so I had no way of knowing it was coming. I'm proud of you."

"No more talking," said Dave. "Place the chest down and free Spidroth, or this backpack goes into the lava, along with your potion of weakness and the golden apple. You'll spend the rest of your days as a mindless zombie."

"I guess I don't have much choice," said Mad Mulligan. "Looks like you win, Dave."

Mad Mulligan placed the ender chest down on the ground where it immediately grew to full-size, but instead of opening it, he quickly grabbed his crossbow from the holster on his belt and fired an arrow. The arrow went right through the strap of the backpack that Dave was holding and through Dave's hand as well. The arrow stuck in his hand, pinning the backpack to his palm.

"Arg!" Dave shouted.

Mad Mulligan charged forward. He grabbed the backpack and yanked it away, pulling the arrow out of Dave's hand at the same time. Dave fell to the ground, clutching his hand in pain. Immediately, Mad Mulligan opened his backpack and pulled out a bottle of potion, pouring it over his head. Then he took out a gold apple from his bag and gobbled it down before breathing a big sigh of relief.

"You nearly beat me there, Dave," Mad Mulligan grinned. "But I can be unpredictable too. Now come on, have some healing potion for that hand."

Mad Mulligan reached into his backpack and took out another bottle of potion. Dave scowled, but took the potion in his good hand, pulled the cork out with his teeth and drank it down. Immediately, the arrow hole in his hand began to heal.

Mad Mulligan walked over to the red ender chest and punched it until it turned into a tiny block again, then he placed it back in his backpack.

"Escaping to the Nether," Mad Mulligan grinned, "that was a good plan. I'll have to remember that one; it might come in useful sometime. I'd heard the Nether had changed, but it looks the same as it did before."

"It has different biomes now," said Dave, getting to his feet. "This is just a biome that looks like the old Nether."

"Nice," grinned Mad Mulligan. "Maybe once this is all over I'll have to explore the Nether properly. It seems like a cool place. Maybe I could create an empire here as well. That would be pretty neat, wouldn't it? If I ruled over both the Overworld and the Nether."

Dave said nothing. He was disappointed with himself: he'd thrown away his one chance to defeat Mad Mulligan and free Spidroth.

"I guess we'll wait here for a little while before going back into the portal," said Mad Mulligan. "Then we can return when the sun is up, and all the zombies will be dead. I hope Big Bessie survives the night. It was pretty mean of you to leave her all alone like that, Dave."

"You really do love the sound of your own voice, don't you?" said Dave.

"I do," said Mad Mulligan. "But I need you to listen to me now, Dave — I'm starting to lose my patience with you. Yes, I need you to open the end portal for me, but if you try something like that again, I might get so angry that I can't help myself. Do you understand?"

Dave said nothing.

"Come on," said Mad Mulligan, placing down a smoker. "It must be nearly morning now. I'll cook you some breakfast."

I almost had him, Dave thought bitterly. *I almost got him to open that chest. I hope you're okay, Spidroth. I'll get you out — I promise.*

CHAPTER TWO
Spidroth Takes Flight

"Come on, Spidroth, jump!" Noer the cow woman shouted from down below.

"Do I need a running start?" Spidroth shouted back.

"No," Noer replied, "just jump, shake your shoulders, and the wings should open. And then you can just glide."

Spidroth was standing on the roof of the only three-story building in Mulligan town, with Noer, Big Nose, and a few of the other residents gathered below to watch. She had a pair of silvery-blue elytra wings attached to her shoulders. According to the legends that Spidroth had heard, the Old People used to use these wings to travel. They were extremely rare, and Spidroth had never used them before.

Spidroth wasn't afraid of heights, but she was afraid of messing up and looking like a fool in front of the others. Spidroth had never been comfortable with people laughing at her: her father had always taught her that if people laughed at you, it showed that they didn't respect you. That was what Spidroth found so annoying about Carl the creeper – he was constantly teasing her and making fun of her, and because it annoyed her, he kept doing it. Every time Spidroth thought that she might change her mind about Carl, the creeper made another stupid joke, and she found herself annoyed with him once more.

Right, Spidroth thought to herself, *here goes.*

She jumped off the side of the building and began plummeting towards the ground. She shook her shoulders, and at first, nothing happened. The ground was rising to meet her fast, and Spidroth began to panic, but then she shook her shoulders again, and this time the elytra opened. Just before she was about to smash into the ground, she swooped upwards. She was soaring straight towards another building, so she swerved to the side and ended up sweeping through the gap between two buildings.

So, this is what flying feels like, thought Spidroth. Despite all her troubles, she found herself grinning. This feeling was like nothing she had ever experienced before — it felt like true freedom. She had always envied her brother Necroth, who'd been able to turn into a giant phantom and fly, and finally, she was experiencing flying for herself. It wasn't true flying, as she was merely gliding with the wings, but it still felt amazing.

Spidroth curved back around and swooped between the buildings again. Below her, she could see the residents of Mulligan town looking up at her.

"You're doing great, Spidroth!" Noer shouted.

Spidroth swooped towards the gap in between the inn and the building next to it. The gap was only one block wide, but she was determined to try and make it. She held her arms tightly by her side and tucked her wings in.

WOOSH! She flew through the gap. It was so narrow that her boots brushed the wall of the inn, but somehow she made it. With a big smile on her face, Spidroth curved back around and then landed gracefully in front of Noer, Big Nose and the others.

"Impressive," grinned Big Nose, walking over to her. "Most people just land flat on their face or end up flying into a building on their first go."

"Well, I am not most people," said Spidroth.

"Now you can try it with some fireworks," said Noer excitedly. "I'll go and get some."

The cow woman ran off into one of the buildings.

"I never thought I'd say this," said Big Nose, "but I'm starting to get my hopes up about this plan. No doubt it will still go wrong, and you'll end up struck by lightning and falling to your doom like most of the other poor souls who have tried this, but part of me thinks you might succeed."

"Of course, I'll succeed," said Spidroth. "I do have some questions, however. First of all, if Mad Mulligan caused that crack with his sword, how come it's still there? Normally if you hit a block and don't destroy it, it fixes itself."

"It's something to do with Mulligan's sword," said Big Nose. "That ruby sword of his leaves scars and cuts in blocks that don't heal back up. I don't know if it's because the sword is magical in some way, or that's just what rubies do, but that's the way it works."

"All right then, second question," said Spidroth. "How do you know that exploding a load of TNT in that crack will destroy this chest? And also, if the chest's destroyed, how do you know we won't all be destroyed with it?"

Big Nose laughed.

"Two very good questions," he said. "In truth, we don't know.

But it's the only solid idea we've ever had for escaping this place."

"Haven't you ever tried to escape when Mad Mulligan opens the chest?" Spidroth asked.

"Unfortunately, when Mulligan puts things in the chest or take things out, they just appear or disappear," said Big Nose. "The sky doesn't open up, or anything like that. So, if Mulligan opened this chest to get his elytra, they would simply disappear and reappear in the Overworld. That happened while one of our group was attempting to blow up the crack before. She flew up and was doing a good job of swerving around all the lightning, but then, suddenly, the elytra disappeared, and she plummeted to her doom."

Spidroth felt a cold rush of fear. She couldn't imagine anything worse than being up that high and suddenly having your wings disappear. That would be a bad way to go.

A door swung open, and Noer came rushing over with an armful of red and white striped rockets.

"Fireworks," the cow woman said excitedly.

"So, how do you use these?" Spidroth asked. "Do you strap them to the back of the elytra?"

"No," said Noer, "you hold a rocket in your hand and squeeze it to blast yourself forward. And when that rocket runs out, you use another one. To get yourself up to the crack, you'll have to use rocket after rocket to get enough height."

"I see," said Spidroth. It sounded incredibly dangerous: holding firework rockets in her hand to blast herself up into the sky while wearing a pair of wings that could be teleported away by Mad Mulligan at any moment. Still, it didn't look like she had much choice. As unlikely as this plan was to work, it was the only plan she had. The only alternative was staying in this chest forever, and Spidroth had no desire to do that.

"I suppose I ought to get practicing," said Spidroth, taking one of the firework rockets from Noer. It felt lighter than she thought it would. She shook it and heard something powdery inside, which she assumed must be gunpowder.

Spidroth looked up at the glowing white crack in the sky. It only looked small from down here, but from what she'd been told, she knew that it was much bigger up close and was surrounded by fierce lightning storms. Flying into a lightning storm with gunpowder-filled explosives in your hands didn't seem like a good idea to Spidroth, but she knew that she had no choice.

If I die, at least I'll die risking my life like a true warrior, Spidroth thought. As foolish as flying into a lightning storm with a pair of rocket-powered wings was, at least it wouldn't be a boring death.

Spidroth held the firework rocket in her hand, then squeezed it. Immediately, the rocket went off, and Spidroth was propelled into the sky. She shook her shoulders, and her elytra opened as she soared upwards. She flew much higher than she had last time, with the firework allowing her to get much greater height than she had with the elytra on their own. Finally, the firework rocket ran out of power, and Spidroth tossed the empty shell away before sweeping down in a graceful arc and landing back on the ground in front of the others.

"That was great, Spidroth," said Noer. "Do you want to try that again?"

"No, that's enough practicing," said Spidroth. "Give me the rest of those rockets and get me some TNT. It's time to destroy that crack and get us all out of here."

CHAPTER THREE
A Surprise in the Night

The sun was starting to go down, so Porkins and Mayor Grady built themselves a small house with two beds. They were traveling through an area of the badlands with lots of hills made from different color layers of terracotta. They built their house in the shadow of one of the hills, putting it behind a few cactuses, in an attempt to make it as hidden as possible. Normally, Porkins would have put some torches outside to keep away mobs, but they didn't want any of Mad Mulligan's soldiers to find them, so they only put torches inside and didn't give the house any windows.

Neither Mayor Grady nor Porkins felt sleepy yet, so they sat by the netherrack fireplace and talked for a while. Mayor Grady told Porkins about his youth growing up on the villager continent and how he'd been a member of a criminal gang.

"I used to rob and steal and do all sorts of bad stuff when I was young," said Mayor Grady. "But then some of my friends in the gang began taking things too far. There was one in particular, this kid my age called Xander. He seemed to enjoy the criminal life a bit too much, and he had no morals at all – as long as a job paid, he would do it, no matter how horrible it was. I'd never been that close friends with him, but we had grown up in the same village, and I was shocked to see the monster he was becoming. Eventually, he took over our gang, and that's when I decided to leave. I left in the middle of the night, without saying goodbye to anyone. Eventually, I decided to cross the ocean and ended up here in the badlands, where I could start a new life."

Mayor Grady sighed sadly.

"I founded Dead Bush, and I thought it would be a fresh start – a place where I could safely raise a family. But then Mad

Mulligan and his gang arrived. They took over the entire area, forcing all the towns and villages to pay them 'protection money,' as they called it. At first, a few people tried to fight back, but I'd seen what fighting back against criminals could do, so I kept Dead Bush out of the conflict. Maybe if I'd helped to rebel against Mad Mulligan back then, things might have been different. Maybe if we'd all banded together, we could have defeated him."

"Or maybe he would have destroyed your town," said Porkins. "You did what you thought was best, dear chap. There's no point digging through the past, trying to think about what you would change. Trust me, I know."

"You're right," sighed Mayor Grady. "Still, I can't help but worry. We've found a new place to build a town, but what if Mad Mulligan's soldiers find our new home?"

That was something that Porkins had been thinking about as well. The zombified piglins had slain Marie and her soldiers in the Nether, but Porkins suspected that Mad Mulligan probably had many soldiers left. And from what he'd seen of Mad Mulligan, it didn't seem like he was going to give up easily.

"Once we've saved your daughter, we can figure out where to go from there," said Porkins. "Maybe you chaps should build your new town even further away, to make sure Mad Mulligan never finds it."

"That might be a good idea," said Mayor Grady.

Suddenly, Porkins heard a noise. It sounded like something had landed on the roof above them.

"What was that?" asked Mayor Grady.

"Sssh," said Porkins, holding a trotter up to his lips. He picked up his bow, being careful to make as little noise as possible. It was probably just a spider, but they couldn't be too careful.

Then, suddenly, the wooden door to their house was kicked open, and Porkins saw a crossbow aimed right at his head. With lightning reflexes, he ducked, and the arrow plunged into the wall behind him. Porkins notched an arrow, pulled back the string of his bow and was about to fire when Mayor Grady shouted:

"Wait! Stop!"

Mayor Grady ran forward, standing in between Porkins and his attacker. For the first time, Porkins noticed that the person with the crossbow was a cow woman.

"Grady?" said the cow woman, looking confused.

"Hello, Sonu," said Mayor Grady. Then, to Porkins's surprise, the two of them hugged.

"What's going on here?" asked Porkins. "That chapette just tried to shoot me."

"I'm sorry," said the cow woman, turning towards Porkins. "We saw the building here, hidden away on the side of the hill, and we assumed you must be some of Mad Mulligan's troops."

"Porkins, this is Sonu," said Mayor Grady. "She's the mayor of Blue Sky Village."

"Well, I used to be," said the cow woman, looking sad. "Until Marie and her goons burnt it down."

"I thought you'd been slain," said Mayor Grady. "Marie implied that she'd wiped all your people out."

"She tried," said Sonu darkly. "Many of us were slain, but some escaped. I would have fought to the bitter end, but I was knocked out in the battle, and some of my citizens carried me to safety. I thought you'd been slain too — we went to Dead Bush, and it was nothing but a ruin."

"Yes, Marie tried to wipe us out as well," said Mayor Grady. "But thanks to Porkins and his friends, most of us managed to escape."

"That's good," said Sonu. "If any of your people are still willing to fight, we could do with their help for the rebellion."

"Rebellion?" said Mayor Grady, looking confused.

"Come," said Sonu, and she walked out of the door. Mayor Grady and Porkins followed her, and, to Porkins's surprise, outside was an enormous army. Most of them were cowmen, but there were a few illagers as well. Most of them were wearing iron armor.

"After we escaped Blue Sky Village, the other survivors and I decided that enough was enough," said Sonu. "We've been going from village to town, asking people to join us. That's why we went to Dead Bush, to see if any of your people wanted to join the fight."

"I think many of my people will," said Mayor Grady, looking out at the huge army. "I'll have to go back and get them."

"Good," smiled Sonu. "Because we've heard that Mad Mulligan has gone off on a mission, and Marie lost a lot of her troops. There will never be a better time for us to fight back."

"So, what's the plan?" Porkins asked.

"Simple," said Sonu, "we're going to march straight to Mad Mulligan's base and destroy his forces once and for all. It's time to bring freedom to the badlands."

CHAPTER FOUR
Prison Break

Creepo Jones was slightly disappointed that he was not dead. After his heroic sacrifice, electrocuting all the illagers to save Milo and the others, Creepo had assumed that the illagers would slay him. But instead, they'd captured him and brought him back to Mad Mulligan's base. Creepo would have welcomed an epic hero's death, but instead, he'd been shoved back in the same cell he'd been in before. And this time, he didn't even have Milo with him. As foolish and annoying as the cowman could be, Creepo missed having Milo around. It was good to have someone to shout at sometimes.

Creepo walked over to one of the windows and tried to jump up to see through the metal bars. Not for the first time, he wished he had his old suit back. He missed having arms and being tall. After a few attempts, Creepo managed to grab hold of the window ledge with his mouth and pull himself up. Once he was up, he was able to look through the bars and could see what was going on in Mad Mulligan's base. The morning sun had begun to rise in the east, covering the base with a warm orange glow. Creepo was surprised to see that there were very few soldiers in the base. The guards standing outside his cell seemed to be the only ones left.

Where has everyone gone? Creepo wondered. Before, Mad Mulligan's base had been a hive of activity, with illagers everywhere. And now it was like a ghost town.

Creepo saw a cloud of dust in the distance and saw a lone illager on horseback riding past the empty guard towers and tents towards the base. The illager rode right up to the prison, and the illagers standing guard walked over to speak to him.

"New orders," the illager on horseback said. "Marie wants the yellow creeper dead."

"I thought Mad Mulligan wanted him alive?" asked one of the illager guards.

The illager on horseback shrugged.

"Marie's in charge now," he said. "She gives the orders. She wants the yellow creeper dead, and then we're to take all Mad Mulligan's weapons and treasures to her."

"Fair enough," said one of the other guards, taking out his sword. "It'll be good to get revenge on that little yellow brat, after what he did. Getting electrocuted hurt."

The illagers turned towards the prison cell, and Creepo Jones quickly jumped down from the window.

What am I going to do? he wondered. He could hear footsteps as the illagers walked towards the door of his cell. In a second, they would walk through and try to kill him.

Come on, Creepo Jones told himself. *You are the great Creepo Jones. These idiots can't stop you!*

Creepo waddled over and stood by the side of the door, preparing himself.

"Put that sword away, you idiot," he heard one of the illagers outside say. "Do you want to get electrocuted? You need to use a bow."

"That won't work either," said another voice. "Yellow creepers can zap arrows out of the air."

"Well, how are we going to kill him then?" said a third voice.

"There's some wood in the storage room over there," replied one of the illagers. "We'll just build ourselves some wooden swords. Wood doesn't conduct electricity."

"Wooden swords are for noobs," said another voice.

The illagers argued like this for a while, until finally, they decided that using wooden swords was the best option. After they'd visited the storage room, Creepo Jones heard them approaching his cell once more. He assumed each of them must now have a wooden sword.

You're only going to get one chance at this, Creepo, Creepo Jones told himself. *Don't mess it up.*

Creepo heard the click of a redstone switch, and the iron door of his cell swung open.

"Here, little creeper," said the first illager guard, as he walked in. "We've got some food for you."

Creepo charged into the illager's legs, blasting him with electricity.

"YAAAA!!!!" the illager screamed, and he fell to the side, knocking himself out on the door frame. Immediately, Creepo jumped over his unconscious body and charged into the next illager. The illager tried to swipe at him with his wooden sword, but Creepo dodged to the side and electrocuted the illager's legs. There were three more illagers left, and they all ran towards him. One slashed his sword forward, but Creepo jumped over the blade, charging into the illagers stomach and electrocuting him. Then he dodged out of the way as the other two illagers tried to hit him with their wooden swords. One of the illagers ended up hitting the other one in the face.

"Arg, my nose!" the illager who'd been hit in the face yelled. Creepo Jones took advantage of his distraction and electrocuted the illager's legs. The illager went flying backward and landed in a horse trough. The final illager started to run away, but Creepo Jones ran after him, charging headfirst into the back of his legs. The illager fell to the ground, dropping his wooden sword. Creepo Jones jumped onto his back.

"Tell me where my suit is, or I'll fill you with enough electricity to take out a ravager," Creepo Jones hissed.

"S-suit?" said the illager. "I don't know what you're talking about!"

"The suit I had when they captured me the first time," said Creepo Jones. "It's got two arms, two legs and no head."

"O-oh, that," said the illager. "It's in that storeroom over there."

He pointed to a red sandstone building across the courtyard.

"Much obliged," said Creepo Jones. The *ZAAAAP,* he blasted the illager with electricity, knocking him out. All five of the illagers were unconscious now, with only the horse left standing. It had been tied with a lead to a fence post.

"I'll be back for you in a second," Creepo Jones said to the horse. He waddled over to the storeroom, which had a sign on the door that said *Mad Mulligan's Storeroom: Keep Out.* There was a button next to the door that was too high for Creepo to reach, so he jumped up and tried to head-butt it. It took a few attempts, but finally, he managed to hit the button, and the door swung open. Waddling inside, he was amazed to see a room packed full of strange weapons and odd treasures. And there, sitting in the middle of it all, was his suit. Creepo went over and jumped into the suit's neck hole, taking control of it. He flexed his arms and legs and was pleased to see that it was still in full working order.

"While I'm here, I might as well get a decent weapon or two," Creepo said to himself, looking around the room. He settled on a diamond sword with a blade twice as long and thick as usual, a bow that looked like it was made from emerald, and a quiver full of strange-looking arrows. Creepo had no idea what the arrows were, but he was looking forward to trying them out. Finally, he left the room with his weapons and was about to walk over to the horse when he remembered that the illagers had been ordered to bring the weapon stash to Marie. Creepo couldn't let that happen. He'd seen some TNT blocks inside the storeroom, so he picked them up, spread them evenly around the storeroom, then lit them with a piece of flint and steel. Then he rushed out of the door.

KATHOOOOOM!!!!! The storeroom exploded behind him. Creepo turned and saw that the room and all its contents had been blown to bits. He supposed that some of the weapons and artifacts in the room had been explosive as well, as the explosion had been much bigger than he had expected, and the ruins of the storeroom were now burning with different color fires: blue and green and purple, as well as the usual orange. The fire had begun to spread as well, and the other buildings in Mad Mulligan's base had begun to burn.

Maybe I should have taken more of those strange weapons and objects, Creepo thought. *There were probably some very rare treasures there that I could have brought back to Spectrite City Museum.*

Still, it couldn't be helped. Right now, Creepo had to do what he always did – defeat the bad guys and save the day.

The explosion had been so loud that some of the illagers had begun to wake up.

"What happened?" one of them groaned, sitting up and rubbing his head.

"You were defeated by the great Creepo Jones," said Creepo, jumping onto the back of the horse. He released the lead connected to the horse's muzzle, then tugged at its reins, galloping off into the distance.

"No, wait!" the illager shouted. "Somebody stop him!"

But it was too late — Creepo had taken the only horse, and he had made his escape.

CHAPTER FIVE
What Do We Do Now?

Carl put a golem hand on Milo the cowman's shoulder.

"How you doing, dude?" Carl asked.

"I'm okay," said Milo, smiling sadly. "The best thing I can do now is live on, so I can tell everyone how amazing Master Creepo was and how he died to save the world."

"Uh, yeah," said Carl. He thought that saying that Creepo Jones had died to save the world was a bit of an exaggeration, but now was probably not the best time to point that out.

Carl, Milo, Liza and Alex were resting next to a small oasis in the middle of the badlands. The horses were standing under the shade of a lone oak tree, sipping from a pool of water.

"So, what do we do now?" Alex asked. "We have no idea where Dave, Spidroth, Porkins and the others are."

"When Mad Mulligan beat Dave in the fight outside of Dead Bush, did he give any indication of where he was going?" Carl asked Alex and Liza.

"I couldn't hear that clearly," said Liza. "When we were tied up, we were lying quite far away from them."

"Yeah," said Alex. "All I heard Mad Mulligan say was that he was going to take Dave to an end portal. So, who knows which direction they went?"

Carl gave Alex a frustrated look.

"Alex," he said, "if they're heading to an end portal, we know exactly which direction they went."

"We do?" said Alex, looking confused.

"Alex, do you remember what the purpose of our journey is?"

Alex thought for a moment.

"Oh!" she said. "We're trying to find an end portal!"

Carl sighed.

"So I guess if Mad Mulligan is heading towards an end portal, it's probably the same one we're looking for," said Alex. "The one the ender eyes are leading us towards."

"Yes," said Carl, glad to see that Alex had finally worked it out.

"You and your friends are heading towards an end portal?" said Milo. "Master Creepo would have loved to have found an end portal. He believed that they'd all been destroyed."

"Most of them have," said Carl. "But we've been heading towards one, and I guess Mad Mulligan must know where it is."

"And where is it?" asked Liza.

"West," said Carl. "I guess if we head west, we'll eventually catch up with them."

"And what about my father and Tom and all the other people of my town?" Liza asked. "We need to find them too."

"Unfortunately, we've got no idea where they are," said Carl. "But they're with Porkins, and he should be able to lead them to safety. Dave and Spidroth are the ones who need rescuing. I mean, if I had the choice, I'd only rescue Dave, but I suppose it can't hurt to rescue Spidroth as well."

After resting a bit longer, they got back on their horses and started riding west, across the badlands. Carl didn't have a horse, as he was too heavy, so he just ran alongside them in his golem suit.

Don't worry Dave, we're coming to save you, Carl thought to himself. He was eager to get all this Mad Mulligan business behind them once and for all. It seemed like there had been nothing but trouble ever since they'd arrived in the badlands, and Carl was fed up with it. He was looking forward to biffing Mad Mulligan in the face and teaching him a lesson.

Eventually, the flat plains ended, and they found themselves riding through an area full of hills made from stripes of different color terracotta. The route through the hills was full of slopes and tight paths, so they had to go slowly. As he walked, Carl occasionally thought he spotted people watching them from the top of the hills, but every time he looked up, there was no one there. He thought he was seeing things until Alex said that she saw them as well.

"We're being watched," Alex whispered, looking up at the hills.

"Do you reckon it's Mad Mulligan's forces?" Carl whispered to Liza.

"Maybe," said Liza. "Or it might be some bandits. There are a lot of outlaws in this area."

"Everyone be ready," Carl whispered. "If those idiots start to fire arrows at us from above, we're gonna to have to ride away quickly. We won't be able to fight them from down here."

Then, as soon as Carl had spoken, hundreds of figures suddenly appeared on the tops of the hills, all of them aiming bows and crossbows down at them. There were so many that even if they'd started to ride off at full speed, they would have been peppered full of arrows.

Carl was surprised to see that the archers weren't illagers; they were cowmen.

"Don't shoot," Carl said, raising his netherite golem arms in the air. "We're just passing through."

"Carl?" said a voice. Carl turned and saw that one of the archers was someone he recognized. Someone he recognized very well indeed.

"Porkins?" Carl laughed. "I'm glad to see you're not dead. What are you doing with these morons?"

"Everyone lower your bows," said Porkins. "These chaps are my friends."

And, to Carl's surprise, the cowman archers all lowered their bows.

"Liza?" said another voice. This was another person that Carl recognized — Mayor Grady. He was standing on the top of the hill next to Porkins. There were some illagers and cowmen standing next to them who Carl recognized as well — they were some of the townsfolk from Dead Bush who Carl had fought alongside in the battle against Mad Mulligan's forces.

"Dad!" Liza said, her eyes filling with tears. "I'm so glad you're okay!"

"Okay, we can do the emotional reunions in a minute," said Carl. "What's going on here?"

"We're the resistance, old boy," said Porkins. "We're going to war – and we're going to give Marie and her chaps a jolly good thrashing."

CHAPTER SIX
Visions

Dave was pleased to see that Mad Mulligan was in a foul mood. He seemed distracted and was barely saying a word — which was unlike him. Most of the time, the illager's eyes would glaze over as if he wasn't really there.

He's using the Sight, Dave realized. *He's using the Sight to check up on his forces, and he's not happy about what he's seeing.*

Dave had seen time and time again how Mad Mulligan was better at using the Sight than he was and a much better warrior, but Dave hadn't given up hope of defeating the illager just yet. With Mulligan so distracted, Dave was certain that he'd eventually get an opportunity to defeat him and force him to free Spidroth from the ender chest. He wasn't sure exactly how yet, but that was probably a good thing — as Mad Mulligan would only be able to be defeated by a sudden and unpredictable plan that came out of nowhere so that he didn't see it coming.

The two of them were making their way across a flat open badlands plain on foot. By the time they'd gone back through the nether portal, Big Bessie the ravager had been slain, and there was nothing left on the top of the tower but bits of rotten flesh from the zombies who had burnt up in the sunlight. With no horses and no ravager, they had no choice but to walk.

"How far is it to Bedrock City?" Dave asked.

Mad Mulligan scoffed.

"Far," he said. "Travelling on foot, it'll probably take us a few weeks."

Good, thought Dave. The longer it took, the more chances he'd get to outsmart Mad Mulligan.

While they were walking, Dave was making the most of the

time by practicing using the Sight. Dave didn't know if he'd be able to contact Spidroth since she was in the ender chest, so instead, he tried to reach out to Carl. After trying and failing for a while to reach his friend, Dave instead tried to look into his future, to see if he could get any clues about what lay ahead and how he'd be able to stop Mad Mulligan. Again, he didn't have any luck. The closest thing he got to a vision was a brief glimpse of a figure with glowing yellow eyes sitting in a prison cell, but the vision ended almost as soon as it began.

They walked across the red sand until the sun began to set, then Mad Mulligan built them a small house with two beds. As he laid down in his bed, Dave tried once more to reach out to his friends but had no luck. Then he drifted into a deep sleep.

Dave hadn't had any bizarre dreams for a while, but that night his dreams were full of strange images. He saw the figure with glowing yellow eyes again, sitting alone in a prison cell. Then one of the walls of the prison exploded, and the prisoner was free. Then that scene vanished, and Dave was standing in a barren landscape made from pale yellow stone. Above him, the sky was jet black, and a shadow with huge wings and glowing purple eyes flew overhead, circling him.

The dragon, Dave thought.

"I'm not here to hurt you!" Dave shouted at the dragon. "I wish you no harm!"

But the dragon just laughed: Deep, booming laughter that echoed across the empty yellow plains. Then the beast opened its mouth. Before Dave could react, a jet of purple flames blasted out of the creature's throat, and he was engulfed in fire.

Dave closed his eyes, holding his arms up to protect himself. The flames seemed to have stopped, and he couldn't hear anything, so he cautiously opened his eyes. He was standing in a gigantic black void, and standing next to him, was Spidroth. She was wearing a pair of silvery elytra wings.

"Spidroth?" said Dave.

"Dave?" said Spidroth, looking confused.

"Wake up!"

Dave woke to find Mad Mulligan shaking him. Light was pouring in from the windows, and Dave was back in the little house.

"That was a deep sleep you were having," Mad Mulligan grinned. "Let me guess — the Sight was giving you visions?"

Dave didn't reply.

"Come on," Mad Mulligan said, tossing Dave his backpack. "It's morning now. Let's get a move on."

Mad Mulligan took the house apart and put the blocks in his backpack, and then the two of them resumed their journey, walking across the endless Badlands plains. The sun was especially hot today, and Dave wore the straw hat that he kept in his bag to protect his bald head from getting burnt.

Mad Mulligan started the day in a good mood, but as the day went on, his high spirits seem to fade, and he walked along in silence with an angry look on his face.

"Are things still going badly for your troops?" Dave asked.

Mad Mulligan scowled but said nothing.

They walked until midday, then stopped in the shade of a lone oak tree to have lunch.

"I'm a bit short on food," said Mad Mulligan, looking in his backpack. "Most of my food was in Big Bessie's satchels, so I assume those zombies must have eaten it after they slew her. We're gonna have to eat some of your food for a change."

Dave opened his backpack and had a look. He had a few bits of raw beef, so he reached in to take them out but accidentally dropped his bag. Some of the contents spilled out, including, Dave was horrified to see, an eye of ender. The thin eye-shaped disc rolled across the ground before falling onto its side. Dave looked up and saw Mad Mulligan looking at the disc.

"Relax, Dave," grinned Mad Mulligan. "You don't think I didn't check your backpack when I captured you? You've got three of those eye-disk things in there — the same eye things that fit into the frame of an end portal. Unfortunately, my end portal is missing five of those discs. If you'd had enough discs in your bag, I would have just killed you and taken them. But unfortunately, I'd be two eye-discs short, so I need you alive to make more of them for me."

"You must know that I'd never do that," said Dave.

"As I said," said Mad Mulligan, "I've seen a vision of you opening the end portal, and I've seen a vision of myself riding on the back of the ender dragon. So, at some point, you're going to change your mind. I don't know how or why, but it's going to happen."

Mad Mulligan picked up the eye of ender and studied it.

"So," he said, "do these have another use, other than just slotting into the end portal frame to activate it?"

Dave said nothing.

"Fine," said Mad Mulligan, "keep your secrets." And he threw the eye back to Dave. But before Dave caught it, the eye of ender rose into the sky. It hovered there for a moment, then zoomed off towards the west.

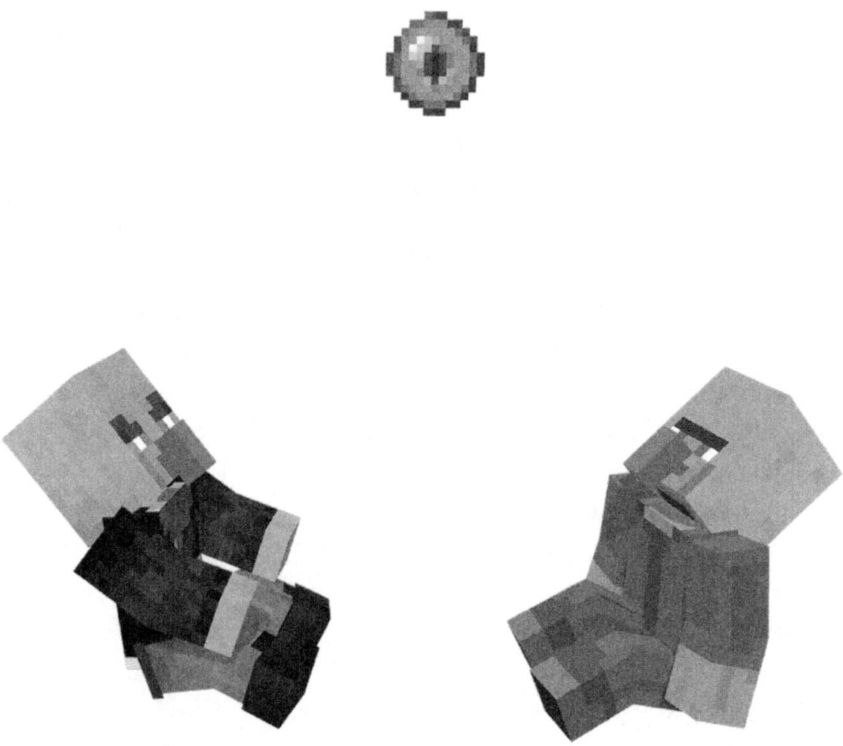

Mad Mulligan laughed.

"I see," he grinned. "They show you which direction an end portal is. That's so clever! Those Old People really knew what they were doing, didn't they?"

After they'd eaten, Dave and Mad Mulligan resumed their journey, walking across the badlands. For a while, Dave thought that the badlands might never end, but soon they caught sight of some snow-peaked hills in the distance.

"We're going to miss Big Bessie when we're trudging through that snow," said Mad Mulligan. "Hopefully, we can find some horses soon, or we're gonna have very sore feet by the time we get to Bedrock City."

And maybe the snow and your sore feet wall give me another chance to distract you and defeat you, Dave thought hopefully.

CHAPTER SEVEN
War Council

Now that Mayor Grady had brought over his volunteers from Dead Bush, the rebel army was bigger than ever. Most of the rebels had iron armor and weapons, but some had to make do with leather armor or stone swords. Even so, Porkins knew that spirit was one of the most important things in a battle, and all the rebels had plenty of spirit. It was clear from talking to them that they were fed up with being pushed around by Mad Mulligan and his goons, and now they wanted to fight back.

Most of the rebel army was made up of cowmen, but there were a few illagers, from Dead Bush and a few other towns and villages with an illager population.

From what Porkins had seen of Mad Mulligan's forces, they mostly wore diamond armor and had diamond weapons. Few members of the rebel forces had diamond armor and weapons, so it would not be an easy battle. Still, Porkins was quietly confident. He'd seen before what a small band of underdog rebels could do. He thought back to how the citizens of Greenleaf had defeated Herobrine's zombie pigman army. That had seemed like a hopeless fight at the time, but in the end, they'd been victorious.

Porkins made his way through the tents and makeshift houses that the rebels had built outside the ruins of Dead Bush to house their troops. The town had been almost completely destroyed, seemingly by a mixture of fire and TNT, leaving nothing but scattered ruins and holes in the ground. Still, it was a fitting base to launch a rebellion from — as the ruined town acted as a constant reminder of Mad Mulligan's barbarism.

In the center of the rebel camp was the command building — a house made from oak wood planks with a red wool block roof.

There were two cowmen guards in iron armor standing outside the door, and they both nodded to Porkins. Porkins nodded back and opened the door. Inside, Alex, Carl, Mayor Grady, Sonu and the other mayors and leaders from the badlands settlements were gathered around a map.

"We've had reports that Marie and her army are on the move," said Sonu. "According to our scouts, Mad Mulligan's base has burnt to the ground."

"Why would Mulligan's forces burn their own base?" asked a cowman in scarlet robes.

"From what I've seen of Marie, some of the blocks in her head are missing," shrugged Carl. "She probably just burnt it down because she's crazy."

"Maybe," said Mayor Grady. "But that seems a bit too crazy, even for her."

"Well, whatever the reason, we know that Marie has gathered her entire army together and is marching across the badlands," said Sonu. "Apparently, they've been marching from village to village, burning them to the ground."

"Thank goodness we got all the settlements to evacuate," said the cowman in scarlet robes. "Why is Marie doing this?"

"I told you," said Carl, "she's crazy."

"Crazy or not, this provides us with a unique opportunity," said Sonu. "Before, we thought we'd have to storm Mad Mulligan's base. It's normally heavily guarded, with watchtowers, high walls and soldiers everywhere. But now that Marie and her army are out in the open, at least we can fight them on level footing."

"They're still far better armed than we are," said another cowman. "Plus, they have ravagers."

"Oh, ravagers aren't that bad," said Carl. "You should see Porkins punch them in the face with his metal arm."

"That's one thing I was going to talk to you three about," said Sonu, turning towards Porkins, Carl and Alex. "From what Mayor Grady has told me, you three are such amazing fighters that you can take on armies all by yourself."

"Well, I wouldn't quite go that far," said Porkins.

"I can take on armies all by myself," said Alex. "The trick is not dying. And thankfully, I can come back from the dead!"

The other leaders, including Sonu, all gave Alex strange looks.

"Alex can respawn," Porkins explained. "When she dies, she reappears back in the same bed that she last slept in."

"Like the hero Steve in the old stories?" said the cowman in the scarlet robes.

"Yes!" said Alex excitedly. "I'm actually a clone of Steve."

"It's a long story," said Carl.

"Anyway," said Sonu, "I've come up with a strategy, so I want to see what you think of it. I was thinking that our main forces would attack Marie and her army head-on, but at the same time, you three would sneak around the back and launch a surprise attack on them from behind. Then we can cause chaos in their ranks as they struggle to fight a battle on two fronts."

"Sounds like a jolly good idea," said Porkins. "But surely they'll have lookouts everywhere, so it may be hard to take them by surprise."

"Not if we travel by nether portal," said Alex. "We can go into the Nether, travel to the right place, then build another nether portal to come back into the Overworld right behind Marie's army."

"Yeah, but how are we going to work out where to build the second nether portal?" asked Carl. "Distance in the Nether is pretty complicated."

"I'll be able to work it out," said Alex. "I've done it before, lots of times."

"When?" said Carl, giving her a suspicious look.

"I'm not sure," said Alex. "I guess they must be old Steve memories, but I definitely remember doing it."

"If Alex retains fighting skills from her previous lives, I suppose it makes sense that she retains some tactical skills too," said Porkins.

"Yeah!" said Alex, a big dumb grin on her face.

"I can't see this ending well," sighed Carl. "But go on, we'll give it a try."

"Good," said Sonu. "If the information our scouts have given us is correct, Marie's army should be arriving at Dead Bush sometime tomorrow morning."

"Why are they heading here?" Porkins asked. "Those blaggards have destroyed the town already, so why come back?"

"Maybe they're looking for survivors," said Mayor Grady darkly. "It looks like they're trying to wipe all of us off the face of the earth, so I guess it would make sense if they came back here to check we're all dead."

"Well, we'll be waiting for them when they do," said Sonu. "If all goes well tomorrow, we can put an end to Mad Mulligan's reign of terror once and for all."

"What about Mad Mulligan himself?" asked Carl. "Has there been any word on him or Dave?"

Mayor Grady shook his head.

"I'm afraid not," he said.

Porkins could see that Carl was worried about Dave. He was worried about Dave too. Dave was a good warrior, but it seemed that Mad Mulligan completely outclassed him. He'd beaten Dave in a split second, without even raising a sweat.

"I'm sure Dave is fine," said Carl, putting on a brave face. "I'm sure he'll be back here soon, being as annoying as ever."

"And hopefully Spidroth will be back too," said Alex.

"Yeah, I guess it would be good to see her as well," said Carl. "Then I can make fun of her for getting her butt kicked by Mad Mulligan."

CHAPTER EIGHT
The Crack

The other exiles had gathered around Spidroth as she prepared to take flight. She had a bunch of firework rockets in one hand and more in her backpack, along with a load of TNT blocks. If someone had lit a fire at that moment, she would have gone up in a colossal explosion.

"Good luck, lady Spidroth," said Noer the cow woman.

"Yeah, good luck, m'lady," said Big Nose, giving Spidroth a nod. "I'm sure you'll probably get blown to pieces by lightning, but if anyone can do this, it's you. I've never seen anyone take to the elytra so quickly."

"Stand back, fools," said Spidroth. She shook her shoulders, and her elytra wings unfurled. High above her, she could see the crack, glowing with white light against the black sky.

Here goes nothing, she thought. She put all of the firework rockets under her left arm, keeping one in her right hand. Then she gripped the rocket in her hand tightly and squeezed it.

FWOOOOOOOOOSH!!!!!

Sparks gushed out of the bottom of the rocket, and Spidroth was propelled into the air. Once the rocket ran out of juice, Spidroth tossed the empty shell to the side, then grabbed another rocket from under her arm and squeezed that. Sparks poured out of the bottom of that rocket, propelling her even higher up. She used rocket after rocket, propelling herself higher and higher into the sky. The higher she got, the bigger the crack became. She could see it more clearly now: a huge cut in the sky hundreds of blocks wide, glowing with white light. She couldn't see the lightning yet, but she was still quite far away.

Spidroth looked down and immediately regretted it. Mulligan Town was no more than a tiny speck, far, far below. She was much higher than she'd thought she was, but it still wasn't high enough.

Spidroth squeezed another rocket and went blasting further up. She was trying to conserve the rockets so that she wouldn't run out, but the elytra were only really useful for gliding – using the rockets was the only way to get more height. When that rocket was used up, she threw it to the side and used another, and finally, she was able to see the lightning. The white glow around the crack was a glowing white mist, with constant lightning bolts shooting down from the opening. The lightning was constant: and after every flash, a few seconds later, Spidroth heard a tremendous crack of thunder. She'd seen fierce storms before, but nothing like this. Normally,

Spidroth's confidence knew no bounds, but she felt a rush of fear and hopelessness wash over her.

There's no way I can do this, she thought to herself. How was she going to avoid getting hit by lightning? It didn't seem possible.

The last firework rocket she'd squeezed sputtured out its last few sparks, and for a moment, Spidroth floated in midair, neither rising any higher or falling any lower.

Maybe I should give up and go back down to Mulligan town, she thought. *Maybe this whole thing is complete foolishness.*

But no, this was her only hope, Spidroth reminded herself. Her only hope of getting free from this chest.

Her only hope of seeing Dave again.

Spidroth gritted her teeth with determination, then grabbed another firework rocket.

"Come on," she muttered to herself, "you can do this."

FWOOOOOOOOOSH!!!!! Spidroth squeezed the rocket and went flying upwards. When that rocket ran out of juice, she grabbed another and squeezed it as well, then another, then another. Finally, she was at the same height as the crack. A few blocks above her, she could see the roof of the void — an enormous black ceiling that stretched off in every direction.

She spread her elytra wings and began gliding forward now, moving sideways instead of heading up. Ahead of her, she could see the crack in all its majesty, with lightning blasting out of it constantly. Spidroth twisted her backpack around as she flew, so the backpack was hanging the wrong way, with the bag resting against her chest. The plan was to fill the crack with as much TNT as she could, but she didn't want it to go off immediately, so she had to stop the TNT blocks from getting struck by lightning. Spidroth wanted to fill the crack with a load of TNT, then set it off at the same time. Her hope was that the explosion would be so big that it would cause a chain reaction, destroying the entire chest and setting her and the other exiles free. Of course, none of them knew if it would work. It was all theoretical, but it was the only hope they had.

As she neared the crack, Spidroth reached into her backpack and took out some tiny TNT blocks. She swooped upwards, the bright white light from the crack almost blinding her. A bolt of lightning blasted down, and she quickly barrel-rolled to the side to avoid getting hit, then she shoved one of the TNT blocks against the inner wall of the crack. With a *THUNK,* it immediately grew to full-size, sticking to the wall. Then she flew along the crack, placing as many TNT blocks against the inner wall as she could – *THUNK, THUNK, THUNK, THUNK, THUNK* – before swerving out of the way of another bolt of lightning.

The lightning bolts were coming out of the middle part of the crack, so Spidroth placed the TNT blocks along the sides so that they wouldn't get hit. It was going well, and she had covered about half the length of the crack with TNT, but she suddenly had a sobering thought. When TNT was activated, it took a few seconds for it to explode. And during those few seconds, it no longer stuck to walls and was affected by gravity. As soon as the TNT blocks she'd placed in the crack were activated, they would fall down, exploding far below where they were supposed to.

What am I going to do? Spidroth wondered. She continued to fly along the edge of the crack, placing TNT blocks against its inner walls – *THUNK, THUNK, THUNK, THUNK, THUNK* – but she had no idea how she was going to keep the TNT from falling once she lit it.

KRA-KOOM!

Suddenly a lightning bolt flashed through the sky, coming so close to Spidroth that she barely managed to roll out of the way. But as she turned and continued her flight along the edge of the crack, she began to have trouble with the elytra wings. They kept veering to one side, and she was losing height. Spidroth turned her head around and saw, to her horror, that her right wing had a massive scorched hole in it.

The lightning must've hit it, Spidroth thought. She was just about managing to stay up, but she was losing height every second. Spidroth quickly put the tiny TNT block she was holding back in her backpack, then pulled out a firework rocket, squeezing it to propel herself upwards. She placed some more TNT blocks inside the crack but immediately began losing height again, so she had to use another firework to launch herself up. She only had a couple of firework rockets left now, and with her broken elytra, she wouldn't be able to maintain her height without them. She was going to have to act fast.

Spidroth had only placed TNT blocks along the inner edge of about three-quarters of the crack, but it was going to have to do. She needed to get the TNT to explode before she ran out of fireworks and was forced to glide back down to the ground.

How am I going to stop the TNT from falling? she thought desperately. *Think, fool, think!*

Then she realized what she had to do. The only way to stop the TNT from falling was to place other blocks underneath it. Spidroth opened her bag to see what she had. There was an assortment of different blocks in there — cobblestone, netherrack, wood and a few others. She used another firework rocket to propel herself upwards, then began placing the other blocks under the TNT— *THUNK, THUNK, THUNK, THUNK, THUNK.* She felt herself losing altitude, so she took out her last firework rocket and squeezed it, propelling her upwards once more. She placed a load more blocks underneath the TNT, but then she found herself starting to drop once more. She hadn't managed to place blocks under all the TNT, but she didn't have any choice – without any more firework rockets to keep her and her damaged elytra in the air, she was going to have to blow the TNT now. Spidroth swooped back around, pulled out her flint and steel, and lit one of the TNT blocks. The TNT block was held up by a block of cobblestone, so it didn't fall when it started flashing white.

KRA-KOOM!

Suddenly another lightning bolt hit Spidroth, sending her flying. She began falling down, down, down, towards the ground. She tried to glide with her elytra, but they wouldn't work. She turned around and saw that both wings were now in shreds. She was falling, and there was nothing she could do to stop herself. She twisted around and found herself looking up at the crack as she plummeted towards the ground.

Please let this work, Spidroth thought.

For a moment, nothing happened, then, with a horrible sound like crunching metal, the crack exploded. More glowing white cracks began appearing, snaking their way across the black sky like the branches of an enormous white tree. The entire black void was covered in glowing white crack lines now, and more of them were appearing every second.

Then, with noise that almost destroyed Spidroth's eardrums, the void exploded with a brilliant blast of white light...

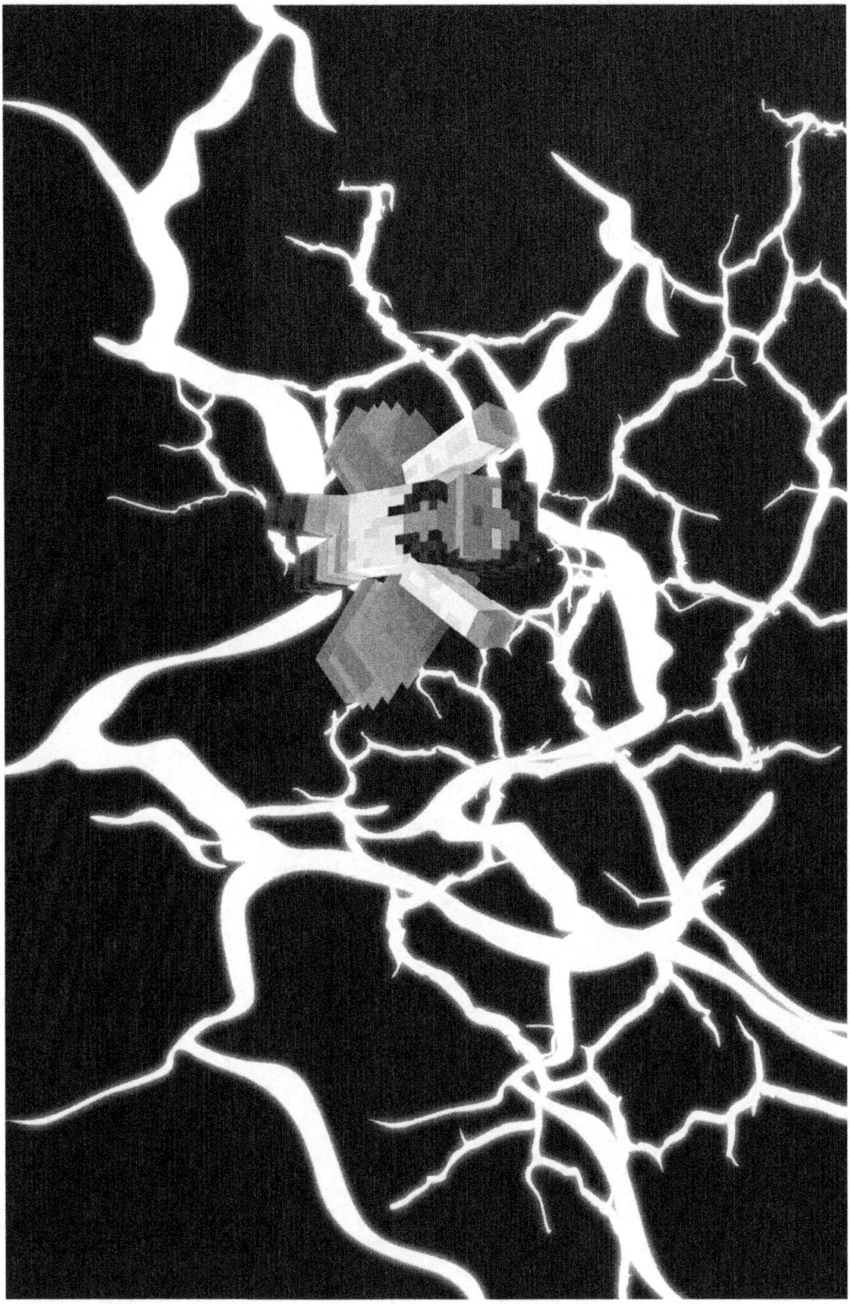

CHAPTER NINE
Doing Something Unexpected

Dave was exhausted, and his feet were aching, but Mad Mulligan insisted that they kept going.

"It's going to take us at least twice as long to get to Bedrock City without Big Bessie," said the illager, "so I don't want to waste any more time. We keep walking until the sun goes down, and that's final."

The path through the snowy mountains was steep and dangerous, with big drops and pools of lava in unexpected places. There were polar bears too, and Mad Mulligan make sure to keep well away from them. As powerful a warrior as the illager was, it seemed that he was still keen to avoid getting attacked by bears if possible.

As the sun began to set, Dave caught glimpses of strange skeletal creatures in rags, watching them from the shadows and caves of the mountain.

Strays, he thought. He'd last seen strays on a frozen ocean biome when he and his friends had been crossing the ocean. They were pale-gray skeleton creatures who wore rags and lived in cold places, and just like skeletons, they used bows. But the arrows the strays used were extra dangerous, as they inflicted a slowness effect on whoever they hit.

The last light of the sun was still stretching across the mountains, and the strays were waiting for the sun to disappear so they could come out and attack.

"Do you see them?" Dave whispered to Mad Mulligan.

"The strays?" Mad Mulligan asked. "Of course, I do. We'll set up camp in a minute. There's a nice area of flat snow up ahead, next to that pool of lava."

If Dave was in charge he would have built a shelter to hide from the strays now, before it was too late, but Mad Mulligan, as ever, didn't seem worried. Dave supposed that the Sight had told Mad Mulligan everything was going to be alright that night.

They reached the flat area of snow, and Mad Mulligan built them a house using the blocks in his backpack. As usual, the house had two beds, and Dave wasted no time climbing into his. His feet were exhausted, and it felt good to get his boots off.

Outside, Dave could hear the sound of bones rattling as the strays made their way across the snow, but he knew that they wouldn't be able to get into the house. Mad Mulligan had built the house from cobblestone and hadn't added any windows. The door was made from iron as well, so the strays would be unable to break through.

"How is your army doing now?" Dave asked Mad Mulligan. He

liked asking the illager that because it always seemed to annoy him.

But, for once, Mad Mulligan told him what was going on back in the badlands.

"It seems that there's going to be a battle," said Mad Mulligan. "Marie and all my soldiers on one side, and your friends and some rebels on the other."

Dave felt nervous. He didn't want to ask the next question, but he did:

"And who's going to win the battle?"

"It's hard to tell," said Mad Mulligan. "Battles are always difficult things to predict unless one of the sides is a lot stronger than the other. There are so many variables in a battle – so many different decisions going on at once. Anyway, it looks like it's going to take place tomorrow morning, so I guess we'll have our answer then."

Mad Mulligan grinned.

"Want to place a bet on it?" he asked Dave. "How about fifty emeralds."

"People are going to get killed, and you want to make jokes?" said Dave. "Some of your troops will probably get killed."

Mad Mulligan shrugged.

"Troops are replaceable," he said. "There are always plenty more idiots willing to fight for emeralds. Even if all my forces get wiped out, I'll have no trouble getting more recruits for my army once I come back with a dragon. People respect power, Dave. You'd do well to remember that. It's not about whether you're good or bad; it's how much power you have."

Dave said nothing and just turned to face the wall. He found it hard to get to sleep that night, as he was so worried about his friends. He didn't know what had happened since he and Mad Mulligan had left Dead Bush, but it seemed that it was all going to be settled tomorrow in an all-or-nothing battle. Dave tried using the Sight to contact his friends or see what was going on, but, once again, he was unable to.

When he finally managed to drift off to sleep, Dave's dreams were full of glimpses of the battle. He saw Alex, Carl and Porkins fighting alongside Mayor Grady, Liza and a load of other illagers and cowmen, fighting Marie and her forces. Dave was surprised to see that Marie was holding a green trident — the Trident of Emeros. Also, she was missing an arm. The snippets of the battle that he saw were only fleeting, and it wasn't enough to give him an indication of which side was going to win.

In the morning, Dave and Mad Mulligan got out of bed, and then Mulligan destroyed the house, as usual, putting the blocks in his backpack. They were so close to the pool of lava that Dave was half-tempted to shove Mad Mulligan in. But he knew that if he did that, Spidroth would be lost forever. Thinking of Spidroth made Dave sad. He hoped that one day he would see her again.

"Right," said Mad Mulligan, putting the last of the blocks into his backpack, "I guess we ought to start —"

FWOODOOOOOSH!!!!!!!!!

Suddenly Mad Mulligan exploded in a blast of white light. Dave was sent flying backward, skidding across the snow on his back. When he finally pushed himself to his feet, he was amazed to see Mad Mulligan lying on the ground with his backpack torn to pieces and a huge group of illagers and cowmen standing over him, all of them looking very confused. Dave had no idea who any of them were, but then he spotted someone who he did recognize.

"Spidroth!" Dave gasped happily.

Spidroth looked confused too, and she was wearing a pair of tattered elytra wings on her shoulders. Dave wanted to rush right over and hug her, but then he realized that there was something more important that he had to do. Mad Mulligan was on the ground looking confused, but his confusion wouldn't last very long. This was Dave's perfect opportunity — an unexpected event that Mulligan hadn't seen coming. Dave dashed over as fast as he could, pushing through the crowd of illagers and cowmen. Mad Mulligan had started to get his bearings now and was pushing himself to his feet, but Dave got to him first, snatching the illager's red sword out of his belt. Before Mad Mulligan knew what was going on, Dave had pointed his own netherite blade and Mad Mulligan's ruby blade at the illager's head.

"Don't move," Dave said to Mad Mulligan, who was still on his knees. The illager scowled.

The other illagers and the cowmen had started to get their bearings now and had noticed Mad Mulligan.

"Well, well, well," said an illager with a white beard and an eye patch. "It's good to see you again, Mulligan."

"Dave," said Spidroth, smiling. "Um... how have you been?"

"Um, good, good," said Dave awkwardly. He felt his cheeks start to glow pink. But then he shook himself out of it and turned back to Mad Mulligan, who was still on his knees with Dave's swords pointed at him. Thankfully, all the illagers and cowmen gathered around them seemed glad to see Mad Mulligan defeated.

"Chop his head off," one cowman told Dave. Dave was half tempted, but he stopped himself. Unlike Mad Mulligan, he wasn't a killer.

"No," said Dave. "He's going to have to stand trial, like the criminal he is."

Mad Mulligan laughed.

"Dave, do you really think you're gonna be able to bring me all the way back to the badlands without me escaping or killing you?"

"Yes, he is," said the illager with the eye patch. "Because we'll be there to guard you. And if you try and run away, you're gonna get an arrow in your back."

"That's big talk coming from you, Big Nose," grinned Mad Mulligan. "Don't you remember how easily I defeated you the last time? In fact, I've defeated all of you. I don't know how you all escaped my ender chest, but even together, you won't be able to hold me."

Then, moving so fast that Dave didn't have time to react, Mad Mulligan tackled Dave's legs. Dave went flying backward, letting go of both of his swords. Mad Mulligan jumped up and caught them, and now he had the netherite blade in one hand and the ruby blade in the other. Suddenly the smiles on the faces of all the illagers and cowmen disappeared. It was clear that all of them knew how dangerous Mad Mulligan could be.

"I hope you've all enjoyed your few minutes of freedom," Mad

Mulligan grinned, "because now I'm going to slaughter you all."

Something fast and red charged towards Mad Mulligan from behind. It took Dave a moment to realize that it was Spidroth, holding an iron sword. She slashed the iron sword down, aiming at Mad Mulligan's head, but the illager raised his ruby sword behind him, blocking the blow without even looking. Then he turned and kicked Spidroth with his boot, sending her flying backward.

The other illagers and cowmen all charged towards Mad Mulligan. Most didn't have weapons, although a few were holding swords. Mad Mulligan dealt with them easily, blocking their blows with his swords and kicking them away with his boots. Before long, they were all injured on the floor, with Mad Mulligan standing triumphantly over them.

"That was fun, guys," Mad Mulligan grinned, "but I am going to kill you now."

I've got to do something, thought Dave. For the first time, he noticed that the ground was covered in random blocks and strange objects. He supposed that they must be objects that were inside the ender chest. Dave had worked out by now that it was the ender chest that had exploded in Mad Mulligan's bag — that had to be the only explanation for how Spidroth had got free. Dave supposed that all the illagers and cowmen had been in the ender chest as well.

On the floor in front of him, Dave spotted a diamond sword and picked it up. Mad Mulligan looked at him with a nasty grin on his face.

"Come on, Dave," he said. "You're not going to try and fight me again, are you? I do need you alive, but that doesn't mean I can't hurt you a lot."

"Come on," said Dave, holding his diamond sword up. "You've taught me too well — I'm going to beat you this time."

Mad Mulligan laughed. "Oh, I'm going to enjoy this."

Then Mad Mulligan charged towards Dave with his two swords.

Okay, what now? Dave wondered. He needed to do something unexpected: so unexpected that Mad Mulligan would never see it coming. But what? He racked his brains but couldn't think of anything.

But then, suddenly, he knew the answer.

Dave was standing next to the pool of lava, so he decided to do the one thing that Mad Mulligan would never have expected: He leaned back and let himself fall towards the lava.

"No!" Dave heard Mad Mulligan scream. The illager needed Dave alive to open the end portal for him, so he didn't want him to die.

For a moment, Dave thought he'd made a terrible mistake. He could feel the heat of the lava rushing up towards him and knew that in a split second, he would land inside the orange liquid, and that would be the end of him. But then he felt a hand grab his wrist, stopping him from falling. Dave looked up and saw that the hand belonged to Mad Mulligan. Mulligan was still holding Dave's netherite blade, but he'd dropped his ruby sword on the ground so that he could grab Dave's hand.

Well, I did something unexpected, but it hasn't helped, Dave thought sadly. Mad Mulligan was going to pull him back to safety, and then he'd be back where he started.

Mulligan pulled Dave back onto shore.

"Nice try, Dave," he grinned, but –"

SWOOSH! Something red swiped through the air, hitting Mad Mulligan in the back. To Dave's amazement, he saw that it was Spidroth, holding the ruby blade. Mad Mulligan's mouth dropped open in surprise, as the impact from the sword blow sent him flying forwards towards the lava pool.

"No!" Mad Mulligan had time to gasp, before he landed in the lava. There was a brief *WOOMPH* of fire, and then he was gone.

"You didn't have to slay him," Dave said to Spidroth.

"Yes, I did," said Spidroth.

Dave wouldn't have chosen to have slain Mad Mulligan himself, but he wasn't upset that the illager was dead. It seemed that none of the illagers or cowman who'd been in the chest were very upset either, and a big cheer went up.

"Nice one, Lady Spidroth!" said a cow woman.

"Are you okay?" Spidroth asked Dave.

"I was going to ask you the same thing," said Dave, smiling. "How did you get out of that chest?"

"It's a long story," said Spidroth. "I suppose you've got quite a story to tell as well."

Dave was about to reply in the affirmative when suddenly a vision flashed across his eyes – a horrible vision. He saw Carl, in his netherite golem suit in the middle of a battle. Suddenly a blast of green energy hit him, and Carl and the netherite suit exploded, both of them completely vaporized. Then Marie was standing over him with a big grin on her face, holding the Trident of Emeros.

"Carl!" Dave gasped. The vision was over as quickly as it had begun, but it was so clear that Dave had seen everything.

"What's wrong?" Spidroth asked.

"It's Carl," said Dave. "There's going to be a big battle this morning, and he's going to get slain."

"Then we'd better go and help him," said Spidroth.

"There's no way we'll get back there in time," said Dave sadly.

Spidroth thought for a moment, then she smiled.

"Do you still have those phantom membranes?" she asked

Dave. "The ones you got back at Jean-Cowphio's village?"

"Er, yeah, I think so," said Dave.

"And do you have an anvil?"

"I do. What's this about?"

"According to stories I've heard, phantom membranes can fix broken elytra," said Spidroth, looking at her tattered wings. "There might be no way that we can get back to Carl in time on foot, but maybe we can make it if we fly. We'll need firework rockets as well, so do you have any gunpowder?"

"Probably," said Dave, looking in his backpack. "What are the fireworks for?"

"You'll see," said Spidroth, with a grin. "I just hope you're not afraid of heights."

CHAPTER TEN
The Battle Begins

Carl felt nervous. He always felt like this on the eve of a big battle, and this was no exception. The badlands rebels were getting into position on the outskirts of the ruins of Dead Bush, with Sonu, Mayor Grady and the other generals organizing their troops into units. The soldiers had been divided into blocks. On the front lines, there were blocks of swordsmen in between blocks of archers. One of the generals had suggested putting the archers behind the swordsmen, but Sonu had dismissed this, saying there was too much danger that the archers may hit their own men. Another had suggested that the archers should go at the front, but Sonu had dismissed this as well: saying that the archers would be unable to defend themselves against an enemy charge. Instead, she had decided that both archers and swordsmen should be on the front lines, standing in blocks alongside each other. This would allow them to march forward together, the archers shooting at any foes that came near and the swordsmen there to defend them.

Behind the swordsmen and the archers would be the cavalry units on horseback. The rebels didn't have that many horses, and the ones they had weren't used to battle. Due to the rebels' limited supplies, very few of the horses had armor either. This was why Sonu didn't want them charging into the enemy first: because she knew that the unarmored and inexperienced horses wouldn't stand a chance against Marie's ravagers. Instead, the horses would be kept behind until the battle became more chaotic, when their riders would easily be able to charge forward and take out groups of enemy soldiers who had been separated from the pack.

Carl didn't know much about battle strategy, but as far as he could tell, Sonu's plan seemed to be pretty solid. What he was more worried about was the fact that Mad Mulligan's soldiers were far better armed than the rebels were. Mad Mulligan's troops were getting into formation in the distance, on the red sand across the badlands plains. They were too far away for Carl to see them clearly, but he could see lots of blue – the blue of diamond armor. Few of the rebels had diamond armor, let alone diamond swords. In fact, some were still wearing leather.

And while the main attack was going on, it would be Carl, Porkins and Alex's job to sneak behind Marie's army using a nether portal and launch a surprise attack. It was a good plan in theory, but Carl was still nervous. There were so many things that could go wrong.

"How are you doing, Carl?" Liza asked, riding up to him on her horse. Liza had been given command of one of the blocks of cavalry horses.

"Nervous," said Carl. "You?"

"The same," said Liza. "Do you really think we can win this battle?"

Carl really wasn't sure. The rebels had a lot of heart, but Marie's troops were seasoned warriors with much better weapons and armor. But it would be useless to voice his concerns now, so he just said:

"Yeah. Yeah, I do. We can give those idiots a beating of a lifetime."

Liza smiled.

"Yeah, I think we can," she said. "Good luck, Carl."

Then she tugged at her horse's reins and rode off to join her unit. Carl sighed. He looked around at all the rebel soldiers, hoping that his worst fears wouldn't come true. Hoping they wouldn't all get destroyed.

"Hello, old bean."

Carl turned around and saw Porkins and Alex walking towards him.

"Hello, you two," said Carl. "Is anyone else feeling as doomed as I am?"

"We may be a bit outclassed by the enemy, but I still believe we can win the battle," said Porkins. "We've fought battles with worse odds before and won."

"Yeah, Carl, we'll be fine," said Alex cheerily. "Just because the enemy has more troops than us and better weapons and better armor and more horses and ravagers and more experience doesn't mean they're necessarily going to win."

"Er, thanks, Alex," said Carl. "That makes me feel so much better."

"No problem," said Alex cheerily, missing the sarcasm.

Just then, Sonu walked over to them. The cow woman was one of the few members of the rebels who had a full set of diamond armor, and she had a diamond sword in her hand. Carl thought that that diamond armor would have been far more useful for one of the troops on the front lines, but he bit his tongue and didn't say anything.

"How are you three doing?" Sonu asked. "Do you know what you have to do?"

"You want us to use another portal to pop behind the enemy and bash their butts," said Alex.

"Er, yes," said Sonu. "But wait until I give the order. I want to make sure the battle is well underway before you three attack, so we can surprise the enemy when they are least expecting it."

"As you say, ma'am," said Porkins.

Sonu walked off, leaving the three of them alone once more.

"I don't know about her," said Carl. "I'd feel far more comfortable if Mayor Grady was in charge."

"She seems like a good egg," said Porkins. "And she was the one who founded this rebellion, so I guess it makes sense that she's the leader of it."

"I suppose," said Carl.

He heard the galloping of hooves and turned around to see Mayor Grady riding towards them. The mayor was wearing a set of iron armor.

"What happened to your diamond armor, Mr Mayor?" Alex

asked him.

"I gave it to one of the troops," said Mayor Grady. "They need it more than I will, being on the front lines. I don't have much time, as the battle is about to begin, but I just wanted to thank you three. Whatever happens here today, you all did so much to help my town and my people. If we survive today, we'll never forget it."

"It was our pleasure," said Alex.

"Yeah, we help idiots in need wherever we find them," said Carl.

Mayor Grady grinned, then he galloped off to join the other generals.

Somewhere in the distance, someone blew a horn. Everyone fell silent: the battle was about to begin.

Carl, Porkins and Alex climbed up the stairs of a half-destroyed building to get a better look at the battle. The rebel infantry and archers had started marching forward across the red sand plains, and in the distance, the enemy began marching forward on foot as well, both sides marching towards each other. The enemy units were a sea of blue, all of them wearing diamond armor. The two sides were about to meet when something unexpected happened. The enemy forces all moved to one side, and a huge group of illagers on horseback rode through the gap, heading straight towards the rebels. The horses were all wearing diamond armor, as were their riders.

"Oh my!" Porkins gasped.

The diamond armored horses charged into the rebel front line. The archers tried to fire arrows at them, but the arrows just bounced off the diamond armor. The illagers on horseback pulled out their swords and began attacking the ground troops, causing chaos.

"We need to retaliate with our own horses!" Carl heard one of the generals shout. Sonu, Mayor Grady and the rest of the generals were gathered together on the ruins of another building, a short way away from where Carl, Porkins and Alex were. They were watching the battle from the back, so they could see what was going on and give orders to their forces.

"Send in the horses!" Sonu bellowed. A few seconds later, the rebel horses began charging forward as well, joining the battle. All sense of order had gone now, and the battle was nothing but a mess of swordsmen, archers and horses, all desperately fighting each other. The rebels had committed all their forces to the battle, but Marie had kept her ground troops and ravagers back. But now she was sending her swordsmen in, and they rushed forward, attacking the rebels ground troops, who were still distracted by the horses. Next, Marie's archers stepped forward and began firing indiscriminately, their arrows raining down on the battlefield. Finally, the ravagers charged forward, charging through the soldiers and horses, trampling anything they could.

"What's Marie doing?" asked Porkins. "She's going to end up slaying a load of her own troops."

"I don't think she cares," said Carl. "She is crazy, remember."

"You three, I need you to attack now," Sonu shouted at Carl, Porkins and Alex.

Carl didn't need telling twice. As chaotic as the battle was, it was clear that Marie's illager forces had the upper hand, so he, Porkins and Alex needed to do the best they could to help. The three of them jumped down from the ruined building, then Porkins quickly built a portal out of obsidian and lit it. The purple force field bubbled into life, then the three of them jump through it.

On the other side, they found themselves in a Nether biome that looked a lot like the old Nether, with netherrack hills, clumps of glowstone hanging from the ceiling and huge lakes of lava.

"Okay, Alex, lead the way," said Carl.

"What?" said Alex, looking confused.

Carl rolled his eyes. Sometimes Alex's brain was a bit like mushroom stew: stodgy, thick and full of mushrooms.

"You said you'd be able to work out where we needed to build another portal to reappear behind Marie's forces," Carl reminded her.

"Oh yes!" said Alex happily. "This way!"

She began to run, and Porkins and Carl ran after her.

"Do you think the dear girl really knows what she's doing?" Porkins whispered to Carl.

"I guess we'll find out," said Carl.

But then something unexpected happened: suddenly, from all around them, zombified piglins appeared, stumbling towards them.

"We haven't got time for this," Carl scowled. He charged through the piglins with his netherite golem suit, sending them flying and clearing a path for Porkins and Alex to follow behind him. They ran on, making their way through the endless hordes of zombified piglins.

"This is the place!" Alex shouted suddenly. "We need to build a nether portal here!"

Carl came to a stop. Zombified piglins were still staggering towards them, so he and Alex fought them off while Porkins constructed another portal. Once the portal was lit, the three of them jump through –

– and emerged right behind Marie's army. The army was facing the other direction, so no one noticed them.

"I told you I'd get it right!" said Alex happily.

Carl quickly smashed one of the obsidian blocks with his netherite fists, deactivating the portal. Then he noticed, for the first time, that they were standing right next to Marie, who was clad in diamond armor riding on a diamond armored horse. And for some reason, she seemed to be missing an arm. At first, she didn't notice them, but then she turned and saw them, and her mouth dropped open in surprise.

"You two stick with the plan," Carl said to Alex and Porkins, "attack the army from behind. I'll deal with this crazy illager."

"Bring it on," Marie grinned. She looked even madder than the last time Carl had seen her, and her eyes were practically popping out of her head. As Porkins and Alex began attacking Marie's soldiers from behind, using the element of surprise to their advantage, Carl rushed forward towards Marie's horse, preparing to biff her off of it, when suddenly Marie pointed a green trident at him.

Is that... Is that the Trident of Emeros? Carl had time to think, then *FWADOOOSH,* he was hit by a blast of green energy and sent flying.

Carl went skidding across the red sand, tumbling over and over until he finally came to a stop. He pushed himself back to his feet but saw that his netherite golem suit was badly damaged, with cracks all over it. It was clear that it wouldn't be able to take another blast from the trident. He looked up and saw Marie galloping towards him on her horse, the trident aimed towards him once more. Carl quickly rolled to the side, just in time to avoid getting hit by another blast of green energy. The blast hit the sand instead, creating a huge crater. Carl had no idea how Marie had got her hands on the trident, but he knew she had to be stopped. He tensed his netherite golem arms, turned and charged towards her once more.

CHAPTER ELEVEN
You've Got Me? Who's Got You?!

Dave had never been so terrified in his life. It wasn't just that he was rocketing through the air at a ridiculous speed, it was also that Spidroth was weaving in and out of hills, mountains and trees, and Dave had to keep closing his eyes because he thought they were going to hit something.

"Isn't this fun?" Spidroth said. Dave had never heard her sound so happy — it was like she was actually enjoying herself, which Spidroth didn't do very often. Her face was lit up with one of the happiest smiles that Dave had ever seen.

As they only had one pair of elytra, Spidroth was doing the

flying, and she was holding Dave under his arms. Because she was using both her hands to hold him, it was Dave's job to use a rocket whenever they began to lose altitude. Spidroth did her best to glide for as long as possible, but eventually, she and Dave always began to dip closer towards the ground. When that happened, Spidroth would yell, "rocket!" and it would be Dave's job to squeeze one of the firework rockets, propelling them forward. It was pretty scary and wasn't something that Dave was enjoying.

Still, as scary as their breakneck-speed flight was, in the few moments where he wasn't closing his eyes, Dave couldn't help but marvel at the scenery. From up here, he could see the true majesty of the badlands: the hills and mountains made from different color stripes of terracotta, the occasional water pools surrounded by small oak trees, and the great open plains of red sand, stretching off into the distance.

During their flight, Spidroth told Dave all about her adventure in the ender chest and her harrowing flight through a lightning storm to blast the chest open. Dave told Spidroth the basics of his own adventure: about his journey and all the things that Mad Mulligan had told him.

"Well, at least we know we're finally getting near to an end portal," said Spidroth, when Dave told her about Bedrock City.

"Yeah, Mad Mulligan said that the city was only a few weeks away on foot," said Dave. "Although at the moment, I'm not really thinking about the end portal. All I can think about is that vision I saw of Carl..."

"Don't worry," said Spidroth, "we'll get to him in time. If anyone is going to harm that annoying little creeper, it will be me."

Dave laughed. It felt good to be back with Spidroth. Even though their relationship had been through some ups and downs since their kiss in the Nether, Dave still saw Spidroth as a good friend, and he would have done anything for her.

"Have you had any more visions with the Sight?" Spidroth asked as she swooped through a narrow gap between two mountains. Dave closed his eyes until they were free of the gap, then he said:

"Not yet. That vision of Carl came so suddenly, I guess it was because if Carl died, it would be such a significant thing for me. I think the Sight differentiates between things that are important and things that aren't. Although it gives me some strange visions too, some of which I don't understand."

"You will learn to use it in time," said Spidroth. "From what you've told me, it seems that your trip with Mad Mulligan may have been a blessing in disguise. He's taught you things about the Sight that even I didn't know."

"I guess," said Dave. "I'm still pretty glad he's gone, though."

"Me too," said Spidroth. "He was far too dangerous a foe. Still, it shows you how powerful you could be one day, once you master the Sight for yourself. Mulligan was probably the best hand-to-hand fighter I've ever battled, and that's saying something. He took Alex and me on as if we were nothing more than children with wooden sticks. If you can become even half the warrior that he was, you'd probably be one of the best fighters in the entire world."

Dave had never really wanted to be a powerful warrior — he'd always been more concerned with being an adventurer. Still, being able to fight off bad guys and defend his friends was something that appealed to him. During his adventure, he'd had too many experiences of feeling powerless — where he'd been fighting a foe so powerful that he was unable to do anything. Maybe once he mastered the Sight, that wouldn't be a problem anymore. Dave had never asked for the Sight, but if he could use it to help people, then he would be glad.

Suddenly, without warning, Dave had a vision of the battle taking place. It was a messy and brutal battle, with horses, ravagers and illagers and cowmen on foot all fighting it out on the red sand desert in front of a ruined town. His friends were there too: Porkins running around firing arrows and smashing foes with his metal arm, Alex taking on hordes of illagers at a time with her ninja moves, and Carl fighting Marie in his netherite golem suit. She was firing at him with the Trident of Emeros, and he was doing his best to dodge out of the way.

"I think the battle has begun," said Dave. "I saw a vision... It was so vivid."

"Then we need to hurry," said Spidroth. "Rocket!"

Dave took another rocket and squeezed it. He and Spidroth blasted forward with the elytra, soaring over the red badlands hills below.

Hold in there, Carl, Dave thought to himself. *We're coming to save you.*

CHAPTER TWELVE
The Second Battle of Dead Bush

Alex jumped up, performing a spinning ninja kick and sending the five illagers surrounding her flying backward. Then a diamond armored illager on a diamond armored horse charged towards her, firing a crossbow. Alex jumped out of the way before the arrows could hit her, then kicked the illager off his horse, stealing it for herself. She galloped through Mad Mulligan's forces as they desperately tried to get out of her way.

"Here's your Alex order!" Alex shouted as she scattered a group of illagers with her horse. "Extra Alex and extra cheese — just the way you like it!"

"What's she talking about?" said one illager, looking confused.

"I'm talking about your FACE!" said Alex, and she charged into the illager and sent him flying.

Alex looked across the battlefield and was amazed at what a mess it was. The battle was so chaotic that it was hard to tell friend from foe: it was just a big mass of people fighting. She couldn't even tell which side was winning.

All this fighting because of that Mad Mulligan idiot, she thought angrily. People were getting slain here today, all because of Mad Mulligan, and he wasn't even around to see it. Alex vowed to herself that if she ever saw Mad Mulligan again, she would give him the biffing of a lifetime.

*

Porkins was firing his bow as fast as his trotters could manage, but it still wasn't fast enough. The battle had become such a mess, and Marie's soldiers were pressing in on him from all sides, so he had to switch to his diamond sword instead. Porkins didn't like using a sword when he could avoid it, as he much preferred a bow, but in close quarters combat like this, a bow and arrow was pretty useless.

Porkins raised his diamond sword up, blocking a blow from one illager, but then another illager charged at him from behind, and he had to swing around and block that blow as well.

I should have worn armor, Porkins thought desperately. He was naked, without even clothes to protect him. He'd never expected that the battle would get this messy or that he'd have to fight in hand-to-hand combat like this. Porkins was a great archer, but he was only slightly above average with a sword, so he didn't know how long he'd be able to hold out against Marie's soldiers, most of whom were wearing full sets of diamond armor. Porkins thrust his sword at one of the soldiers, but his blade just glanced off the illager's diamond breastplate.

The diamond armored soldiers began to close in on Porkins from all directions, surrounding him.

"Oh my," Porkins muttered to himself. He had no idea how he was going to get out of this one but knew that he would fight to his last breath if he had to.

Then, suddenly, a horse galloped past, sending some of the illagers surrounding Porkins flying. The other troops tried to attack the person on the horse but were shot with arrows. Porkins looked up and was amazed to see it was Liza on the back of the horse, holding a crossbow.

"Come on," she said, offering Porkins at hand. She pulled Porkins up onto the horse behind her.

"Thank you, my lady," said Porkins.

"Don't thank me," said Liza, "use those amazing archery skills of yours and start shooting!"

Porkins didn't need telling twice. He pulled out his bow and began firing arrows from the back of Liza's horse as she rode around the battlefield.

This is more like it, Porkins thought. He always felt the most comfortable when he had a bow in his hand.

*

POW!

Carl biffed Marie with one of his netherite golem fists, sending her rolling across the red sand. At first, Carl hoped that she'd been knocked out, but then she jumped back to her feet and fired a blast of green energy at him from the end of her trident. Carl jumped out of the way just in time, as the sand behind him exploded in a flash of green light.

Marie had lost her horse and only had one arm, but she was still as good a warrior as the last time Carl had faced her. Carl had taken a few more hits from the Trident of Emeros, and his netherite suit was really starting to crack. At best, he'd be able to take another one or two more blasts from the trident, but after that, it would be game over, Carl knew. He'd managed to biff Marie a couple of times now, but she was wearing a full set of diamond armor, which also looked like it was glowing with some kind of enchantment, and his blows had barely done any damage.

All around them, the battle was raging: an endless sea of fighting and chaos. Carl dreaded to think how many lives must already have been lost, but that was a worry for later – right now, he needed to have his head in the game if he was going to stand any chance of defeating Marie. With Mad Mulligan gone, Marie seemed to be the one in charge of the enemy soldiers, so if Carl could defeat her, maybe he could bring an end to the fighting before more people had to lose their lives.

Even the generals of the rebel forces had got involved now, Carl saw. He caught glimpses of Mayor Grady in the thick of a group of enemy soldiers, attacking them with his diamond sword. He'd even, to his surprise, seen Sonu in the thick of battle, fighting off the enemy. Carl felt bad about doubting her earlier – it was clear that Sonu wasn't the coward he had suspected she was.

"Getting tired yet, creeper?" Marie grinned.

"Only tired of your face," said Carl. He charged towards Marie once again. She fired a blast from the trident at him, but Carl dodged to the side and kept charging.

This is it, he thought to himself, as he raised his arm back, ready for a punch. *This is my chance to take her out once and for all!*

He swung his fist, but Marie rolled out of the way. Carl lost his balance and fell forward onto the red sand. He heard Marie laughing behind him.

FWASSSSM!!!! Marie blasted Carl in the back with the trident. He went rolling across the sand, and when he tried to get up, he couldn't. His netherite golem suit had just about survived the blast, but now it was in tatters, and he was unable to move the limbs. The suit would fix itself eventually, Carl knew, but at the moment he was unable to use it. Marie grinned and aimed the trident at him once more.

"Goodbye, creeper," she grinned. She fired another blast from the trident, and Carl prepared for the worst – but instead, something landed in front of him and blocked the blast of green energy. There was a tremendous flash of green light, and when Carl could see again, he saw Spidroth, standing on the red sand holding Mad Mulligan's red sword out in front of her.

"You?" Marie hissed.

"Me," said Spidroth. She ducked down and did a sweeping kick, kicking Marie's legs out from under her. Marie let go of the Trident of Emeros and fell down onto her back. Spidroth stood over her, pointing her red sword at Marie's face and putting her boot on the illager's stomach to keep her down. For the first time, Carl noticed that Dave was there too, holding a diamond sword. And for some reason, Spidroth was wearing a pair of elytra wings.

"STOP FIGHTING!" Spidroth roared. "I've defeated your leader! Stop fighting!"

To Carl's amazement, the fighting did stop. Everyone – the rebels and Mad Mulligan's forces alike – were looking at Spidroth in amazement.

"Mad Mulligan is dead," said Spidroth. "I have his blade in my hand. And now his second-in-command is defeated. There has been enough death and destruction here today, so stop your fighting!"

Hearing that their leader was dead and seeing Marie defeated on the ground seemed to take all of the heart from Mad Mulligan's soldiers. They began dropping their weapons and putting their hands up in the air, surrendering.

"No," Marie hissed. "I won't let you defeat me!"

Using all of her strength, Marie pushed Spidroth off of her. Spidroth fell to the ground, and Marie pulled a diamond sword from her belt, raising it over her head and preparing to bring it down on Spidroth.

"Die!" Marie shrieked. But then *FWASSSSM!!!!* – Marie exploded in a blast of green energy. When the green light disappeared, there was nothing left of her but dust in the wind. Everyone looked around in amazement and saw Creepo Jones, on horseback, holding the Trident of Emeros. The yellow creeper had obviously rode forward and picked it up off the ground when Marie dropped it, Carl realized. But where he'd come from, Carl had no idea.

"I tried to tell them that this trident belonged in a museum, but they just wouldn't listen," said Creepo Jones.

"Oh, Master!" said a voice, and Carl turned to see Milo the cowman rushing towards Creepo. Carl hadn't even known that Milo had been fighting in the battle, but he was wearing a set of iron armor, so it looked like he had been.

Mayor Grady pushed his way through the crowd. His face was cut in places, and he'd lost some bits of his iron armor, but thankfully he had survived the battle.

"Tie up the prisoners and bring them back to the camp," he announced. "This battle is over."

CHAPTER THIRTEEN
Peace in the Badlands

Mad Mulligan's remaining forces all surrendered willingly, letting the rebels bring them back to the camp as prisoners.

There was no big celebration that night. Yes, the rebels had won the battle, but they'd lost many of their soldiers in the fight. Sonu herself, the rebel leader, had been slain towards the end of the fighting, and Mayor Grady had taken temporary command of the rebel forces.

Spidroth and Dave were asked over and over again what had happened with Mad Mulligan. Mulligan had cast a shadow over the badlands for so long that it was difficult for people to believe that he was finally gone.

Dave and his friends stayed with the rebels for a week or so, to make sure everything was ok. After a few days, some of the exiles from Mad Mulligan's ender chest arrived at the camp, but Big Nose and many of the illagers who'd previously been part of Mad Mulligan's gang were noticeably absent.

Eventually, the leaders of the various settlements took their people and returned home. Many of their villages and towns had been destroyed, but they were all eager to rebuild. With Mad Mulligan gone, it would be a new start for the badlands, and they were all keen to see what the future would bring.

Eventually, Creepo Jones and Milo headed off as well.

"We've got to bring this thing back to Spectrite City Museum," said Creepo, holding up the Trident of Emeros.

"Can't we keep it for a bit?" Carl asked. "It would come in pretty useful, being able to blast bad guys to bits."

"This artifact is thousands of years old," said Creepo Jones angrily. "If you think I'd let you take it off on an adventure and lose it, you've got another thing coming."

"All right, keep your wig on," said Carl.

"I'm not wearing a wig," said Creepo Jones, sounding confused.

Mayor Grady and his people decided that instead of building a new town somewhere else, they would rebuild Dead Bush. And, to Dave and his friends' surprise, they announced they were going to build five very special statues in the center of the town.

"We're going to put up statues of all five of you," Liza told Dave and the others. "You've all done so much for our town and for the whole of the badlands. Without your help, we would have lost everything."

"Can my statue be holding a baked potato?" Carl asked. The little creeper was making a joke, but Dave could see that the idea of having a statue really meant a lot to him.

"I've never had a statue of me before," said Alex. "I mean, back when I was Steve, people built statues of me all the time."

"Wait," said Liza, giving Alex a funny look, "you used to be Steve? I thought you were a clone of Steve?"

"Yes, but I'm a clone of him with all his memories," said Alex cheerily. "Although most of those memories I've forgotten."

"It's all very complicated," Dave explained.

As Dave and his friends rode away from Dead Bush on horses they'd been given, Dave couldn't help but smile. After all the bad things that had happened over the past few days, the idea that there was going to be a statue of him filled him with happiness. Back when he'd first thought about going on an adventure, the idea that people would one day build statues of him seemed like an impossible dream, and now it had actually happened. Maybe he really was becoming a hero?

When they made camp for the night, building a house next to a small pool of water, Dave and his friends sat around the netherrack fireplace, just talking. They'd been through so much over the past couple of weeks, so it was good to just relax and chat. As usual, Carl made jokes, Spidroth scowled, Porkins said funny phrases and Alex... Well, Alex was Alex. Dave was glad to be back on the road once more, heading west to Bedrock City, where they would finally find an end portal and complete their adventure. It had been a long time coming, but it looked like at last, they were finally going to reach the End.

Dave had just climbed into bed and was looking forward to a good night's sleep when there was a flash of purple light from outside the windows.

"What now?" Carl groaned.

They all jumped out of bed and made their way out of the house. Carl was so sleepy that he didn't even bother putting his netherite golem suit on. Next to the house was a lit nether portal with a purple force field.

"Everyone go and get your weapons," said Dave, his muscles tensing. Could it be that the Empress had returned? Was she sending more of her piglin soldiers after them?

And then a figure walked through the force field. It was a piglin, wearing a black suit, white shirt and a top hat.

"Boggo?" said Dave in disbelief.

"Machine work!" said Boggo excitedly. "Boggo use Empress machine to find you. Boggo smart!"

"What do you want, Boggo?" sighed Carl.

"Boggo getting married!" said Boggo excitedly. "And Boggo want Carl to be best man!"

Carl's mouth dropped open. For once, the little creeper seemed to be at a loss for words.

"I'm sure Carl would love that," Spidroth grinned, reaching down and rubbing Carl's head. "Wouldn't you, Carl?"

"Where's Mad Mulligan when you need him?" Carl scowled.

"Come on," said Boggo. "Follow Boggo. You all invited to Boggo wedding."

Then, suddenly, Boggo began to shake.

"Er, Boggo, are you okay?" Dave asked.

"Boggo no feel so good!" said Boggo. Suddenly he turned a paler shade of pink, and some of his flesh fell off, revealing green mold and bone underneath.

"BURR!" said Boggo, his voice deep and lifeless.

"Er, I think your friend has just turned into a zombie," said

Alex.

"Porkins, get your bow and put an arrow in his head," said Carl.

"Carl!" said Porkins, outraged. "Boggo just asked you to be his best man! We need to try and save him."

Carl sighed, his eyes rolling back in his head.

"Come on then," he said miserably. "I guess we're going back to the Nether."

Epilogue

It was nighttime in the snowy taiga mountains biome. The moon was covered in clouds, so the only light came from the lava pool in the middle of the snow. Suddenly there was a *POP,* and a figure appeared by the side of the pool, lit by the orange glow of the lava.

I'm alive, thought Mad Mulligan. Judging by the fact it was night, he had been dead for several hours, but now he was back.

He reached into the inner pocket of his jacket and pulled out a small statue. The statue was in the shape of an illager with its arms outstretched. It was made from ruby, with two emerald eyes. He held the statue for a moment, and then it crumbled to dust, leaving nothing behind. The statue had been a *Totem of Never Dying,* another treasure that he'd found in Bedrock City long ago. Unlike the far more common *totem of undying,* you didn't have to be holding the Totem of Never Dying for it to bring you back to life when you died. A regular totem of undying brought you back straight away, so it was of little use if you fell in lava, but the Totem of Never Dying was smarter than that and would bring the user back in a safe place. Mad Mulligan had kept it in the pocket of his jacket for all these years, on the off chance that he would get killed unexpectedly. Now, finally, the totem had done its job. Spidrothbrine had killed him, pushing him into the lava with his own sword, but now Mad Mulligan was back, and he was going to have his revenge.

He checked his other pockets and was disappointed to see that his suspicions were right – all his belongings were gone, destroyed in the lava, no doubt.

It's no matter, he thought to himself. *Empires can be rebuilt. Especially when you have a dragon.*

Mad Mulligan reached out with the Sight. As he expected, he

saw that his army had been defeated and Marie had been slain. All his soldiers were currently in captivity in Dead Bush.

Let them rot in jail, Mad Mulligan thought. His empire may be gone for now, but once he took control of the Ender Dragon, he would build a bigger and better empire than before. Perhaps he would conquer the villager continent as well, declaring himself king over villagers and illagers alike. The thought of that made him grin.

Mad Mulligan stood up. It was still night, but he didn't want to waste any more time. He began walking west, beginning the long journey to Bedrock City. That was where Dave was heading, he knew, and when the villager got there, Mad Mulligan would be waiting for him...

To be continued...

BOOK 35

Boggo's Wedding

CHAPTER ONE
The Groom

"Have you got him secure?" Dave asked.

"Yep," said Carl. "This little pig isn't going anywhere."

"ROKK!" snorted Boggo.

Carl was back in his golem suit and was holding Boggo under his arm. The piglin, who was now a zombie with moldy flesh and bits of bone showing, was struggling but wasn't strong enough to break free from Carl's grip.

"I must say, I do object to you calling Boggo a 'little pig,'" said Porkins. "That's a bit offensive, old chap."

"How about 'little piglin'?" Carl asked. "Is that less offensive?"

"Everyone, just be quiet a moment," said Dave. "Now come on – let's bring Boggo back to the Nether and see if there's any way to fix him."

"To be honest, I don't see much difference," said Spidroth. "He was a fool before he even became a zombie."

"I agree that Boggo isn't the sharpest tool in the chest, but we still have to help him if we can," said Dave. "Especially as he's supposed to be getting married."

"And Carl is going to be the best man," grinned Porkins. "You'd better hurry up and write a speech, old chap."

"I can help you write some jokes for the speech," said Alex. "People are always laughing at me, so I must be funny."

"Pah," said Carl.

"Come on," said Dave, walking towards the portal. "Let's go and see what we can do for Boggo."

"BURR," said Boggo.

"Maybe Boggo's wife-to-be won't notice the difference," said Carl, looking down at the zombified piglin. "As Spidroth said, he's not that different than he was before. If anything, he sounds a bit more intelligent like this."

I can't believe there's another distraction to stop us from getting to the End, Dave thought to himself. He knew that they had to help Boggo, but he couldn't help feeling a bit disappointed. They were so close to an end portal now – only a few weeks away if Mad Mulligan could be believed. They were finally reaching the end of their quest, and Dave was eager to reach the End, and finish the mission he'd started all that time ago.

"Here we go," said Dave, taking out his diamond sword. Because they didn't know what kind of reception they would face in the Nether, he was wearing his netherite armor. Porkins was wearing a set of diamond armor, Carl had his golem suit, and Spidroth and Alex, as usual, weren't wearing any armor at all. Both of them were such good fighters that they rarely wore armor, as they could move much more freely without it. Dave agreed that sometimes armor could be a bit clunky, but he felt much safer with it on. Maybe once he became an expert with the Sight, he would feel safe enough not to wear any armor at all, but he preferred to have it on for now.

“Come on, hurry up,” Carl said to Dave. “Let’s get this over with.”

Dave took a deep breath and walked through the Nether portal.

CHAPTER TWO
The Bride

Dave walked through the nether portal and emerged in a large room with purple nether brick walls. There were lots of strange screens and contraptions around the room, many of them making whirring sounds; it was obviously some kind of laboratory. Standing in front of the portal was a piglin in a wedding dress.

"Saggo?" said Spidroth, who had just walked through the portal after Dave.

"Hello Dave, hello Spidroth!" said Saggo happily. "Saggo pleased to see you!"

Then Carl stepped through the portal with Boggo under his arm, and Saggo's smile disappeared.

"Boggo!" she yelled, running over to him. Carl held up a netherite golem hand and held her back.

"You don't want to get too close to him," Carl said. "Not unless you want to get turned into a zombie as well."

Saggo began to sob.

"My poor Boggo!" she blubbed.

"Hi, I'm Alex; nice to meet you!" said Alex, oblivious that Saggo was crying.

"Don't worry, Saggo, we'll fix Boggo," said Dave.

"Gold apples and splash potions of weakness were unable to turn zombie pigmen back to normal, but perhaps they might work on zombie piglins?" Porkins suggested. "There are over a million years of evolution between pigmen and piglins, so our biology has to be quite different."

"I'm afraid that won't work," said a cheery female voice. At first, Dave couldn't see where the voice was coming from, and then he noticed a silver robot with glowing pink eyes. The robot was in the shape of a pigman — or rather, a pig woman.

"This is P1Go," said Saggo. "This is robot that helped me and Boggo get Empress's machine working."

"You were built by Chops?" Porkins asked the robot.

"Yes," said the silver robot. "Chops, or the Empress as she preferred to be known, built me as her own personal assistant. I was by her side for almost one million years before she left the Nether."

"Left the Nether?" said Carl, raising an eyebrow. "That's one way of putting it. She was blown to smithereens."

"If you say so, sir," said P1Go.

"So P1Go, are you saying that using a splash potion of weakness and a golden apple won't turn Boggo back to normal?" asked Dave.

"Yes," said the robot. "That treatment has proven to be

ineffective in curing zombified piglins."

"Why did Boggo turn into a zombie anyway?" Carl asked.

"The Empress speculated that piglins who stayed in the Overworld too long would turn into zombies due to their bodies not being used to the colder environment," said the robot.

"Fool, we've seen other piglins go to the Overworld without turning into zombies," said Spidroth. "The Empress sent an army of piglins to capture us when the Nether stopped fast-forwarding, and none of them turned into zombies."

"Yes, ma'am, but that was because the Empress administered them all with a special potion," said P1Go. "The potion allowed them to stay in the Overworld for several hours without a zombie transformation taking place."

"Wait," said Saggo, wiping the tears from her eyes, "you knew Boggo would turn into zombie, but you didn't tell us?!"

"You never asked, ma'am," said P1Go.

"Poor Boggo," sobbed Saggo. "He just wanted to come to Overworld to ask Carl to be his best man. Carl was Boggo's best friend. Best friend in all the world."

"Er... Yeah, of course," said Carl.

"P1Go, is there any way we can turn Boggo back?" Dave asked.

"Let me check my databanks," said the silver robot. For a few seconds, the lights in her pink eyes flickered, and then they turned back to normal again. "Yes, there is. Years ago, the Empress developed a special potion that could transform zombified piglins back into regular piglins. She abandoned the project as most zombified piglins were born as zombies, so even if you turned them into piglins, they rarely had the power of speech of cognitive thought. However, the potion was found to be 100% effective in all cases."

"Well, give us some of that potion then, rust for brains," said Carl.

"I'm afraid it is not that easy," said P1Go. "The laboratory where the Empress kept that potion is far away from here, in a location heavily affected by the zombie plague."

"What's the *zombie plague?*" Alex asked.

"Recently, zombified piglins have been causing trouble in the Nether on an unheard-of scale," said P1Go. "Normally, zombified piglins only get violent when they are attacked, but recently they have been attacking unprovoked. Some areas have become completely inhospitable to regular piglins. As of yet, I have yet to deduce the source of this plague."

"So zombified piglins are going crazy, and we're going to have to go to an area with loads of them," said Carl. "That's just great."

"That not great," said Saggo. "That very bad."

"I believe Carl was using a form of speech known as sarcasm, ma'am," said P1Go. "When he claimed that this situation was *great,* he actually meant the opposite. Isn't that right, Carl?"

"This robot better not be coming with us," said Carl. "Her shtick is going to get old real fast."

"Don't worry, Saggo," said Dave, putting a hand on the piglin's shoulder. "My friends and I are going to go to that other laboratory and fix Boggo. You'll still have your wedding, I promise."

"Saggo hopes so," sobbed the piglin. "Saggo already paid for catering."

CHAPTER THREE
The Venue

Before they left on their quest, Saggo wanted to check on the wedding preparations. Dave told her that she didn't need to come with them on the quest, but she insisted.

"Boggo is love of Saggo's life," she said defiantly. "Saggo must help save him."

Saggo didn't want to alarm any of the guests for fear that it would ruin the wedding, so they had to keep Boggo's condition secret.

The wedding was taking place outside in a warped forest biome, so Carl stayed with Boggo behind a large blue-green mushroom as the others joined Saggo to check on the ceremony.

The wedding was much larger than Dave expected, with crimson wood tables and chairs set out for the meal and rows of crimson wood seats for the wedding ceremony itself. Many piglins were busy decorating.

"Dave!" said a piglin, walking over to them. "Wroxo glad to see you!"

"Er, good to see you too, Wroxo," said Dave. The good thing about piglins was that they always said their own name out loud, so even if you didn't remember which one was which, you could soon work it out. Dave would have hated to admit it, but all the piglins looked pretty much the same to him – even the women.

"Where is Boggo and Carl?" asked another piglin. "Groggo want to see Carl. Carl Groggo's good friend."

"Boggo and Carl are working on their speeches for the ceremony," said Porkins. "You chaps are really in for a treat – they are jolly good speeches."

"Groggo no like speeches," said Groggo. "Speeches boring. Groggo looking forward to wedding meal. Groggo likes eating."

"Wroxo likes eating too," said Wroxo. "But Wroxo likes dancing too. Wroxo hoping that pretty piglin girl will dance with him. Then maybe next wedding will be Wroxo's."

"No one will marry Wroxo," said Groggo. "Wroxo is not handsome like Groggo."

"Groggo no handsome!" said Wroxo. "Wroxo handsome. Dave, who is more handsome — Wroxo or Groggo?"

"Er, you're both equally handsome," said Dave. Technically he wasn't lying — he thought both piglins looked pretty much the same.

Saggo walked over to a piglin who was cooking something in a smoker.

"Saggo have to go get ready for a few hours," Saggo told the piglin. "But Saggo will be back in time for ceremony with Boggo."

"Zaffro will look after things until then," said the piglin at the smoker, who Dave realized was female.

"Thank you, Zaffro," said Saggo. "You are good friend."

The two piglins hugged, then Saggo walked back to join Dave and the others.

"Ceremony is soon," said Saggo. "We must hurry and fix Boggo."

"Fix Boggo?" said a voice. "What do you mean?"

Dave turned and saw another piglin behind them.

"Hello, Dave and Dave's friends," said the piglin. "Poffo glad to see you again."

Dave couldn't recall ever meeting Poffo before, but to be polite, he said:

"Hello, Poffo. Great to see you."

"Is anyone else a bit confused?" Alex whispered. "All these piglins look really similar, and they all have similar names as well."

"And they're all similarly stupid," whispered Spidroth.

"Poffo ask again," said Poffo. "Why did Saggo say Saggo needs to fix Boggo? What is wrong with Boggo?"

Saggo sighed.

"Saggo tell Poffo secret, but Poffo must not tell anyone else. Agreed?"

Poffo nodded. Saggo told Poffo what had happened to Boggo and about their mission to go to the laboratory to get the potion.

"Poffo come too," said Poffo. "Poffo didn't help when Boggo tried to rebel against Empress. Poffo make big mistake then, and Poffo want to make up for it. Please let Poffo come?"

"Dave, can Poffo come?" Saggo asked.

"Er, yeah," said Dave. "The more, the merrier."

"Thank you, Dave," said Poffo. "Poffo will be brave. Brave like hoglin."

"Come on, that's enough messing about," said Spidroth. "If we're going to save your husband and get him back in time for the wedding, we need to get moving."

"Saggo agree," said Saggo.

"You might want to change out of that wedding dress, Saggo," said Alex. "It's not really an appropriate outfit for an adventure."

"Saggo keep wedding dress on," said Saggo. "It took Saggo long time to get on. Wedding dress complicated. Saggo no have time to take off and get changed."

"It must be so cool and romantic getting married," grinned Alex. "Is it cool and romantic, Saggo?"

"It was cool and romantic," said Saggo, "before Saggo's husband-to-be turned into zombie. Husband-to-be turning into zombie isn't very romantic."

"No," said Alex. "I suppose it's not."

CHAPTER FOUR
Death From Above

They rejoined Carl and Boggo and then made their way through the warped forest biome, with P1Go leading the way. Even though she'd been built by the Empress, the silver pig woman robot seemed friendly enough.

In total, there were nine in their party: Dave, Carl, Spidroth, Porkins and Alex, the three piglins, Saggo, Poffo and Boggo (who was still a zombie and had to be held under Carl's arm) and P1Go. Dave would have preferred if he and his friends had gone alone, leaving the piglins behind, but Saggo and Poffo insisted on coming, and they had to bring Boggo as P1Go wasn't sure if the potion had to be drank fresh or not.

"Have you been to this laboratory before?" Dave asked the silver robot.

"Oh yes," said P1Go. "As the Empress's assistant, I went with her to all her different bases and laboratories. She was always working on plans to get revenge on the Overworld."

"She sure was one crazy lady," said Carl.

"That crazy lady was a good person once," said Porkins, a sad look crossing his face. "But a lot of bad things happened to her, and the poor thing couldn't handle it."

"A lot of bad things have happened to me," said Carl, "and to you, and to all of us. But you don't see any of us turning into evil supervillains."

"I suppose not," said Porkins.

"Sometimes, there can be a fine line between what makes someone a good person or a bad person," said Spidroth. "Trust me, I know."

Dave thought about Robo-Steve and how he'd almost become a villain who'd wanted to rule the world. The Robo-Steve who Dave knew had been kind and gentle, but Future Dave, a version of Dave from an alternate timeline, had known a different Robo-Steve — a Robo-Steve who had caused countless death and suffering.

Suddenly they reached the end of the warped forest biome, and Dave was shaken from his thoughts. In front of them was a huge river of lava.

"How are we going to cross this?" Alex asked.

"We ride striders," said Saggo, pointing at some red creatures wading in the lava.

"Wow," said Alex, "those things are cool — they can walk in lava without burning up!"

Dave was surprised to hear that Alex had never seen a strider before, but he supposed that they hadn't been in existence very long. It had only been a few weeks, or maybe months (Dave had lost track of time) since the Nether had fast-forwarded, changing beyond all recognition. The old Nether had been a barren place full of endless netherrack and lava, but the new Nether contained different biomes and strange new creatures like these striders.

Dave had ridden on the back of a strider before, but he wasn't looking forward to repeating the experience. Even though riding striders seemed safe enough, he still didn't like the idea of crossing lava on the back of some strange creature.

Saggo reached into her white dress and pulled out a handful of fishing rods.

"Saggo sneak these away from wedding," the piglin said proudly. "Warped fungus on stick was for wedding guests to cross lava river to see fireworks, but fixing Boggo more important."

She handed them each a fishing rod. Dave saw that each rod had a blue-green mushroom with orange spots on the end of it – warped fungus.

"Cool," said Alex, looking at her rod. "Do those strider things like these mushrooms then?"

"Striders love warped fungus," said Saggo. She walked to the edge of the lava river and dangled her rod towards the striders, shaking the warped fungus on the end of it. "Dinnertime striders! Come get dinner from Saggo!"

The striders quickly spotted the warped fungus and walked over towards Saggo. Dave had seen striders before, but he still couldn't get used to them – they were such unique creatures, unlike anything else in the Nether or the Overworld. Bright red, their bodies were large squares with far apart eyes, drooping mouths and wisps of thin, string-like hair on their temples. They had no arms, just two long red legs. The bottom of their legs were grey and crusty, which Dave supposed came from a lifetime of walking in lava.

Saggo walked backward, forcing the striders to come on land to get the fungus. The striders hesitated a moment, then walked out of the lava. Immediately their skin turned purple, and they began to shiver.

"Striders don't like being out of lava," Poffo said. "Striders get cold."

How the striders could ever be cold in the Nether, where it was always warm, Dave had no idea. He supposed that if they normally lived in lava, they were used to quite high heats.

Saggo put her warped fungus on a stick away before the striders could get it, then she pulled some saddles out from somewhere in her dress and placed them on the striders. Once all the striders had saddles, she turned towards Dave and the rest of the group.

"You can ride striders now," she told them. "Get on saddles and use warped fungus to guide them."

"Oh, I get it," said Alex. "It's like using a carrot on a stick to guide a pig."

"Saggo no know what is carrot on stick," said Saggo. "Saggo no know what is pig."

Even though Alex had never ridden a strider before, she easily clambered onto hers, and within seconds was guiding it around using the warped fungus on the end of the fishing rod.

"This is fun!" she said happily, then she walked her strider straight into lava, without a care in the world.

"Er, how am I going to ride a strider?" Carl asked. "The last time I rode one of those things, I didn't have my golem suit – thanks to Boggo."

"Just get on strider and ride," said Saggo.

"My golem suit might be a bit heavy for it," said Carl. "It is too heavy for horses."

"Saggo no know what is horse, but strider is strong," said Saggo. "Strider can carry Carl."

"If you say so," said Carl reluctantly. "But don't blame me if I squish this strider flat."

Carl still had Boggo under his arm, but his golem suit was so tall that he easily climbed onto the strider's saddle without needing to pull himself up. For a moment, the strider wobbled, but then it seemed perfectly fine. As Saggo had said, it was able to take Carl's weight, and Carl was sitting on it with no problem.

"Saggo told Carl," grinned Saggo. "Strider strong."

"So, this is what riding feels like," said Carl, with a grin. "It's kind of cool."

Keeping Boggo under one arm, Carl held the warped fungus on a stick in the other hand, dangling it in front of his strider. The strider walked forward, walking into the lava.

"Carl be careful not to drop Boggo in lava," said Saggo, giving Carl a concerned look.

"I make no promises," said Carl.

"BURR," said Boggo.

Everyone else had led their striders into the lava now, so Dave did the same, dangling the warped fungus out in front of it using his fishing rod.

"CRRURP," said the strider, then it walked forward. As the strider began walking across the lava, Dave could feel the heat all around him.

Just one slip-up, and I'll be dead, Dave thought, looking down at the lava all around him. He knew he was secure on the saddle, but it didn't stop him from feeling scared. He didn't think he'd ever get used to riding across lava, no matter how many times he did it.

"Come on," said Saggo. "Follow Saggo."

Saggo began leading her strider across the lava lake, and the others followed behind her. As they got closer to the opposite shore, Dave saw that it was a basalt delta biome – a bleak gray biome made from hills of basalt and blackstone. Of all the new Nether biomes, it was certainly the least welcoming.

"Isn't there a more scenic route we can take?" Carl asked. "Those basalt biomes aren't very inviting."

"There are alternate routes, sir, but they will take much longer," said P1Go.

"So how come you're good now anyway?" Carl asked the robot. "Or is this one big evil plan to lead us into a trap?"

"I am neither good nor bad," said P1Go. "I am programmed to obey orders and offer assistance. My primary function is to serve the Empress above all others, but because she's gone now, I can serve anyone who asks me for assistance."

"Dear boy, when you say 'gone,' you do mean 'dead,' don't you?" Porkins asked. "The Empress is dead, isn't she?"

"I do not believe so," said P1Go. "The last time I saw her, she was starting to build a new golem army amongst the ruins of her castle, then she disappeared. My scanners have been unable to detect here, so I suspect she has left the Nether."

Dave didn't like that news one bit. He and the others had believed the Empress had died when Steve had destroyed her castle, but it looked like she'd survived. Whatever she was up to, he was sure that it was nothing good.

Finally, they reached the shore of the basalt delta biome. They walked their striders up onto the land and climbed off the saddles. The striders were all purple and shivering. Saggo reached into her pockets and pulled out some warped fungus, throwing them to the striders, who caught the mushrooms in their mouths.

"You go now, striders," she said. "Saggo grateful for striders' help."

The striders all walked off back into the lava, where their skin immediately became red again and they stopped shivering.

"Riding those things was fun," said Alex. "They're like lava horses."

"What is horse thing everyone keeps talking about?" said Saggo, looking very confused.

"Come on," said Dave. "We should get a move on."

Saggo walked over to Boggo, who was still zombified and held underneath Carl's golem arm.

"Don't worry, Boggo," Saggo said softly. "We fix you soon."

"RURRK," said Boggo.

They began their journey across the basalt delta. Unlike the warped forest biome, where they could walk casually through it, the hills of the delta were so steep that they had to climb most of the way, squeezing between gaps and clambering up and down jagged peaks. Before long, Dave's arms and legs were aching from the strain. It didn't help that the air was thick with fog and ash, making it difficult to breathe. They had to go slowly, as there were constant drops and chasms, many of them with lava down below. There were lava waterfalls as well, the orange liquid pouring from the gray ceiling of the biome, high above them.

They were clambering across a particularly steep hill when Alex held up a hand, indicating that they should all be quiet.

"Can you hear that?" she whispered.

Dave could hear it too now, a thudding sound coming from somewhere above them. He looked up, and for a moment, he couldn't see anything, just jagged peaks of basalt and blackstone above them, but then a huge square creature bounded into view on a cliff above them.

"Magma cubes!" Poffo shouted, the panic rising in his voice.

The magma cube was a dark red color — so dark that it was almost black. Like a slime, its body was a perfect cube, with no arms and legs, just two glowing orange eyes.

The cube jumped and fell through the air towards them.

That thing is huge! Dave had time to think.

"Everyone scatter!" Spidroth screamed.

They all got out of the way as best they could, which was difficult as they were on a jagged peak of rock without many places to go. Dave clambered down the rock face just in time as the magma cube landed above them. It was so heavy that the peak shook, and Dave almost lost his grip. He looked down and saw that there was a stream of lava far below him that he hadn't seen before. If he fell, he would be doomed.

The magma cube jumped again and fell straight towards Dave. This time there was nowhere for him to go – he was on a narrow crop of rock with nowhere to move to.

"Dave, grab my hand!"

Dave turned. It was Carl – the creeper was standing on a nearby ledge, holding out one of his golem arms for Dave. He was still a couple of blocks away, so Dave was going to have to jump. He took a deep breath, then leaped through the air, just as the magma cube smashed onto the ledge behind him. Dave grabbed hold of Carl's golem arm, clinging on for dear life. He looked behind and saw that the magma cube was too big for the ledge, and it toppled off, falling down into the lava below.

Carl lifted Dave and dropped him safely on the ledge next to him.

"Thanks, buddy," Dave said, wiping the sweat from his forehead.

"Don't thank me yet," said Carl, looking up. "Our troubles aren't over!"

Dave looked up and saw that Carl was right — more magma cubes were leaping off ledges above them, raining down from the sky.

"Everyone, keep moving!" Dave shouted. "We need to find shelter! We need to get out of here!

As the magma cubes fell down all around them, Dave and the others all made their way forward as fast as they could, clambering around jagged rocks while avoiding getting squished. Every time a magma cube landed, the ground shook, so they had to be careful not to lose their grip.

Dave was just about to jump from one steep spiral of rock to another when a magma cube fell through the air just in front of him. He breathed a deep sigh of relief – if he'd jumped any sooner, the cube would have landed on him in mid air and the two of them would have fallen into the lava pool below.

"Poffo no like adventures anymore!" whined Poffo, clinging on to the side of a jagged basalt pillar. "Poffo scared!"

Dave joined him on the pillar and put a hand on the piglin's shoulder.

"It's okay to be scared, Poffo," he said. "But we need to keep going if we're going to avoid getting squished."

To illustrate his point, a magma cube slammed into a pillar just above them. It turned to face them, then jumped again, falling right towards them.

"Jump!" Dave shouted.

Poffo jumped to the next pillar, and Dave jumped after him, both of them escaping just in time to avoid getting squished by the magma cube.

"There's a cave!" Alex shouted from somewhere ahead. Dave looked over and saw that she was far ahead of all of them. With her ninja skills, she'd been able to jump from pillar to pillar with ease. Behind Alex, Dave saw the entrance to a cave cut into the side of a huge gray mountain.

Up ahead, Poffo and Saggo were jumping from basalt spire to basalt spire, heading towards the cave, when suddenly, Saggo slipped. She fell and just managed to hold onto a ledge by the tips of her trotters. Far below her, a pool of lava surrounded the foot of the spire. If she fell, she would get fried.

"Help!" Saggo screamed. "Saggo no want to die!"

Spidroth, Alex and P1G0 were ahead, and Carl and Dave were behind, and they all began rushing forward to help Saggo. But before they got there, Poffo reached down a trotter.

"Poffo save Saggo!" said Poffo. "Grab Poffo's trotter!"

Saggo reached down and grabbed Poffo, who then pulled her up. The two of them sat on the ledge, breathing heavily.

"Poffo save Saggo," said Saggo. "Poffo is hero."

Poffo blushed.

"Poffo just saving friend," said Poffo.

"Hurry up, fools," said Spidroth. "Get to the cave!"

They all rushed forward, jumping from spire to spire until all of them were safely in the cave. Dave looked out and saw that more magma cubes were raining from the sky, slamming into the pillars or landing straight in lava.

"I hate this biome," said Carl.

"How's Boggo doing?" Dave asked.

Carl looked down at the zombified piglin under his arm. Boggo still looked as gormless and zombified as before. Although Dave had to admit he was the smartest dressed zombie he'd ever seen — there weren't many zombies who wore wedding suits.

"I think he's fine," said Carl, "although he's starting to smell a bit. It must be all the moldy flesh."

"Poor Boggo," said Saggo, walking over to her husband-to-be. "Saggo will save you, my love. Saggo promise."

"Come on, you guys," said Alex, who had gone slightly ahead in the cave. "I think the basalt biome comes to an end here. I can see some kind of weird red forest up ahead."

"A crimson forest biome," said P1Go. "In general, those are far safer than basalt delta biomes."

"Well, as long as there aren't any giant cubes raining from the sky, that's good with me," said Carl. "Now, let's hurry this up — Boggo is really starting to stink."

CHAPTER FIVE
Zombified Piglins

After the chaotic spires, cliffs and lava pools of the basalt delta biome, the crimson forest biome seemed like a haven. Giant crimson mushrooms grew all around them, many of them with strange lamp-like glowing blocks inside them that P1Go said were called shroomlights. Red vines hung down from the giant mushrooms, and smaller mushrooms littered the ground. The ground itself was made from a squishy red material a bit like grass, called nylium.

Dave was starting to think that this biome would be a pleasant place to live, but then he caught sight of some hoglins in the distance – huge, pig-like creatures with fierce tusks. Dave had fought hoglins before and did not care to repeat the experience, so they kept as far away from the huge beasts as possible.

After walking for a while, they began to feel hungry. It was hard to know how much time had passed in the Nether since there were no days or nights, so Dave had no idea if it was actually lunchtime, but from the growling of his stomach, he guessed that it must be near. So they all picked some mushrooms, then Porkins and P1Go cooked them in smokers. Dave was a little worried that the smell of cooking mushrooms might attract hoglins, but thankfully none of the huge beasts approached them. The group all sat down, eating their mushrooms and chatting.

Carl tried to feed Boggo some mushrooms, but the zombified piglin just spat them back out.

"HAHOO!" grunted Boggo.

"Zombified piglins do not need to eat," said P1Go. "At least regular zombified piglins don't."

"What do you mean, 'regular'?" asked Dave.

"Most zombified piglins aren't former piglins like Boggo," explained P1Go. "Most of them were born that way. For generations, zombified piglins have bred in the Nether, so most of the zombified piglins you see here have parents who are zombies as well. A regular piglin rarely gets bitten by a zombified piglin, as zombified piglins normally only attack when provoked."

"I'm not sure about that, old chap," said Porkins. "Every time I've bumped into zombified piglins, those blighters have always been jolly aggressive. They wiped out an army of illagers, and they tried to attack Carl, Alex and I as well."

"Yes, recently zombified piglins have been unusually aggressive in the Nether," said P1Go. "As I said before, I am currently unaware of what the reason for this is. But we should try to avoid zombified piglins if possible. They are fairly weak but usually congregate in vast numbers."

"We should avoid crazy zombie piglins," said Carl, "got it."

"Why did Boggo transform into a zombie?" Alex asked. "He wasn't bitten."

"As mentioned before, the Empress correctly theorized that piglins who went to the Overworld would transform into zombies," said P1Go. "That is why when she sent her piglin soldiers to capture your group, Steve and Herobrine, she gave the piglins a special potion to stop them from transforming. She also theorized that a hoglin that went to the overworld would become zombified as well."

"A zombie hoglin," said Carl. "I don't like the sound of that."

"The Empress called this theoretical creature a 'zoglin,'" said P1Go.

"That is a pretty cool name," said Carl. "I know the Empress was crazy and evil, but it sounds like she was good at naming stuff."

After they'd eaten, they started walking through the crimson forest again. Dave decided to make the most of his time in the forest by collecting some of the unique blocks and items. He used his diamond axe to chop some blocks of crimson wood from the stems of the huge mushrooms (P1Go informed him that the proper name for the blocks was 'crimson stems' rather than 'crimson wood'). He also picked some of the red mushrooms with orange spots that littered the ground. P1Go informed him that these crimson fungus were useful for breeding hoglins (although why anyone would want to breed hoglins, Dave had no idea) but that warped fungus, the cyan mushrooms with orange spots found in warped forest biomes, could be placed in plant pots to keep hoglins away, as the huge beasts had a strange aversion to them. Whenever a group of hoglins began to walk too close towards them, P1Go would place some warped fungus down on the ground to keep them away.

Stiff, stringy plants called crimson roots grew on the ground as well, so Dave put some of them in his bag, even though P1Go told him they didn't have many practical uses. He collected some of the crimson vines that hung down from the mushrooms as well. P1Go was more positive about these, saying that they grew down from blocks if placed correctly and could be used as makeshift ladders.

Dave's favorite block in the crimson forest were the shroomlights. They were squishy orange cubes that grew on the underside of the giant mushroom cups, and they emitted light without being attached to a redstone circuit. Dave was sure they'd come in useful, so he tried to collect as many as possible.

The walk through the forest was so pleasant that Dave almost forgot that they were on a quest to save Boggo, and it was only the occasional *"BURR"* from Boggo that reminded him.

I could actually imagine living here, Dave thought to himself. *I could have a nice house made from crimson stem, with plant pots with warped fungus all around the house, to keep away the hoglins. If I had a nether portal next to my house, I could go back and visit the Overworld whenever I liked.*

It was just as Dave was in the middle of these pleasant daydreams that he heard a not so pleasant sound coming from his left. He turned and saw that something was going on in the distance.

"What's going on over there?" Spidroth asked, peering in the same direction. Some sort of creatures were moving towards them, but there were so many giant mushrooms and vines in the way that it was hard to see what they were.

Carl squinted. The creeper had the best eyesight out of any of them.

"Oh no," said Carl, his black eyes going wide. "Zombie piglins!"

"Their official name is zombified piglins," said P1G0.

"I couldn't care less what you call them," said Carl, "hundreds of them are coming this way!"

"Poffo run!" shouted Poffo before running off between the giant mushrooms.

"I think that fool has the right idea," said Spidroth. "Everyone run!"

They all began dashing through the forest, weaving their way past the giant mushrooms and around roots and vines. As they ran, Dave turned and saw that the zombified piglins were gaining on them. He'd never seen zombies moving that fast.

"Do zombified piglins always move that quickly?" Dave asked P1G0.

"No," said the robot. "Ever since they've become more aggressive, they seem to have become faster as well. It really is perplexing."

"Well, if they catch us, it's going to be perplexing how dead we are," said Carl.

"I do not believe that is a proper use of the word perplexing," said P1G0.

Carl rolled his eyes and kept on running.

Finally, they ran out of the crimson forest and found

themselves on the shore of a huge lava river. On the other side of the river was a colossal black castle. It looked like it had been abandoned for some time, with parts of its towers broken in places. There was a narrow black bridge leading across the river to the castle.

"That's a bastion remnant," said P1Go. "One of the castles that used to be controlled by the Empress during the time of the Bastion Empire. They were abandoned long ago."

"Will it be safe in there?" Dave asked.

"I do not know," admitted the robot.

"Well, it will be safer than here," said Carl, turning around and looking at the zombified piglins rushing through the crimson forest towards them.

Dave had to agree. If they didn't escape now, zombified piglins were going to get them. He didn't like the look of the bastion remnant one bit, but there didn't seem to be any other choice.

"Come on, we'll cross the bridge and destroy it behind us!" Dave shouted.

They all ran towards the bridge. The bridge was long but only four blocks wide, with walls on either side to stop anyone from falling off into the lava. Dave and the others all ran across the bridge, crossing the lava river. When they reached halfway, Dave turned and pulled out some blocks of TNT. He placed the TNT across the bridge as quickly as he could.

"Everyone stand back!" Dave shouted. He pulled out some flint and steel and lit one of the TNT blocks. It flashed white. Dave ran away from the TNT as fast as he could, then heard it explode behind him.

KADOOOOOOM!!!!!!!

The explosion was so large that Dave was sent flying forward and landed on his front. He pushed himself to his feet and turned around. The bridge had broken, and the zombified piglins were on the other side, snorting angrily that they couldn't get across.

"See you later, losers!" Alex shouted at the zombified piglins.

"We will have to see them later," said P1Go. "We're going to have to come back this way when we return to the wedding."

TNT
TNT

"Oh," said Alex. "Er, sorry about calling you losers, guys. No hard feelings."

"Come on," said Dave, looking up at the huge black castle. "Let's make our way through this place as fast as we can. I don't like the look of it one bit."

"Saggo scared," said the piglin, looking up at the black castle. "When Empress alive, piglins used to go into bastion remnants and not come out. Bastion remnants scary places."

"I'm sure it will be fine," said Dave. "The Empress is gone now, remember?"

"Saggo suppose so," said Saggo, although she sounded very unsure. Dave was very unsure himself, but he tried to put on a brave face.

"Weapons at the ready," said Dave. "Let's make sure we're ready for whatever we find in here."

"I think that's a jolly good idea, old chap," said Porkins, looking up at the castle. "A jolly good idea indeed."

CHAPTER SIX
The Bastion Remnant

As they walked through the entrance to the colossal black castle, a chill went down Dave's spine. The bastion remnant was like something out of a horror movie, with black walls and lanterns hanging down from the ceiling with chains. The walls were made from black bricks, some of them cracked in places. They were in a large hallway, but there were gaps in the walls, the ceiling and the floor where they could see through to other rooms. Porkins almost fell into a hole in the floor, but thankfully P1Go grabbed his arm just in time.

"Good gosh," said Porkins, looking down at the hole. "You saved my bacon there, dear chap."

Dave walked carefully over and looked down into the hole. Below was a pool of lava. If P1Go hadn't stopped Porkins, the pigman would have fallen straight into it.

"Watch your footing, everyone," said Dave.

The layout of the bastion remnant was very confusing, with passages and stairways going off in lots of different directions. It was made all the more confusing by all the gaps in the walls, so it was hard to know where one hallway or staircase ended and another began.

"Wait," said Carl, who was walking slightly ahead of them, "is that gold?"

Dave walked over to him. Carl was looking at one of the black blocks in the wall that had thin lines of shiny yellow material running through it.

"Gold!" said Poffo excitedly. He pulled out a golden pickaxe and immediately began hacking at the block. Once he'd destroyed it, some gold nuggets fell to the ground. Poffo quickly picked them up and stuffed them into his pockets.

“Was that some kind of gold ore?” Dave asked.

“Yes,” said P1GO. “Those blocks are known as *gilded blackstone.* They sometimes appear in the walls of bastion remnants and are a good place to mine gold from.”

Dave looked around and saw that there were other black blocks with veins of gold running through them. Poffo was running around, mining as much gold as he could. Dave had seen before that piglins liked gold, but it was as if Poffo was caught in some sort of frenzy – he was obsessed with getting every little bit of gold that he could. Dave turned around and saw that Saggo was looking at the gold with envious eyes. It was clear that she wanted to mine it too, but she managed to hold herself back.

“That’s enough of that,” said Spidroth, grabbing Poffo’s pickaxe arm. “We are on a mission to save your friend, don’t forget.”

“Oh yeah,” said Poffo, looking around at Boggo, who was still zombified and underneath Carl’s arm. “Poffo forgot.”

It was like Poffo had come out of a trance. He looked sleepy and was rubbing his head.

Piglins seem to be almost addicted to gold, Dave thought to himself.

They walked on, weaving their way through narrow hallways, doing their best not to fall through gaps in the floor into pools of lava. Poffo finally seemed to be over his thirst for gold, but then they came across something that made the piglin’s eyes go wide: a solid gold block right in the middle of one of the walls. Poffo dashed over and ran his trotters along the smooth gold surface. There were a couple of other gold blocks in the walls nearby as well, Dave saw.

“A solid gold block!” Poffo said, tears in his eyes. “Poffo always dream of having solid gold house!”

“Well, keep dreaming, pig face,” said Carl, giving Poffo a light whack on the back of the head. Poffo immediately shook himself out of his trance, but he still couldn’t keep his beady white eyes off the gold block.

They came around another corner, and this time there was a small wooden chest against one of the walls. Dave opened the chest and saw that it was full of a variety of different items and blocks. There were blocks of blackstone, a few tools made from both diamond and iron, some chains, some porkchops and a set of golden armor. Dave pocketed most of the items, but he gave the golden armor to Poffo.

"Thank you, thank you, thank you," said Poffo, quickly putting the armor on.

"Fool," said Spidroth. "Do you know how easily gold armor breaks?"

"Poffo no care," said Poffo. "Poffo look cool."

There was a spare golden helmet, so Dave gave it to Saggo. She looked very odd, wearing a full white wedding dress and a golden helmet on her head.

"Does Saggo look pretty?" she asked Dave.

"Er, yes, very pretty," said Dave. He noticed Spidroth giving him a suspicious look, so he quickly said: "let's keep moving, shall we?"

They walked down a short staircase and found themselves in a large open area, with several hoglins roaming about. There was a patch of brown soul sand on the ground with red nether wart growing out of it, and some of the hoglins were grazing on the nether wart. Like the rest of the castle, this area was ruined and decayed, with walls missing and gaps in the ceiling and floor. Looking around the room, Dave guessed it had once been a stable of some kind, with pens for the hoglins. The pens were all broken now, and the hoglins were roaming about wherever they pleased. Dave and the others kept as far away from the hoglins as they could, walking around the edge of the room and trying their best not to attract attention. A couple of the hoglins looked at them, but thankfully they didn't attack.

After walking through a few more broken hallways, they reached the biggest room they'd seen so far. It was a tall room, many stories high. Far below them, the floor of the room was covered in lava, with a few blackstone blocks placed in the lava in a grid pattern. Dave and the others were on one of the upper floors of the huge room. On the other side of the room, Dave spotted the first living creatures he'd seen since they'd entered the bastion remnant — some piglins wearing black rags. Each of them had a huge gold belt buckle and a strange gold gauntlet strapped to one of their arms. There were about five of them, and they were holding golden axes. They seem to be patrolling, walking back and forth around the room.

"Piglin brutes," whispered Saggo darkly. "Those are bad piglins."

"What's a piglin brute?" Alex asked.

"Piglin brutes were the Empress's top commandos," said P1Go. "They were highly trained warriors and very dangerous. The Empress trained them to obey her every command, and since her disappearance, most of them have stayed loyal, guarding her bases and castles for when she returns."

"Oh, come on," said Carl. "How dangerous can a few piglins be?"

"Do not underestimate them, sir," said P1Go.

"Piglin brutes very tough," whispered Poffo. "If they catch us, we in big trouble."

"More like 'pig trouble,'" said Carl, grinning.

Everyone looked around at him.

"What?" said Carl. "It was a funny joke. You lot just don't appreciate good humor."

The piglin brutes had gathered on a walkway on the right to have a chat, Dave saw. The path along the left side of the room was completely unguarded.

"Now's our chance," Dave whispered. "Come on."

Dave led the way, walking quickly and quietly along the walkway. He tried not to look down at the lava pool a few stories below them.

Who would build a massive room with a pool of lava at the bottom? Dave wondered. He couldn't see what practical use a room like this had, but everything in the bastion remnant was so decayed and ruined that maybe the room had made sense at some point.

Up ahead of them was a doorway. If they could reach the doorway before the piglin brutes saw them, they could leave the massive room safely. Dave glanced to his left and saw that the piglin brutes still hadn't noticed them.

Dave stood by the doorway, ushering the others through. Spidroth and Alex went through first, followed by Porkins, Saggo and Poffo, then P1G0 the robot, and finally Carl, with Boggo still under his arm. Carl ducked his head down and was just about to go through the doorway when Boggo let out a groan.

"HORR!"

Immediately, Dave heard angry snorts behind him. He turned and saw the piglin brutes on the other side of the room had finally noticed them. They had their golden axes in their hands and were rushing around the edge of the room towards them.

They may be tough, but there's only five of them, Dave thought, taking out his diamond sword. *We'll easily defeat them.*

Then he heard snorting behind him. He turned around and saw more piglin brutes rushing towards him from the other side of the room as well. Down on the other floors of the huge room, he could see piglin brutes running up staircases, all of them heading in the direction of him and Carl.

"It looks like we're going to be running for our lives again," said Carl. "Just like old times."

"It looks that way," agreed Dave. "RUN!!!"

CHAPTER SEVEN
Battle with the Brutes

Dave and Carl ran through the doorway, where the others were waiting for them in a ruined hallway.

"What's going on?" Alex asked. "What's all that snorting?"

"The piglin brutes are coming for us," said Dave. "And there are a lot of them."

Alex took out her two diamond swords, Spidroth took out her red sword, and Porkins notched an arrow on his bow.

"I've never been to a wedding before," said Carl, flexing his golem arms, "but I can confidently say that this is the worst wedding of all time."

"Carl, don't be rude about Saggo's wedding," said Saggo crossly.

"Come on," said Dave. "We need to get out of here."

Dave began running down the hallway, but then he heard snorts coming from up ahead of them. It seemed that the piglins were closing in on them on all sides.

"It looks like we don't have any choice but to fight," said Dave, gripping his diamond sword tightly. He wished he still had his old netherite blade, but that had been destroyed in the lava when Spidroth defeated Mad Mulligan.

Dave didn't have much faith that either Saggo or Poffo would be much use in the battle, but then he remembered P1Go.

"Can you fight?" he asked the robot.

"I do have self-defense protocols," said P1Go. "If I am attacked, I'm programmed to defend myself."

"Well, you're about to be attacked," said Carl. "So get defending."

A hatch slid open in the middle of the silver robot's chest, then

P1Go reached inside and pulled out a netherite sword.

"Defense mode initiated," she said, holding the sword out in front of her. Her eyes began to glow red.

The horde of piglin brutes, all wearing black rags and holding golden axes, ran through the doorway, out of the large room that Dave and the others had just left. Simultaneously, a horde of piglin brutes ran towards them from the other end of the hallway.

To Dave's surprise, Poffo had taken out a netherite sword and was standing next to him, ready to fight the brutes.

"You know how to use a sword, Poffo?" Dave asked.

"Poffo was in Empress's army," said Poffo. "Poffo may not be as well trained as a piglin brutes, but Poffo can still fight."

Dave was even more surprised to see Saggo holding a crossbow. She looked quite the sight, in her white wedding dress and gold helmet.

"Saggo will defend her true love Boggo," said Saggo defiantly.

"Are you going to be all right fighting with Boggo under your arm?" Dave asked Carl.

I'll be fine," said Carl. "I only need one arm to beat up these bozos."

"BURR," said Boggo.

"We need to defend from both directions," Dave told them all. "Carl, P1Go and Poffo, you stay on this side with me, and Spidroth,

Alex, Porkins and Saggo, you four stay on the other side."

"Got it, old chap," said Porkins. "Let's give these blaggards a darn good thrashing. Pip pip, tally-ho, chocks away!"

"Porkins say funny words," said Saggo. "Does Porkins's brain work properly?"

"Here they come!" said Dave.

"Yes, I can see that," said Carl, rolling his eyes. "I am standing right next to you."

The piglin brutes rushed into them from either side, and the battle began. Immediately the brutes began hacking away at Dave with their golden axes, much more viciously than Dave would have expected. He raised his diamond sword to block the blows but was unable to block all of them. Thankfully, his netherite armor was able to block the blows as well, but the brutes were hitting him so fast that he wasn't sure how much more his armor would be able to take before it broke.

Next to him, Carl was swinging his right arm at the brutes, sending them flying, while continuing to hold Boggo under his left arm. However, after a few of them had been sent flying, the piglin brutes wisened up to Carl's attack strategy and began ducking out of the way of his arm swings, then rushing over and swinging their golden axes into the golem suit. Carl kicked and punched them away as best he could, but more of them kept coming.

Poffo was fighting surprisingly well, swinging his netherite sword to block the blows from the golden axes. However, a few of the brutes managed to hit him on his golden chest plate, and it broke, leaving his middle exposed.

"Poffo, get behind Carl!" Dave shouted. "You can't fight them without your armor!"

Poffo reluctantly did as Dave said, standing behind Carl to keep safe.

Of the four warriors on Dave's side, P1Go was putting up the best fight. The silver pig woman robot was swinging her sword so fast that it was a blur, blocking the blows from the piglin's axes, then slashing away at them until they went *POOF*. Her fighting style reminded Dave a lot of Robo-Steve's, and he felt a sharp pang in his chest when he remembered that his old friend was gone. He shook the thought of Robo-Steve from his head, remembering that he needed to concentrate and continue to fight on. It took all of Dave's concentration to block the axe blows, so he needed his wits about him.

Out of the corner of his eye, Dave could see the other four warriors fighting off the piglin brutes that were attacking from the other end of the hallway. Alex and Spidroth were swinging their swords at the piglin brutes, fighting them off as best they could. Dave was surprised to see that even Alex and Spidroth weren't able to take the piglin brutes down easily. Normally, the two women could cut down enemies as if they were nothing, but the brutes were fierce warriors.

Porkins and Saggo were behind Alex and Spidroth and had built themselves small towers, two blocks high. They stood on the towers, shooting arrows down at the brutes: Porkins from his bow and Saggo from her crossbow.

Dave turned back to focus on his own battle. A piglin brute swung its axe down at him, and Dave raised his diamond sword to meet the blow. Once he'd blocked the attack, Dave quickly swung his diamond sword back, then stabbed it forward at the brute's chest. The brute staggered backward, flashing red, then swung his axe at Dave once more. Dave ducked down, so the brute just swung at the air, then slashed his sword at the brute once more. When the blow connected this time, the brute exploded in a puff of smoke – *POOF*.

Some of the brutes had climbed up onto Carl's golem suit and were hacking away at it with their golden axes. Carl was doing his best to shake them off, but he'd had to duck down into the suit to protect his head, and he'd shoved Boggo into the suit as well, to protect the piglin. Dave was going to go over and help Carl, but before he could, Poffo ran forward, hitting the piglin brutes with his sword to get them off Carl. P1Go ran over as well, grabbing the brutes by the shoulders and yanking them off of Carl. Once all the brutes were off his golem suit, Carl reached into their head hole and pulled Boggo out, putting him back under his arm, then his little creeper head popped out. Carl charged forward towards the brutes once more, swinging his right arm and sending them flying.

Finally, almost all of the piglin brutes had been slain. The few that remained ran off, snorting angrily.

"You are traitors to Empress," one of the brutes said angrily. "When she returns, you be in big trouble!"

"Empress not coming back," said Saggo angrily. "Empress gone forever."

The brutes grunted, then disappeared back down the hallways. When they were gone, Dave and the others were alone once more.

"Come on," said Dave. "Let's get out of this castle before more of them turn up."

CHAPTER EIGHT
The Island

They wandered through the confusing maze of ruined black hallways until finally they found the exit. They walked out of the bastion remnant and found themselves in a biome full of red netherrack hills and lava. It looked just like the old Nether before it had changed. In the distance, Dave could see huge white ghasts floating in the sky and herds of red striders walking through the lava.

"A nether wastes biome," said P1Go.

"Back in my day, all the Nether was like this," said Porkins sadly.

P1Go looked at him strangely.

"The Nether hasn't been like that for over a million years," said the robot. "Surely you can't be that old?"

"It's complicated," said Carl. "It involves a lot of weird time stuff."

"Wait," said P1Go, looking at Porkins, "you're a pigman, aren't you, sir? Just like Empress Chops?"

"That's enough talking," said Dave. "We need to get moving."

Dave knew that the subject of the old Nether and the Empress was a sensitive one for Porkins. He didn't want P1Go to upset his friend by talking about the past.

"So how much further?" Spidroth asked as they walked along.

"Not long," said P1Go. "We should be at the laboratory in a couple of hours."

After they were a safe distance from the bastion remnant, they all sat down to have lunch. Or it might have been dinner or breakfast; Dave wasn't quite sure. As always, Carl ate baked potatoes, but instead of his usual two, he only ate one.

"Don't tell me you're finally running out of potatoes?" Dave asked him.

"I don't want to talk about it," said Carl grumpily.

Alex came over with some paper, and she and Carl started chatting, whispering to each other and drawing pictures.

"Are those fools still working on that comic?" Spidroth asked disapprovingly.

"It looks like it," said Dave. "Hey Carl," he shouted, "how's the comic going?"

"We're working on the chapter where Carl went down to the Phantom Realm to save you and Spidroth," said Alex.

"Er, I think you've got it the wrong way round," said Dave.

"I'm the main character in the book," said Carl. "We have to change some of the events to make sure I'm always the hero. It's just common sense."

"Ooo, and in our version of the story, Robo-Steve comes back from the Phantom Realm with you," said Alex. "I know it didn't happen in real life, but we're going to honor his memory by having him come back in the comic. Although when he comes back, he's going to get a cool new body."

"I was thinking jet black with red eyes," said Carl. "And his catchphrase is: 'I came back from the dead, and now you're going to get hit in the head.'"

"He says that to bad guys before he hits them in the head," Alex explained.

"That sounds nice," Dave smiled. "Not the hitting in the head part, but the Robo-Steve part."

"What is comic book?" asked Poffo, picking up one of Carl and Alex's pages.

"It's like a normal book, but it tells a story with pictures instead of words," said Alex. "Well, there are some words, but less than in a normal book. I don't really know how to explain it."

"Comic book look fun," said Poffo, studying the page. "Who is green worm in picture?"

"That's Carl," said Alex.

Poffo looked at the picture, then at Carl, and at the picture again, then at Carl again.

"Picture not good," said Poffo. "Does artist have small brain?"

"Give me that," said Carl, angrily grabbing the page off Poffo. "Some people just don't appreciate art."

Dave was having fun watching the others bicker, but he knew that they ought to get moving. Carl had climbed out of his golem suit, but Boggo was still underneath the golem's arm, squirming and *BURR*ing. Saggo was looking sadly at her husband-to-be. She looked like she wanted to cry.

"Come on, everyone," said Dave, standing up. "Let's go and save Boggo."

He put a hand on Saggo's shoulder. She looked up and smiled at him.

They resumed their journey, walking across the netherrack hills and making sure to keep well away from any ghasts. P1Go said that zombified piglins often roamed the nether wastes biomes, but thankfully there didn't seem to be any nearby.

Dave found himself walking next to Saggo. She still looked sad, but there was a look of determination on her face as well.

"How are you doing, Saggo?" Dave asked her.

"Saggo okay," said Saggo. "Saggo just hope we can save Boggo. Saggo miss him."

"So, have you two been in love long?" Dave asked, trying to make conversation.

"Not long," said Saggo. "Saggo and Boggo got talking after you help us defeat Empress. Boggo very clever and very handsome, so Saggo fall in love."

"Er, how lovely," said Dave. 'Clever' and 'handsome' weren't words he would have used to describe Boggo, but maybe it was true by piglin standards.

"Saggo was sad after Saggo's brother died," said Saggo, "but meeting Boggo made Saggo happy again."

"Oh, I'm sorry to hear about your brother," said Dave.

"Conko was good piglin," said Saggo. "Empress forced him to be in army, then he went on mission and never came back. Saggo was very sad."

Dave knew that the Empress had been Porkins's friend once, but the more he heard about her, the more horrible a person she seemed. It seemed she'd shown no respect for the lives of the piglins at all, using them as her slaves and her soldiers without caring if they lived or died.

They came over a hill, and Dave saw a huge lava lake at the bottom of a valley, with an island in the middle. The island was covered in blue-green mushrooms and vegetation – another warped forest biome. In the middle of the forest was a tower made from gold, rising high above the mushrooms.

"That tower is the laboratory," said P1Go. "That's where the cure will be."

"Island should be safe," said Poffo confidently. "Warped forest biome is safe normally. Only bad guys are endermen, and those are safe if you don't look at them."

"I'm not so sure about that," said Carl, squinting. "I can see some things between the mushrooms that don't look like endermen. They look more like zombified piglins."

"But zombified piglins no live in warped forest!" said Poffo.

"Let's just all be careful," said Dave. "If the Empress had a laboratory here, there's no telling what weird things we might come across. We'll try and sneak through the forest to the laboratory without attracting any attention, but we may need to fight if we get spotted. Have your weapons ready at all times."

They made their way down the netherrack slope towards the lake. There was an old ruined bridge made from blackstone bricks that went from the shore to the island. Dave and the others crossed the bridge, keeping their eyes peeled in case they were attacked. Once they reached the forest, there was a cyan haze in the air, and blue-green vegetation in every direction: huge mushrooms the size of trees with cyan caps and purple stems with blue veins running through them, blue-green vines that twisted in spirals down from the mushroom heads, stringy roots growing up from the ground, and instead of grass the ground was covered in a squishy blue-green material.

Dave led the way as they all walked through the forest, taking care to be as quiet as possible.

"Have you seen any more zombified piglins?" Dave whispered to Carl.

"Yeah, I can see a few in the distance, hidden by the vegetation," Carl whispered back. "Thankfully, it doesn't look as if they've spotted us yet."

The only positive about there being zombified piglins in the forest seemed to be that they had scared off all the endermen – or, at least, Dave never saw any endermen. As they got nearer to the center of the island, even Dave, whose eyes were nowhere near as sharp as Carl's, spotted some zombified piglins through the overgrowth. The nearer they got to the laboratory, the more zombified piglins there seem to be.

Finally, they could see the golden tower up ahead of them, through the vines and mushrooms. At the foot of the gold tower was an iron door with a button next to it. Unfortunately, there were also lots of zombified piglins wandering aimlessly about around the tower.

"We can take those zombies on," said Alex. "There's only about fifteen of them."

"The trouble is, once those ones see us and start snorting, all the other zombified piglins in the forest will know we're here too," said Dave.

"Good point," said Alex sadly.

"We need a distraction," said Spidroth. "Carl, you need to distract the zombified piglins."

"Er, what?" said Carl.

"In your golem suit, you're the fastest out of all of us," explained Spidroth. "You can easily outrun those zombies, and you can lead them away from the bottom of the tower. Then the rest of us will be able to enter without getting spotted."

"So, you want to sacrifice me to the zombies, do you?" said Carl. "That's just great."

"Don't be such a fool," snapped Spidroth. "Once you have escaped from the zombified piglins, you can run back around and join us at the tower. With the speed your suit can go, it should be easy. Or, if you'd prefer, I can put the golem suit on instead and show you how it's done."

"Okay, okay, I'll do it," said Carl, rolling his eyes. "But if it all goes wrong and I get killed, I'll be waiting in the Phantom Realm to beat you up."

"Fool," snapped Spidroth.

"All right, calm down, you two," said Dave. "That does seem like a good idea. You sure you're all right doing that, Carl?"

"Yeah, I guess so," said Carl, "but someone is going to have to carry Boggo."

"My strength is superior to the average organic being," said P1Go. "I can carry him if you like, sir."

Carl took Boggo from under his arm and handed him to the robot. She held him in her arms like a big ugly baby.

"ROOK," said Boggo.

"ROOK to you too," said Carl. "Right, wish me luck. And if I die, I want you all to know that you're big idiots."

"Thanks, Carl," said Alex cheerily.

Carl rolled his eyes, then began walking towards the golden tower. Dave and the others watched from behind some giant mushrooms as the creeper walked up to the tower in his golem suit.

"Hey, zombie idiots!" Carl shouted, waving his arms to get the zombified piglins' attention. "Delicious creeper here, all ready to be eaten. Come and get it!"

Immediately, all the zombified piglins in the area began rushing towards Carl. Carl legged it back into the warped forest, running off in a different direction from where Dave and the others were hiding. As he ran, more and more zombified piglins began to chase him until a whole horde of them were behind him.

I hope he doesn't trip up, Dave thought to himself, as Carl and the zombified piglins all disappeared into the forest, hidden by the vegetation.

"Right, come on, this is our chance," said Dave. "The tower is unguarded, so let's go in and get that cure for Boggo."

"BURR," said Boggo.

CHAPTER NINE
The Laboratory

They ran up to the golden tower. Dave pressed his hand on the button, and the iron door swung open. They all ran inside, and the door slammed shut behind them.

The floors, walls and ceiling of the laboratory were all made from gold blocks. There were some shroomlight blocks in the ceiling to light up the room. Around the edges of the room were crafting blocks that Dave was familiar with, such as crafting tables, furnaces and anvils, but there were also lots of strange computers and devices that he didn't recognize. He supposed they must all be things that the Empress had built. There were two stairways as well, one leading up and the other leading down. Since they were on the ground floor, Dave supposed that the tower must have a basement as well, or maybe several floors of basements.

Suddenly, the door swung open, and Carl squeezed through the doorway into the room. The door slammed shut behind him.

"I've lost the zombies," said Carl. "We should be safe. Probably."

"I hope you did it properly," said Spidroth, giving Carl a suspicious look. "If you messed up and led them back here..."

"I'm sure Carl did do it properly," said Dave, quickly saying something before Carl and Spidroth started arguing again. "Now, P1Go, where can we find this cure?"

The robot went over to one of the computer terminals and placed her robotic hand into a hole. Suddenly her eyes went from pink to green and began flickering. After a few seconds, her eyes turned back to normal, and she pulled her hand out of the hole.

"What was all that about?" Carl asked.

"I was interfacing with the local computer," said P1Go. "It

seems that the cure is on the bottom floor of the tower — floor minus five."

"Minus five?!" said Carl. "Are you telling me there are five floors below us?"

"yes, I am," said P1Go.

Dave didn't like the idea of going deep underground in this tower, but it seemed like they had no choice.

They made their way down the stairs. The stairway was lit by shroomlights embedded into the walls. They passed another floor of the laboratory, which was set out in a very similar way to the one above, but there were huge bones scattered about the floor — rib cages that were far too big to be any creature that Dave had ever seen. He had seen fossils like this before, though, scattered across the Nether.

They went down another floor, then another, then passed a floor where the lights had broken so they couldn't see anything, then finally they reached the bottom floor. The shroomlights on this floor were flickering, giving the laboratory a creepy quality. Dave had a shock when he saw what he thought were bits of bodies on some tables, but on closer inspection, they turned out to be bits of robots. The robots looked just like P1Go — silver pigmen.

"This place is giving me the creeps," said Carl, picking up a severed robot head and looking at it.

Suddenly a green image flickered into life in the middle of the room. Dave had seen an image like this before — it was a hologram. The hologram appeared to be of an elderly pig woman. She looked ancient and was using a walking stick.

"Chops," said Porkins sadly, looking at the hologram.

"I have been trapped in the Nether now for sixty-five years," said the hologram. "Despite my best efforts, I am unable to return to the Overworld. It seems that the Nether is still fast-forwarding, and until it slows down, travel to the Overworld will be impossible. I've tried building portals across the Nether to see if the fast-forwarding is only limited to some areas, but it seems that all of the Nether is in the same situation. I have no choice but to wait and build up my army. I have devised a computer system that allows anyone on the planet to be tracked, so as soon as the Nether stops fast-forwarding, I will be able to track down that traitor Porkins and the others who may be a threat to my plans. Once they are dealt with, my invasion of the Overworld will begin. Villagers and illagers alike will regret the way they treated the pigmen."

The image flickered and then disappeared.

"It's some kind of hologram diary," said Spidroth.

"Poor Chops," said Porkins. "She was so consumed by hatred. I can't believe she fell so far."

The hologram flickered into life again, but this time the elderly pig woman was sitting in a chair. Judging by her wrinkled face, she was much older than before, and bits of her body had been replaced by robotic parts. Her legs were both robot legs, and one of her arms was completely robotic too. The arm that wasn't robotic was withered and rested weakly on her lap.

"I have now been trapped in this forsaken place for one hundred and ten years," the hologram of the pig woman said bitterly. "I have had to use technology to prolong my life, but each year my body gets weaker. My empire is getting stronger though, and I now have fortresses all across the Nether. I will wait as long as it takes for the Nether to stop fast-forwarding, and when it does, I will have my vengeance!"

"She waited all that time to have her revenge, and then she messed it up," said Carl. "What a loser."

"Be quiet, Carl!" Porkins snapped. Dave was surprised — the pigman never normally got angry about anything.

The hologram flickered again, and this time the elderly pig woman was replaced by the version of the Empress that Dave had seen before — a grey floating skull surrounded by white blaze rods.

"It has been over half a million years now," the Empress hissed. "Without these hologram diaries, I believe I would have gone insane by now. I have no one to talk to. The piglins are all fools, and my robots are all sycophants who just do whatever I say. I feel my mind slipping, but I must keep going. I have tried everything to keep my body and my mind alive, and this form seems to be the best one so far. Blazes were developed by the Old People, who had far superior technology to our own. By combining my body with the blazes, I should no longer age. I miss having arms and legs, but I have my robots and my piglins to do things for me. It has been so long, but my mind is still focused on my revenge. When the time comes, I will have my vengeance. All the pain I've gone through will be nothing compared to what I do to the Overworld. Nothing!"

The hologram flickered off once more. They waited to see if it would turn on again, but it seemed to have finished.

"That was when she'd been in the Nether for half a million years," said Spidroth. "So it was another half a million years before we met her again. She must have been so lonely."

Dave was surprised to see Spidroth feeling such sympathy for someone else, but then he remembered that she had been in a similar situation — trapped in the void beneath the bedrock for countless years.

"Okay, this is all getting very gloomy," said Carl. "Where is the cure for Boggo?"

"Here," said P1Go. The silver pigman robot was standing next to a chest with a bottle of bubbling purple potion in her hand. "A couple of drops of this should turn Boggo back to normal."

"Then what we waiting for?" said Saggo, running over. P1Go had left Boggo on the ground, sitting up against the wall. He was staring around blankly, making the occasional snorting sound.

Saggo took the bottle from P1Go, then knelt down next to Boggo. He looked at her with blank eyes.

"Burr?" he said, sounding confused.

"Poffo, please hold Boggo's mouth open," said Saggo.

Poffo came over, knelt down next to Boggo, and used his trotters to hold Boggo's mouth open. Then Saggo tilted the bottle, letting a few drops of purple liquid fall into Boggo's mouth.

The change was almost immediate. Boggo started vibrating, and the green mold on his flesh began to disappear. Then pink flesh began to grow back over his exposed bits of bone until finally, he was back to normal again.

"Boggo had strange dream," said the piglin, rubbing his head.

"Oh, Boggo!" said Saggo, giving him a big hug.

"Aw, isn't it romantic?" said Alex.

"I suppose so," said Carl. "If you like that sort of thing."

Dave met Spidroth's gaze, but then the two of them quickly looked away from each other. Dave could feel his cheeks burning.

"Carl!" said Boggo, noticing the creeper for the first time. "Have you written best man speech for Boggo's wedding yet?"

"Written the speech?" said Carl incredulously. "No, I haven't; I've been too busy saving your life!"

"Thank you for saving Boggo's life, but don't forget to write speech," said Boggo. "Best man speech should be highlight of wedding, with good jokes and lots of emotion. But make sure it's not better than Boggo's speech. This is Boggo's wedding, so Boggo needs to be star."

Dave had a horrible vision of having to sit through hours and hours of piglins giving speeches. It was not a happy thought.

"Come on, it's time we were going," said Spidroth.

"Yes, we must get back in time for wedding," said Saggo.

"What time is the wedding?" Alex asked. "How do you tell time the Nether, anyway?"

"Piglins not very good at telling time," said Poffo. "That's why piglins always late for things."

"Yes," said Saggo. "Wedding should actually have been three days ago, but Boggo kept changing his mind about his suit."

"Boggo couldn't figure out whether he looked better in black or navy," said Boggo.

"Do you mean we've been rushing around this whole time, and the wedding was delayed anyway?" asked Carl. He rolled his eyes.

They made their way back up the stairs until they reached the ground floor again.

"Someone should check to see if there are any zombified piglins out there," said Carl.

"I'll do it," said Spidroth, walking up to the iron door. She pressed the button next to it, and the door swung open. She looked around the door, then pulled her head back. The door slammed shut.

"Well?" asked Carl. "Are there any there?"

"Yes," said Spidroth, her cheeks going pale. "By my estimate, at least three hundred, maybe more. The tower is completely surrounded."

CHAPTER TEN
The Staircase

They made their way up the staircases to the top of the golden tower. When they got there, they climbed out of a trapdoor onto the roof and looked out across the island. There were hundreds of zombified piglins surrounding them in every direction, all of them standing perfectly still.

"Is it just me, or do the zombified piglins look a lot more organized than they were before?" Carl asked.

"I hate to say it, but you're right," said Spidroth. "Before, they were just a mindless horde, attacking anything they saw. But now it seems like they're waiting for us."

Looking down at the zombified piglins, Dave noticed something strange. One of them didn't look right – standing a few rows back from the golden tower was a normal piglin. He seemed to be holding something, but Dave couldn't make out what it was.

"Carl, look at that piglin down there," said Dave, pointing. "Is that a normal piglin rather than a zombie? And what is it holding?"

Carl squinted. Then his eyes went wide with surprise.

"Yep, it's a normal piglin all right," he said, "and he's holding a staff. A golden staff with an emerald on the top."

Dave's mouth dropped open in shock.

"You mean..."

"Yeah," said Carl, "it looks just like the one that Herobrine gave to Trotter. The one he used to control the zombie pigmen."

"But that staff was destroyed," said Porkins. "Didn't it go in the lava and explode?"

"It did," said Dave, "but what was to stop Herobrine building another one?"

"Fascinating," said P1Go. "If someone has been controlling

zombified piglins with magic, that would explain why they've been acting so strangely lately."

"This is very confusing," said Boggo, scratching his head with a trotter. "Boggo's brain hurt."

Suddenly the normal piglin looked up, spotting them.

"Oh no," said Alex, "I think we been seen."

"Well, at least we're safe here," said Dave.

The normal piglin slammed the golden staff on the ground, and the emerald began to glow green. Suddenly the zombified piglins all began to move, getting on each other's shoulders and forming some kind of structure.

"They're building stairs!" said Alex.

Dave realized she was right: zombified piglins had arranged themselves into a staircase, getting higher and higher every second. Finally, the staircase was finished, and the top of it reached the roof of the golden tower. The normal piglin began walking up the staircase towards them.

"Anyone got some TNT?" asked Carl. "Let's blow this weird staircase to bits and that piglin with the staff too."

"No, wait!" said Saggo, looking over the top of the tower. "Don't hurt that piglin!"

"Why not?" Carl asked.

"Because it's my brother!" shouted Saggo. "It's Conko!"

CHAPTER ELEVEN
The Leader

The normal piglin reached the top of the staircase. He was wearing netherite armor, apart from his helmet was missing, and his eyes were glowing green.

"Conko!" shouted Saggo. She ran forward towards her brother, but he aimed the golden staff at her and sent her flying backward with a flash of green energy. She landed in Boggo's arms.

"Why Conko hurt sister?" Boggo asked angrily.

Conko smirked. He ignored the piglins and instead turned to Dave.

"Hello, Dave," said Conko, in a very un-piglin-like voice.

Dave's blood went cold; he'd heard that voice before: it was a voice he hoped he'd never have to hear again.

"Herobrine!" he gasped.

Spidroth drew her red sword. "I don't know how you've returned, father," she snarled at Conko, "but I will strike you down right now!"

"Relax, daughter," grinned Conko. "I'm not really Herobrine. Well, I am sort of. I'm a *shade*."

"I don't want to sound stupid, but what's a shade?" Carl asked.

"He is a copy of Herobrine," said Spidroth angrily. "Or at least a copy of Herobrine's personality. Back when his empire stretched across the world, Herobrine used to put his mind into other beings, so he could rule from afar. The beings were an exact copy of Herobrine's personality at that exact moment. He couldn't manipulate them from afar or see what was happening to them, but because they had his personality, he knew that they would do things the way he wanted."

"So Herobrine made a copy of his personality and put it in the brain of this poor piglin?" asked Alex.

"Correct," Conko grinned. "This fool of a piglin was part of the army that the Empress sent to capture me. I slew his comrades and then took the information I needed from him. I was going to slay him as well, but then I saw a better use for him. I gave him this staff and told him to start gathering together all the zombie pigmen in the Nether. Then, if I ever needed them, I would have an army ready and waiting for me."

"Those chaps aren't zombie pigmen," said Porkins angrily, aiming his bow at Conko. "They're zombified piglins."

"Well, whatever you want to call them, they're my army," said Conko, shrugging.

"Not anymore," growled Spidroth, "I'm going to cut you down!"

She dashed forward, lifting her red sword, ready to strike it down on Conko.

"No!" Saggo shrieked.

Spidroth stopped just in time, her blade just above Conko's forehead. She looked like she wanted to strike Conko down more than anything, and it was taking all her own willpower to stop her.

"You've become soft, daughter," Conko said, smiling mockingly at Spidroth. "The old you would have struck me down no matter whose body I was wearing."

"Listen, you Herobrine copy or whatever you are," said Carl, "the real Herobrine is gone. He's trapped in a dead dimension with no way out, so there's no point in you gathering a big army for him. He's not coming back."

"You lie," said Conko. His smile disappeared for the first time, replaced by a scowl.

"It's the truth, father," said Spidroth. "You have been banished from this universe for good. You are the only remnant of Herobrine that is left — a cheap copy in a weak body."

"Is that so?" Conko growled. "If that is true, then I will launch a new empire with this body. This piglin may be weak, but I can enhance him with magic and make him strong."

"Get out of Saggo's brother's body," Saggo sobbed. "Get out, you big meanie!"

"This has been fun, but I will leave you now," said Conko. "I spotted you all earlier in the blue forest, so I waited until you got inside the golden tower and then ordered my soldiers to surround it. In this body, I may be too weak to defeat you all, but there are over a thousand of these disgusting zombie creatures on this island. They will wait here as long as it takes. Either you will starve inside that tower, or you'll try to escape, and they will slay you. And don't even think about digging underground, as this island's surface is only two blocks thick. Below that is lava. You're trapped, I'm afraid. Of course, I could order my soldiers to let you leave, but only on one condition."

"And what condition is that?" Dave asked.

"You tell me how to find end portals," said Conko.

Dave laughed.

"What's so funny about that?" growled Conko.

"Oh, it's just that I told the real Herobrine that already," said Dave. "Well, I didn't tell him exactly, but he sucked the information from my brain. If he knew that information, how come you don't know?"

"It's because this shade only has Herobrine's memories from the point that it was created," said Spidroth.

Conko looked angry.

"If the real me got the information about how to reach the End, how is the universe still here?"

He seemed to be talking more to himself than anyone else.

"Maybe the egg didn't do what it was supposed to," Conko muttered. He looked almost afraid. "But if that's true, this has all been for nothing!"

Conko looked up at them with madness in his eyes.

"You," he scowled, looking at Dave. "You wretched villager! Ever since I heard your name, my life has been one problem after another. But it all ends now!"

Conko pulled out a netherite sword and dashed forward towards Dave. Dave was so shocked that he didn't even have time to pull out his own sword. Conko swung his blade through the air, aiming at Dave's chest.

POW!

Carl stepped forward and punched Conko, sending the piglin tumbling down the zombified piglin staircase.

"Conko!" Saggo yelled, running down the staircase after her brother. Boggo and Poffo ran down after her.

"Does anyone else think that staircase doesn't look very safe?" said Carl.

"Come on," said Dave, running down the staircase after the piglins. It was a very weird experience, running down a staircase made from creatures that were still alive — if you could call zombified piglins *alive* — and every time Dave stepped on one of the zombified piglin stairs, they looked at him and made *BURR* noises.

At the bottom of the stairs, Conko was lying on the ground with Saggo kneeling next to him. He looked dazed, and the golden staff had fallen onto the ground. All the zombified piglins were standing around, perfectly still as if awaiting orders. Dave picked up the golden staff.

"Get away, all of you," he said, pointing the staff at the zombified piglins. The emerald on the top glowed green, and then all the zombies began walking away. The zombies that made up the staircase began dismantling the structure as well, climbing off of each other's shoulders. Carl, Spidroth, Alex, Porkins and P1G0 reached the bottom of the staircase just in time before the structure collapsed and all the zombified piglins began walking off back into the forest.

"How are you, brother?" Saggo asked Conko. "Please be okay."

Dave noticed that Conko's eyes were no longer glowing green.

"The shade has left him," said Spidroth. "His fall must have knocked the copy of Herobrine's mind from his brain."

"So, is it gone for good?" Dave asked, looking around them as if expecting to see a ghostly image of Herobrine somewhere.

"Yes," said Spidroth. "Herobrine's shades cannot move from body to body — once they are removed from a vessel, or the vessel they are in is destroyed, they disappear as well."

Dave was glad to hear that. The last thing they needed was a copy of Herobrine taking over someone else's mind.

"Saggo?" said Conko, looking up at his sister. "Is that you? Conko had very strange dream."

"Oh, Conko!" said Saggo, reaching down and giving her brother a hug.

"Why Saggo wearing wedding dress?" asked Conko. "And who is stylish piglin in suit?"

"Conko, meet Boggo," said Saggo. "Boggo is going to be Saggo's husband. Wedding is today."

"Conko like weddings," said Conko happily. "Conko got cool dance moves, so Conko always get lots of kisses from girls."

Saggo and Boggo helped Conko to his feet. He was a bit unsteady at first, then he seemed to be okay.

Porkins pulled out a diamond shovel and quickly dug a hole two blocks deep into the ground. At the bottom of the hole was lava.

"What did you do that for, you weirdo?" Carl asked.

"To do this, dear boy," said Porkins, taking the golden staff off of Dave. He held the staff over the hole then dropped it. It landed in the lava, sunk down below the surface and then there was a

KRAKOOM as it exploded, spraying bits of lava from the hole. Thankfully no one got hit by the spray.

As they walked back through the warped forest island, Dave noticed some zombified piglins roaming about. They were no longer running around like vicious beasts or standing rigidly to attention; instead, they were roaming about aimlessly.

"It seems like the zombified piglins are back to normal now," said P1Go.

"That's a relief," said Alex.

"It will certainly make getting back a lot easier," agreed Dave. "I think I'm just going to build a bed and lie down when we get back to the wedding. I'm exhausted."

"Dave no lie down," said Saggo angrily, bashing Dave on the head with a trotter. "At Saggo's wedding everyone has to dance!"

"Okay, okay," said Dave, rubbing his head. "But I warn you, I'm not a good dancer."

"Poffo show Dave some moves," said Poffo proudly. "Poffo will help Dave get all the ladies, just like Poffo."

"Er, thanks, Poffo," said Dave. "That sounds great."

"Oh, does it?" said Spidroth, raising an eyebrow at him.

"Er, I didn't mean like that," said Dave, feeling his cheeks glowing red. "I just meant it would be good to learn some dance moves."

"Hmmph," said Spidroth, walking on ahead of him.

"I don't think she's going to agree to marry you any time soon after that," Carl whispered to Dave, putting a hand on his shoulder.

"Carl!" said Dave, shoving the creeper's hand away.

"Are you all right, Dave?" Carl asked with a grin. "Your cheeks have gone very red."

CHAPTER TWELVE
The Wedding

The journey back was a lot easier, now that they no longer had to worry about vicious hordes of zombified piglins. They took a long way around to avoid going through the bastion remnant again and managed to avoid passing through the basalt delta biome as well. All those detours meant the journey took a lot longer, but at least it was safe. The only trouble they had was from a few ghasts, but Dave and his friends managed to take them down easily with their bows.

When they finally made it back to the warped forest where the wedding was taking place, everyone had gone apart from an elderly piglin with a grey beard who was asleep on one of the chairs.

Saggo shook the elderly piglin awake.

"Grandpa, where is everyone?" Saggo asked him.

"Hello, Saggo," said the piglin, "everyone got bored waiting, so went home. They thought wedding was canceled."

"Poffo, tell everyone wedding is not canceled," Saggo said. "Tell them wedding is happening now."

Poffo nodded, then ran off. Before long, there were piglins everywhere, all chatting and taking their seats on the two aisles of chairs that had been set out. Dave and his friends took a seat near the back.

"Have you written your best man's speech yet, Carl?" Alex asked.

"Of course I haven't," said Carl. "When have I had time to write that stupid speech with all the adventuring we've been doing?"

"Don't worry," said Alex, handing Carl a piece of paper. "I've written one for you. It's packed full of fantastic jokes and heartfelt comments about Boggo and Saggo."

"Er, thanks, Alex," said Carl. He was about to read the piece of paper, but then a hush fell over the congregation as a piglin in purple robes stepped onto the stage at the front. Boggo was standing at the front too, Dave saw, wearing his wedding suit and top hat.

Music began to play from somewhere, and Dave noticed a piglin standing next to a jukebox by the side of the stage. The music playing didn't seem very appropriate for a wedding – it was good music, though, with a nice beat.

"Pigstep is cool tune," one of the piglins near Dave whispered to their neighbor as they bobbed their heads in time to the music.

Suddenly everyone turned their heads. Dave turned and saw Saggo walking down the aisle in her wedding dress, which had been given a good clean after their adventures in the Nether. P1Go had linked arms with her and was leading her down the aisle.

"Saggo look so beautiful," a piglin near Dave muttered.

"Boggo is lucky piglin," said another.

"Are you crying, Alex?" Carl whispered.

"It's just so romantic," said Alex, using the sleeve of her black ninja outfit to wipe away her tears.

"Pah," said Spidroth.

"Don't pretend you wouldn't like to get married too," Carl teased. "And we all know who you'd like to get married to!"

Spidroth slapped Carl on the side of the head.

"Ow," the little creeper said. "What was that for?"

Saggo reached the front and walked onto the stage, standing opposite Boggo. Boggo reached forward, taking her trotter's in his own.

"Piglin brothers and sisters, we gathered here today for wedding of Boggo and Saggo," said the piglin in purple robes. "Boggo, do you take Saggo to be wife?"

"Boggo do," said Boggo.

"And Saggo, do you take Boggo to be husband?"

"Saggo do," said Saggo.

"Then, by power invested in Zordo, Zordo now pronounce you piglin and wife."

A great cheer went up, all the piglins clapping and shouting happily. Despite himself, Dave found himself caught up in the moment, and even he was clapping and cheering along with the rest of them. Even Spidroth had a slight smile on her face, Dave was pleased to see. She looked almost emotional.

Next came the meal. Everyone sat down around tables, and piglin waiters served the food. There were several courses, although the only ingredients in every dish were pork chops and mushrooms. Dave supposed that there wasn't much variety of food in the Nether compared to the Overworld. Across the table, he saw Carl take a sneaky bite of one of the potatoes he had in his golem suit.

After the meal, it was time for speeches. Saggo's father gave a lovely speech about how happy he was that his daughter was now married and that his son Conko had returned, then it was time for Boggo to give a speech. He stood up, and the guests all fell silent.

"Boggo thank you all for coming today," said Boggo. "This special day for Boggo, as Boggo get to marry his soulmate Saggo. When Boggo first meet Saggo, Boggo think she very pretty piglin, but then Boggo get to know her and realize she is also funny and kind and good friend to Boggo. Then Boggo fall in love."

"Are you all right, Alex?" Porkins whispered.

"I always cry at weddings," said Alex, dabbing her eyes and blowing her nose on her sleeve.

Dave saw Spidroth rolling her eyes at Alex.

"Boggo would also like to thank friends from Overworld," Boggo continued. "Carl and his friends were a big help to piglins, helping us defeat Empress, and now we free." He raised his cup. "To Carl and friends!"

All the other piglins turned towards Dave and his friends, raising their own cups.

"To Carl and friends!" they all repeated.

"And now Boggo's speech is finished," said Boggo. "Boggo would like to invite Boggo's best man and best friend to do speech now. Everyone clap for Carl!"

Everyone clapped. Carl pushed back his chair and stood up in his golem suit. He looked uncharacteristically nervous. He picked up the piece of paper that Alex had given him and began to read.

"Er, having a good marriage is a lot like being a good ninja," Carl read. He gave Alex a furious look, but she just grinned back at him and gave him a thumbs up. Carl took a deep breath and then continued to read. "It takes discipline, patience and sometimes enemies will throw shurikens at your head."

The piglins all gave him confused looks. Carl scrunched up Alex's speech and threw it on the floor.

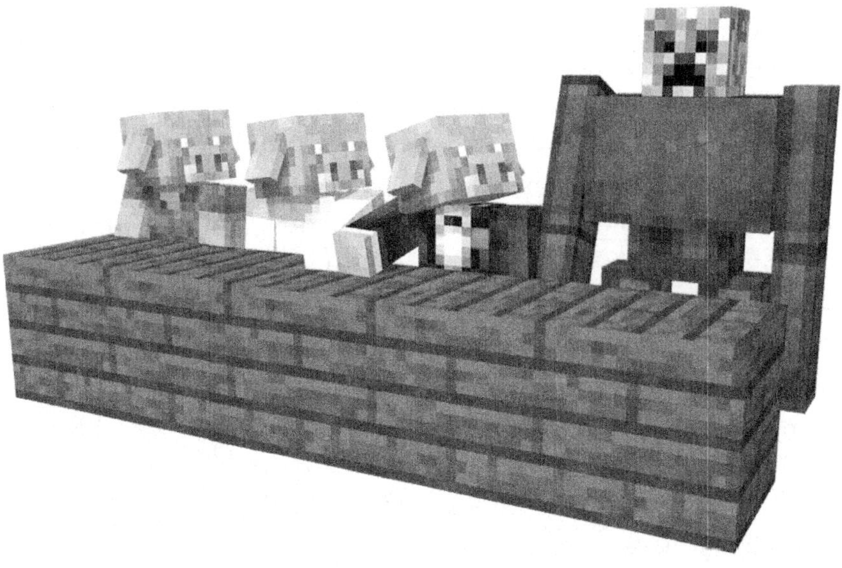

"Right," said Carl, "I don't know much about marriage. In creeper culture, there is no marriage. My mother was a creeper queen with over one hundred thousand children, so I never really knew her. In fact, all my relationships were a bit strange growing up, as everyone I knew eventually blew themselves up. But then I met my friends Dave and Porkins, and later some other friends too. They gave me the family I never had before and showed me what a good family could be like. From what I've seen of Boggo and Saggo, I think they're going to be a good family as well. Saggo risked her life to save Boggo, and if that's not true love, I don't know what is. And Boggo may be an idiot, and he may have destroyed my awesome diamond golem armor, but he's a nice guy, and I know he'll treat Saggo well. Anyway, that's enough rambling on from me. Everyone raise your cups — to Boggo and Saggo!"

"Boggo and Saggo!" everyone repeated.

Carl quickly sat down, and everyone resumed talking.

"Great speech, Carl," said Dave, putting a hand on his friend's shoulder.

"You didn't do any jokes, Carl," said Alex, looking disappointed. "I had loads of good jokes written in my speech. There was one about how piglins look a lot like pigs. It was pretty funny."

"Er, I'm sure it was," said Carl.

Boggo walked over and gave Carl a hug.

"Thank you, best friend Carl!" said Boggo happily. "That speech very great! Although needed more jokes. Best man speech supposed to be funny."

"I tried to tell him," shrugged Alex.

Next, it was time for the dancing. The piglins cleared away the tables, then they put a music disc on the jukebox, and all began to dance. The dancing was jolly and upbeat, with piglins linking arms and swinging each other round and round. Alex and Porkins enthusiastically joined in the dancing, and after some persuading, Dave got up and joined as well. Carl and Spidroth both refused to get involved.

"I have a reputation as a cool dude to maintain," Carl explained to Dave. "Cool dudes don't dance; they just stand at the side of the dancefloor and look cool. Everyone knows that."

"Dancing is for fools," said Spidroth.

Dave had never been much of a dancer, but before long, he found himself having lots of fun, dancing with partner after partner. He danced with more piglins than he could count, including Saggo, Poffo, Boggo and even P1Go. The robot was a surprisingly good dancer.

"I am programmed to be able to pick up any skill through observation," the robot told Dave. "After watching a couple of dances, my systems updated, and I became an expert."

Dave also danced with Porkins a couple of times and Alex. Alex was so full of life when she danced that it made Dave laugh. She swung him around so fast that he got dizzy and almost fell over.

"Isn't dancing fun?" Alex asked happily.

"Yeah, it is," said Dave. He looked over and saw Spidroth and Carl, both of them standing stony-faced on the edge of the dancefloor.

I wish Spidroth would come over and dance, Dave thought to himself.

Alex was just spinning Dave around again when suddenly the music disc changed, and a slow song came on. All the piglins began to dance in a slow waltz, so Dave and Alex followed suit. Dave put his arm on Alex's back, and the two of them were looking right into each other's eyes. He'd never noticed before how green Alex's eyes were. They were as green as emeralds.

Even though he was facing away from her, Dave could suddenly feel Spidroth's eyes boring into his back.

"Er, I think that's enough dancing for me," said Dave quickly, letting go of Alex.

"Oh, okay," said Alex, sounding disappointed.

Dave quickly walked over and joined Spidroth and Carl.

"Having fun, were we?" Spidroth asked Dave.

"Er, yes, although I'm a bit exhausted from all the dancing now," Dave said. "I think I'm just going to sit down for a while."

"You do whatever you want to do," said Spidroth.

Carl looked at Spidroth and Dave, but for once, he didn't say anything. Dave was very thankful for that.

Eventually, the piglins got tired and sat down around the tables, which had been rebuilt on the edge of the dancefloor. Alex and Porkins, both exhausted and covered in sweat, came over and rejoined Dave, Spidroth and Carl.

"That was terrific fun," said Porkins, sitting down. "I haven't had a jolly good laugh like that in a long time!"

"I suppose we ought to be going," Dave said.

"I suppose so, old chap," said Porkins, sounding a bit disappointed.

They all went over to Boggo and Saggo, who were sitting

together holding hands.

"We're all going to go now, back to the Overworld," said Carl. "Great wedding, you guys."

"Thank you, Carl," said Saggo. "But how come Carl wasn't dancing earlier?"

"Unfortunately, I'm allergic to dancing," said Carl. "If I try to dance, I come out in a rash."

"Oh dear," said Saggo. "Poor Carl."

"Aren't you going to stay to see fireworks?" Boggo asked.

"I'm afraid not," said Dave. "We really must be getting back."

"Thanks for everything, Carl and Carl's friends," said Boggo. "You are all good friends to the piglins."

"I'm sure we'll all meet again soon," said Dave.

After saying a few more goodbyes, to Poffo, P1G0 and some of the other piglins they knew, Dave and his friends all walked away from the wedding. In a grove in the middle of some tall cyan mushrooms, Dave built another portal and lit it.

"Well, that's another crazy adventure in the Nether done with," said Carl. "Let's hope we never have to come here ever again."

"Oh, don't be so miserable, Carl," said Alex. "I had a great time!"

"Have you forgotten how we were almost slain by magma cubes falling from the sky?" Carl asked.

"Well, I guess that bit wasn't so fun," said Alex. "But the dancing was great."

"Yes," said Spidroth, raising an eyebrow and giving Alex a suspicious stare. "You certainly looked like you were having fun, Alex."

"Er, let's all get out of here," said Dave.

He walked up to the purple rippling force field, then stepped through it back into the Overworld.

Epilogue

It was nighttime in Bedrock City. Torrents of rain splashed down on the ancient buildings, and the moon was covered by clouds.

Mad Mulligan sat at the top of an old tower, eating porkchops. The part of the tower he was in looked like it had housed a bell once, but the bell was long gone. There was a roof over his head and views in every direction. He knew from past experience that this tower was the best lookout point in the city: it sat at a cross junction and overlooked all the main roads.

Mulligan had a sudden vision; Dave and his friends had returned from the Nether and had resumed their journey once more. Mulligan didn't have a plan for what he would do once Dave reached Bedrock City. He knew that if he planned ahead, Dave would predict his actions with the Sight. No, he would have to come up with a plan on the spot and improvise. That would be the only way to defeat Dave.

I shouldn't have taught him how to use the Sight, Mulligan thought bitterly. He'd been too cocky and confident, and now he was paying the price. He'd lost all his rare magical trinkets and weapons when he'd fallen in the lava, so now all he had were his wits.

This will be my ultimate test, Mulligan thought to himself. *I'm gonna have to defeat a foe who has the same powers as me. It won't be easy.*

Still, Mulligan had never shied away from a challenge. He was confident that whatever happened when Dave reached Bedrock City, he would win out in the end. He would defeat the villager and his friends and then claim the ender dragon for his own. But for now, there was nothing to do but keep his strength up. He took another bite of his porkchop, and he waited...

To be continued...

Have you read *The Jrystal Sword*?

I've written a non-Minecraft book called **The Jrystal Sword**. It's a fantasy book about magic and monsters. It's for a slightly older audience than Dave the Villager, with a few violent bits and a few more adult themes, so I would say it's for **readers age 9+**. For reference, I normally say the DTV books are for readers age 7+. Anyway, it's available on Amazon if you want to read it!

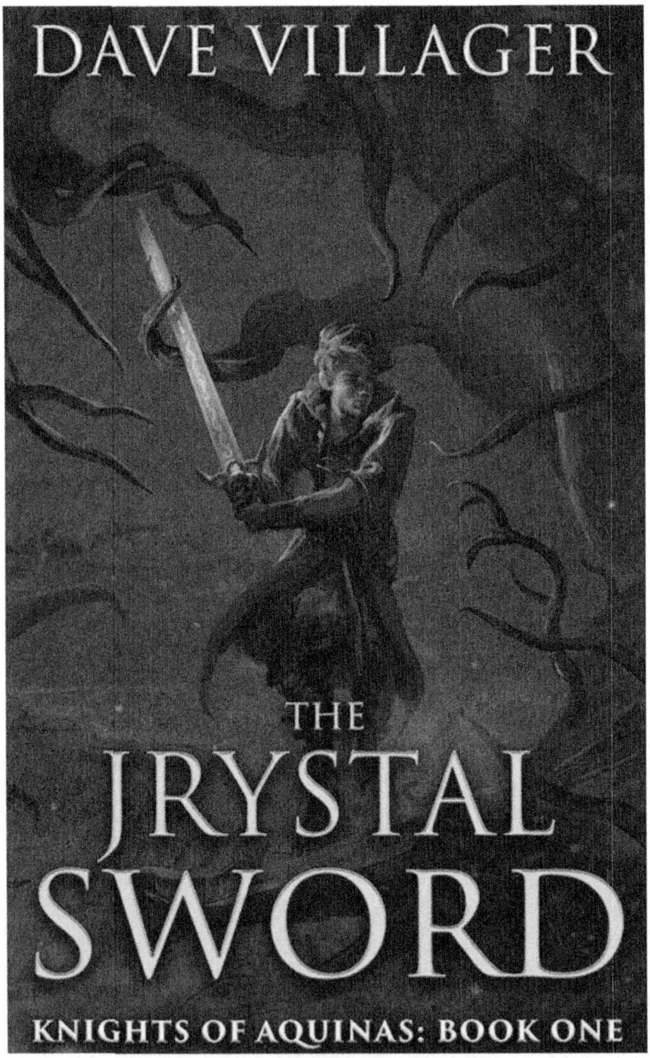

Printed in Great Britain
by Amazon

58194472R00238